W9-AEF-019

The Slave's Rebellion

Blacks in the Diaspora

The Slave's Rebellion

Literature, History, Orature

Adélékè Adéẹ̀kọ́

INDIANA UNIVERSITY PRESS BLOOMINGTON & INDIANAPOLIS

This book is a publication of

Indiana University Press
601 North Morton Street
Bloomington, IN 47404-3797 USA

http://iupress.indiana.edu

Telephone orders 800-842-6796
Fax orders 812-855-7931
Orders by e-mail iuorder@indiana.edu

Library of Congress Cataloging-in-Publication Data

Adéẹ̀kọ́, Adélékè.

The slave's rebellion : literature, history, orature / Adéléke Adéẹ̀kọ́.
p. cm.—(Blacks in the diaspora)

Includes bibliographical references and index.

ISBN 0-253-34596-0 (alk. paper)—ISBN 0-253-21777-6 (pbk. : alk. paper)

1. American literature—African American authors—History and criticism. 2. African Americans—Intellectual life. 3. Nigerian fiction (English)—History and criticism. 4. Slave insurrections—Historiography. 5. Slave insurrections in literature. 6. Oral tradition—Caribbean Area. 7. African Americans in literature. 8. Oral tradition—Africa. 9. Slavery in literature. I. Title. II. Series.

PS153.N5A285 2005

2004028902

1 2 3 4 5 10 09 08 07 06 05

The paper used in this publication meets the minimum requirements of American National Standard for Information Sciences—Permanence of Paper for Printed Library Materials, ANSI Z39.48-1984.

Manufactured in the United States of America

FOR ỌMỌTÁYỌ̀, ADÉBỌLÁJÍ, AND ADÉDIMÉJÌ

contents

ACKNOWLEDGMENTS

In order that I do not become like a stealer of favors, I would like to thank the following for their contributions to the completion of this project. David Simpson, then the chair of the English department at the University of Colorado, Boulder, was the first person to suggest that a paper on slave rebellions and African American literary history that I gave at the Novel of the Americas symposium in Boulder in 1992 touched upon critical issues that deserve a scrutiny far deeper than a conference piece would support. When I revisited this idea six years later, David had left Boulder and could not read the drafts. Other colleagues whose generous collegiality moved this project along, because they read and criticized versions of different parts of the book over the years, include Anna Brickhouse (University of Colorado, Boulder), Adeniyi Coker Jr. (University of Alabama, Birmingham), Tejumola Olaniyan (University of Wisconsin, Madison), and Olakunle George (Brown University). Teju and Kunle listened to me present some of the ideas at several annual meetings of either the African Studies Association or the African Literature Association. A conference Niyi Coker organized at the University of Alabama, Birmingham, in 2000 gave me the chance to speak about slave rebellions and slave narratives to an audience of grade school teachers and college professors. I want to thank Jeff Cox and the University of Colorado's Center for Humanities and the Arts for allowing me to speak about slave rebellions as part of its Work in Progress series. Dr. Duro Oguntebi of Tampa, Florida, read and commented on parts of chapter 6. Chidiebere Nwaubani, my "Naija" colleague at the University of Colorado, Boulder, made his expertise on historiography available to me, patiently answered my many questions about history, and always suggested far more references than I needed. I owe a sea of gratitude to Moyo Okediji, of the University of Colorado, Denver, and Denver Museum of Arts, who without hesitation gave me the permission to use, free of charge, one his paintings for the cover of this book. To all these friends and colleagues, I should serve the warning that I hope to retaliate very soon.

The Slave's Rebellion

INTRODUCTION

No element of modern black history agitates the speculative faculty of writers trying to conceptualize the telos of black struggles more than episodes of historical slave rebellions. Dealing with themes that range from the justness of anti-slavery violence to the unjust inequities that have resulted from the historical misunderstanding of black women's struggles, texts discussed in this book figure the slave's rebellion as something akin to Walter Benjamin's "angel of history," one side of whose "face is turned toward the past" from where we can find the means to "make whole what has been smashed." In these stories, the slave rebel embodies the manifestly unquestionable spirit of restorative justice which each writer's milieu is called upon directly or indirectly to reanimate. But as Benjamin further notes, the past's restless storm can blow the angel of history "into the future to which his back is turned." In many of the stories discussed in this book, accounts of past rebellions are also occasions for historical prognostication on the "turbulence to come," as Arna Bontemps codes it. The intellectual factors that predispose slave rebellions to the task of examining the past and the future are examined in chapter 1.

The second chapter examines the function of the rebel figure in antebellum African American fiction. Against the standard positioning of the autobiographer as the epitome of black "spiritual" aspirations under slavery, it is suggested here that the individualist scope of the autobiographer's self-liberation quest is significantly narrower than the options explored by slave rebels whose visions of freedom encompass the immediate emancipation of the entire community. The protagonists in Frederick Douglass's *The Heroic Slave,* William Wells Brown's *Clotel,* and Martin Delany's *Blake,* I suggest, model a path to freedom that is radically different from the one advocated by the writer-hero of the typical ex-slave autobiography. Unlike the writer-hero who follows a well-known flight plan to the North, Madison Washington, Clotel, and Blake abandon the promises of the North and return to the slaveholding South to force on the class of masters the "recognition" of the right of the enslaved to freedom. The distinct section of early African American fiction constituted by these stories of rebellion, two of them written by autobiographers, expands the modes of cultural agitation for freedom and encourages another form of resistance by converting, self-consciously, the clever heroic fugitive of the autobiography into a thoughtful, fear-inducing insurrectionist. I further contend that Nat Turner's example, one in which the fugitive's run to the North is aborted for a virtuous, but unavoidably violent confrontation with the master, shapes narrative form in early African American fiction and enables the emergence of a literary voice critical of slavery in ways that slave autobiographies could not.

Problems that arose in antebellum presentations of the rebellious black subaltern, I suggest in chapter 3, remain in Charles Chesnutt's critique of the failures of Reconstruction in *The Marrow of Tradition,* the novel Nikki Giovanni describes as "the zero" figure in African American fiction because it repudiates many nineteenth-century conventions of depicting black fictional characters: "Chesnutt wrote the first race riot. . . . The old mammy dies in the riot. The Black folks fight back" (104). Giovanni's naming the novel's unprecedented uprising as a "*race* riot" reveals that after Emancipation the nodal term for articulating black political discontent has changed from eliminating the class of masters to compelling racists to reform their ways. The ramifications of this change in terms, especially as they relate to the difficult birth of black *racial* solidarity, thirty years after Emancipation in the quietly industrializing old South, crop up in the many moral conundrums encountered in the plot resolution. Expressed as race struggles, the goals of emancipatory violence become morally uncertain.

The analysis moves to another historical period in the fourth chapter, focusing on the aims of stories of slave rebellion during the Great Depression (in the United States), an era that also saw the beginning of anti-colonial intellectual movements in Africa and the Caribbean. During this period of social and economic uncertainties compounded by apprehensions about the spread of socialism, white and black writers in the Caribbean and the United States revisited historical black rebellions and re-presented the slave's heroism as foreboding the role black (and other working) peoples would play in the shaping of the (capitalist) future. The chapter examines how Arna Bontemps's *Black Thunder* [1] (1936), a book often described as the first African American historical novel, contemplates, with a reinterpretation of Gabriel Prosser's 1800 slave insurrection plot, the will of desperate (slaving) workers striving for freedom on their own.

Two years after Bontemps, C.L.R. James issued his monumental study of the Haitian slave revolt, *The Black Jacobins,* in 1938. James read the facts of the slaves' plot in Haiti as a sign foreshadowing how late colonialism and industrial capitalism will be fought and defeated. In Africa and the Caribbean, the coming class struggle, James predicted, would mobilize under decolonization and anti-apartheid banners.[2] However, the main focus of analysis in *The Black Jacobins* chapter is not anti-colonial politics but James's inauguration of anti-colonial historiography in the form of what Hayden White calls "realistic historicism." James reinterprets the Haitian War of Independence, I would argue, to outline what is historical in the postcolony and how the historical moment is to be recognized.

The next chapter moves to 1949, by which time the anti-colonial movement foreshadowed by James had begun to coalesce into a major global force. The focus of study in the chapter is Alejo Carpentier's conceptualizing as magical realism the broad outlines of the self-directed aspects of the slaves' mobilization for freedom in Haiti. It is often forgotten in the assimilation of magical realism into postmodernist and postcolonial theories of culture and literature that Carpentier, in his original formulation of that theory, said it was a visit to Haiti in 1943, and the awe he felt on seeing the ruins of the monuments constructed by early leaders of the Haitian war, that revealed to him the structure of thought and action he named American marvelous realism. The "real" American marvel embodied in the Haitian ruins, which Carpentier said he came to know, differs radically from the contrived marvels of surrealism and aesthetic modernism mainly because one practically testifies to the limitless bounds of human possibilities while the other only talks about them. Magical realism's main theme, as shown in *The Kingdom of This World,* the story in which the general formulation is first put to narrative test, is the freedom to experiment with varying forms of knowing for the sake of emancipating the slave's body and mind. Magical knowledge, principally codes of the secret articulations exclusive to slaves, saved the slaves and frightened the masters who are held in thrall for a long time by their enraged servants.

The next two chapters are on Africa, specifically Nigeria, where the problems of slavery and slave rebellion remain minor intellectual preoccupations in cultural work. Although domestic slavery fed the transatlantic trade, examining the moral and political effects of slavery has not attracted sustained attention in modern African critical discourses. The African section of the book proceeds on the premise that domestic African slaves would have resisted their captivity and that the silence of African traditions on this subject demands probing. Hence in chapter 6 I read oral traditions about slavery—specifically *oríkì,* Yorùbá praise poetry—with the intent of isolating the poetics and politics of exclusion that might be responsible for the effacement of slavery in what have become African classical traditions.[3] Poems about two groups that would have played significant roles in slavery in what is now Yorùbá hinterland, the Olúfẹ̀ royal lineage and the Oníkòyí warrior lineage, are studied with a focus on what are not fully said about the relationship between warriors and kings, warriors and captives, royal priests and their human victims of ritual sacrifice, the royal city and outlying locations. The crucial silences observed in the praise poetry of these lineages are contrasted with a close reading of Adébáyọ̀ Fálétí's realistic depiction of human sacrifice in *Ọmọ Olókùn Ẹṣin,* a novel of slave rebellion set in a fictional slaveholding Yorùbá kingdom. In the realistic novel, the meaning of many of the terse claims made in praise poetry about the smooth running of political kingdoms is fleshed out.

In the next chapter, I juxtapose to the textual silences of oral tradition an analysis of the depiction of slaves in a popular Yorùbá play—Akínwùmí Ìṣọ̀lá's *Ẹfúnṣetán Aníwúrà*—about a prominent nineteenth-century Yorùbá woman who was a notorious slaveholder. The discussion relates the slaves' self-description of their condition to Orlando Patterson's concept of "social death." My interpretation of the slaves' words shows that the playwright's attempt to shepherd interpretation toward an allegory of the tragic fate of unhistoricized political underdogs in the hands of an equally unhistoricized powerful class reflects the general pattern of speaking about slavery in modern African literatures. The chapter also analyzes the play's spectacular use of incantations and other "fighting" oral traditions in the confrontation between Ẹfúnṣetán, the heroine, and the male chiefs in her town as a textual feature that conceals the chiefs' hijacking of a rebellion being hatched by Ẹfúnṣetán's slaves. The ruling groups, whose main means of sustenance is slavery, destroy Ẹfúnṣetán because her harsh treatment of her slaves is about to set off a political revolt. The male chiefs ruin Ẹfúnṣetán to protect their own long-term slaveholding interests, but they sell the counter-insurgency to the public as a war against highhanded witchcraft.

The last chapter returns to the Americas. Its main subject is the meaning of slave rebellion after civil rights, and the illustrative text is *Dessa Rose,* Sherley Anne Williams's "meditation" on the historiographic meaning of women's participation in a slave rebellion. After decolonization in the Third World, and the successful massive agitation for the extension of civil rights to the disenfranchised in the First, it should be expected that the interpretation of slavery, and slave rebellion in particular, would take a different turn. William Styron's best-selling novel, *The Confessions of Nat Turner* (1968), undertakes the most aggressively self-conscious reinterpretation of antecedent records. Beginning with a title that quotes Thomas Gray's 1831 pamphlet on the most violent slave rebellion in the United States, Styron questions long-held beliefs about the slave rebel. His story probes literally unreachable parts of Nat Turner's mind and attributes unheroic impulses to the slave rebel's actions. Styron's Turner is roiled by sexual anxieties and impure motivations.

The novel itself straddles several literary, historical, and political moments. On one hand, its focus on Turner's interior and its suggesting a disjuncture between his manifest heroism (for which he is celebrated in popular imagination) and latent baser drives (which propel him into a murderous revolt in the novel) hark back to modernism. On the other hand, the story's self-conscious cannibalization of Gray's pamphlet anticipates the nonreferential allegorical tendencies that will later define postmodern narration. After successful decolonization and civil rights struggles, it seems, an artist in tune with trends in literary and political discourses can question the motives of a historical slave rebel. However, the acrimonious controversy[4] incurred by the imputation of ambiguous libidinal desires to the heroic slave rebel, I would say, forewarned that the slave's struggle for freedom still commanded a great deal of symbolic value in many political and cultural quarters.

Notwithstanding the many tantalizing ways Styron's novel can be used to illustrate the complexities of writing about slave rebellions in the postcolonial and post–civil rights world,[5] I am studying Williams's *Dessa Rose* because the novel's focalization of the activities of a woman rebel brings up critical topics that neither Styron nor any other novelist of slave rebellion considered in depth. The story uses the protagonist's handed-down oral history to rectify the deliberate misdirections she has given a white archivist whose written records are relied upon in texts that archetypally operate like Styron's. The complex interplay of multiple narrative voices in *Dessa Rose* dramatizes the difficulty of accessing the female slave rebel's resistance story and foregrounds the traditionally neglected contribution of the female slave to the cultivation of liberation traditions in modern black New World. The narrative structure insinuates critical questions about what constitutes the proper and readable archive—for example, the meaning of hidden bodily mutilations suffered by the rebellious slave woman of modern black history.

Williams's novelistic commentaries on the construction of the truly judicious historical archives of slave rebellion, I argue, reveal the political acquiescence implicit in the predominantly textualist orientation of black deconstruction. The blackness of black textuality, Williams seems to be saying, cannot be separated from the "Black Experience."

The analysis pursued in this book is ambivalent about unifying theories of the black diaspora. I accept, on one hand, that slavery is a major determinant factor in modern black history. This means that modern black people are related historically and probably share some common cultural consciousness: e.g., the need to always reinterpret the history of slave rebellions as a means of defining modern black existence. I am convinced, on the other hand, that how black people code their common modern experience is circumscribed by local and national circumstances. I am making this point to differentiate my work from contemporary transnationalisms that privilege—prematurely, I think—the universalizing effects of the intellectual products of transatlantic trade *routes* over cultural and political *rites* delimited by national imperatives.[6] Constraints and advantages specific to the United States, for example, shape the use of slave rebellions in the development of black fiction in the nineteenth century. More precisely, the ways early black American novelists, who were also autobiographers, "signified" on the form of slave narratives and on each other's writing are conditioned by developments in American national politics and culture.[7]

When, say, James's *Black Jacobins* is compared to Bontemps's *Black Thunder,* the many abstractions of the former reflect the openness of Caribbean intellectuals—Eric Williams, Frantz Fanon, and Edouard Glissant are well-known examples—to theoretical speculations on the nature of historical motions. Bontemps, like many other American black thinkers and writers of his generation, is not fully at ease with the implications of Marxist telos, although he is intrigued by its pronouncements on the future of capitalism. The difference that national intellectual traditions make to the interpretation of the history of slave rebellion is even clearer when Carpentier's manifesto on magical realism is added to the equation. Unlike Bontemps, who resorts to symbolism to depict the transcendent aims of emancipatory violence, James and Carpentier draw explicitly daring conclusions from the historical slave rebellions they write about.

Colonialism remains the dominant problematic in Africanist discourses. To Achille Mbembe, for instance, to be colonized is to be enslaved, and the theoretical distinction between the two modes of subjugation is immaterial to philosophical analysis. In canonical African literature, the consideration of the consequences of slavery in modern African experience in Ayi Kwei

Armah's and Yambo Ouologuem's "histories" is often regarded as eccentric.[8] The other group of writers in whose works the subject of slavery bears considerable freight are Ama Ata Aidoo, Efua Sutherland, and Buchi Emecheta.[9] However, this topic is usually viewed as an ancillary element of the feminist critique deemed to be more central to these women's writings. As chapter 7 shows, Adébáyọ̀ Fálétí's emphatic conversion of the clear case of vassal slavery that obtained between the Ọ̀yọ́ kingdom and its tributaries into a colonial relationship in *Ọmọ Olókùn Ẹṣin* illustrates the dominance of colonialism in African critical imagination.

The different "national" attitudes toward the historicity of slave rebellions summarized above influenced the reading methods adopted for the study of each region in the book. Beginning with the golden age of deconstruction in the United States in the 1980s, African American literary and cultural criticism has been driven by the problematic of writing as "graphing" and as "voicing," and texts that foreground these issues became main nodal points in influential literary histories such as Henry Louis Gates Jr.'s *The Signifying Monkey* and Robert Stepto's *From Behind the Veil.* Accounts of nineteenth-century literary history suffered most from this approach to black American texts in that antebellum fiction rarely commands a place in systematic explanations of black literary production. Although William L. Andrews bucked that trend in "The Representation of Slavery and the Rise of Afro-American Literary Realism" by connecting developments in antebellum black fiction to the autobiography, the slave rebel figure is not considered an important feature. As the second chapter shows below, heroic slave rebels played hitherto unacknowledged yet significant roles in the politics of textual production in antebellum black fiction. In this chapter and others about American novels the analyses adopt a line of inquiry aimed at revising paradigms of black American literary history.

The analysis of Caribbean texts adopts a philosophy of culture approach. For Carpentier, the Haitian War of Independence constitutes an occasion to meditate on the parameters of understanding culture and history in the Americas. He interprets the Haitian incidents according to the dictates of what he perceives to be the informing epistemic "spirit" of existence in the Americas. For him, Haiti is not an aberration but a fulfillment of the "magically real" situation of the ideas that govern the Americas, a continent where "a drum might be more than just a goatskin stretched across a hollow log" (78). For James, Haiti reveals not an idealistic spirit at play but the adaptation of a materialist ethos by the slaves' avant-garde. The initially weaker side in the dialectics of slavery, in James's narrative, catches up, as it should be expected to, with the stronger side such that the weak becomes the strong.

And nothing, as far as James is concerned, is mysterious here. Every event, we may even say every drumming incident, is subject to a historicizable motive. James's interest is clearly speculative historicism, as he confirms in a 1971 retrospective lecture on the book: "Speculative thought is important, and unless you are doing speculative thought you are not doing any thought at all. You are only playing about" ("Lectures" 74). My discussion of *The Black Jacobins* therefore concentrates on the possibilities which the narrative opened up for anti-colonial history writing in the postwar years. One of the key revelations found in the Caribbean texts is that they foreshadow many of the theoretical concerns of contemporary postcolonial criticism. The hybrid character of cultural formations, the difficulties involved in the writing of subaltern histories, and the indebtedness of anti-colonial insurgence to metropolitan liberal discourses of freedom are all explicit subjects in James.

Dominant literary and cultural practices in Africa regarding the slavery question bear out the truth of Pierre Macherey's critical maxim which says that what is excluded from a text is as meaningful as what is included.[10] The analysis carried out in the Africa section of the book presses on the points of exclusion in both oral and written Yorùbá texts because slaves, it seems in these works, have no socially acceptable "mouth" with which to speak of their condition. Subaltern speech and action have been so thoroughly assimilated into bloodless "culturalism" and "nationalism" that it is difficult to directly locate the feelings of social underdogs such as slaves.

1

HEGEL'S BURDEN

The Slave's Counter Violence in Philosophy, Critical Theory, and Literature

> Ogun layé [Existence is war].
>
> — *Yorùbá proverb*

> What we need to do is kill ourselves.
>
> — M. K. Gandhi, *Hind Swaraj*

> An insurgent is not a subject of understanding or interpretation but of extermination.
>
> — Ranajit Guha, *"The Prose of Counter-Insurgency"*

At the beginning of his very lucid and tightly argued *On the Postcolony,* Achille Mbembe recommends that critics should cease formulating theoretical statements about the possibility of Africa's autonomy and come to terms with the reality that African societies permanently lost their "'distinctive historicity'" when they ceded control to Europe. Since then, nothing important has happened in Africa that is "not embedded in times and rhythms heavily conditioned by European domination" (9). The "particular and sometimes local" concerns of African societies can no longer be honestly perceived outside the worldly orbit into which their dealings with Europe have consigned them. Of course, Mbembe is being a little disingenuous because his book, which he says is intended to lay out "the criteria that African [social and political] agents accept as valid" (7), is about nothing other than "particular and local concerns" of African politics.

A little less than a decade earlier, Paul Gilroy's now deservedly influential *The Black Atlantic* eloquently challenged the self-authorization "resistance" paradigms that have dominated the writing of the intellectual history of black peoples in the New World. Gilroy argued that the manifest antagonism of black thought, at least as it is reflected in literature and popular music, is thoroughly misread if it is classified as an opposition to New World modernity. Idioms of self-constitution such as "nationality, ethnicity authenticity, and cultural integrity" (2) articulated by black thinkers to fight slavery, the deadly path most New World blacks took to modernity, do not contradict modernity's intellectual assumptions. In essence, Gilroy seems to be saying, the basic principles of what we now call modern black thought gestated as questions generated by the contradictions slavery constituted for modernity.

I started by quoting Gilroy and Mbembe, who do not appear to have read each other's work, because their accounts of modern black being (perhaps nonbeing in Mbembe) resurrect the ghost of Hegel's allegory of Lordship and Bondage. For either author, slavery and colonialism constitute the historical "normativity" within which modern black communities in Africa and the New World have evolved in the last four centuries or so, and it is only from inside that "normativity" that black acts of self-constitution can be honestly studied.[1] Gilroy, writing about British and Anglophone American cultural politics, condemns the language of occultic "'cultural insiderism'" that black nationalisms, including both the latent one in black poststructuralist literary criticism and the manifest one in Afrocentricity, use to justify their general assertions and to conceal the fact that the exclusive ethnic space is never the primary category of identification for black thinkers.[2] Writing about Africa in the same valence, Mbembe excoriates theories of a separate African being, historicist or mythical, that fail to reckon with colonization.

The slew of research projects implemented around the "Black Atlantic" theme proposed by Gilroy indicates that the basic terms of writing modern black history may be undergoing some fundamental revisions, and that a distinct body of knowledge is being amassed around the defining impact of the flow of ideas enabled by colonization and modern transatlantic slave trade on the cultures of the African Old World and the American New World. Black Atlanticism represents cultural traffic in black societies in the United States and the Caribbean from the eighteenth century onward as the strategic deployment of ideas that leading writers and thinkers adapt from European philosophers of modernity. Olaudah Equiano, Ignatius Sancho, W.E.B. Du Bois, Edward Blyden, and even the fiercely nationalist Marcus Garvey comment on their societies and generate programs of black advancement by refining the fundamental principles of the Enlightenment to account for black existence. Whatever may be "black" in these formulations cannot, therefore, be uncoupled from the gains of Enlightenment. To complete the argument, it is suggested that a fairly honest account of modernity has to include black peoples' "selective use of the ideologies of the Western Age of Revolution" (Gilroy 44) to make their case against slavery both in theory and in practical politics.[3] In this conception of New World blackness, practices carried over from Africa are to be seen as a spectral presence meaningful only to the needlessly fastidious seeker of ancestral beginnings: "Though African linguistic tropes and political and philosophical themes are still visible for those who wish to see them, they have often been transformed and adapted by their New World locations to a new point where the dangerous issues of purified essences and simple origins lose all meaning" (Gilroy 48).

Some Africanist readers of Gilroy have found his reduction of Africa's link to America into "tropes" and "themes" objectionable.[4] But all we need to do to appreciate the impact of Gilroy's line of inquiry is to turn to Cameroon's Achille Mbembe, who uses phrases that echo Gilroy's, although he does not explicitly align his project with the Atlantic rubric. According to Mbembe, the slave trade "was the event through which Africa was born to modernity" and the story of existence in Africa since the fifteenth century has been dominated by Europe. A true understanding of African historicity should therefore "presuppose a critical delving into Western history and the theories that claim to interpret it" (9). Mbembe diagnoses the maldevelopment of African politics to be a consequence of the normative contradictions of its modern experience:

> It was through the slave trade and colonialism that Africa came face to face with the *opaque and murky domain of power,* a domain inhabited by obscure drives and that everywhere and always makes animality and bestiality its essential components, plunging human beings into a never-ending *process of brutalization.* . . . Underlying the problems of arbitrariness and tyranny . . . lies the problem of *freedom from servitude and possibility of an autonomous African subject.* (14)

The main task of philosophy and policy making in Africa should, given these circumstances, be about calibrating the extent of the regime of brutality immanent to Africa's modern history as a postcolony or, to say the same thing, as an ex-slave farm. Without analyzing the etiology of the "obscure drives," scholars of the African postcolony will be mistaking symptoms for the disease and literality for the sense. The scourge of "tyranny" and "arbitrariness" will not relent unless the fundamental character of servitude which modern history and politics have apportioned to Africa is first analyzed. All existential notions that are derivable from African premodern self-certainties have been suspended by slavery and colonial conquests. Colonialism and slavery, in Mbembe's apt phrasing, tend to "freeze the law of the entity invaded" (183).

The operative syllogism in Mbembe and Gilroy's intellectual transnationalism is that the Atlantic facilitated both the slave trade and the creation of a single historical, philosophical, and, perhaps, cultural unit that supersedes natal notions like ethnicity. (Also implied is the idea that black people did not become Africans until after their conquest.) In order for them to survive in their new environment, New World blacks are compelled by normative forces of modernity to dissolve what may be called their "origins" in favor of a new identity. All the "essential factors" of black being, Gilroy and Mbembe seem to imply, "come into their right in the course of their development" within slavery and colonialism.[5]

The line of argument followed in this book's reading of histories and novels of slave rebellions in the United States, the Caribbean, and Africa departs from the kind of discursive transnationalism being practiced by Gilroy and Mbembe. I am not prepared, yet, to abandon the influence of nationalist and ethnocentric will on black intellectual reactions to slavery and colonialism. Nat Turner, who is not known to have read either Kant or Hegel, was inspired by a millenarian interpretation of the biblical apocalypse; however, the beginning point of his attempt to bring about his new world and new heaven is Southampton County, Virginia. It is from there, he thought, that the liberation of the whole world should begin. Toussaint L'Ouverture knew of the French Revolution, and, unlike Nat Turner, he had read secular texts about worldly freedom like the ones written by Abbéy Reynal. If C.L.R. James is to be believed, and I think he should, Toussaint lost control of the Haitian Revolution because he abandoned Haiti's specific nationalist needs too quickly and tried too hard to make Haiti into a tropical France.

This book's study of the rewriting of the history of black slave rebels in American, Caribbean, and African literary cultures is intended, at the level of abstraction, to interrogate the meaning of what Gilroy has very usefully called the slave's "counter-violence." In practice, the project interprets the uses to which writers, working under diverse "national" literary, historical, political, and intellectual traditions, put the efforts of black slaves who dared to "kill" their masters and break the norms of subjection. This study proceeds on the premise that the central contention in the making of modern black intellectual history concerns how to gauge the meaning of the attempts which black folks have made to cut the normative strings that bound their fate to the will of those who claim to be their masters. I should not be misunderstood as saying that black history and culture are not modern entities; it is an established point, I believe, that black political and cultural thought constituted crucial parts of modernity. Oral poetry, written literature, and history indicate that rebellion and other nonconformities are inherent features of modern slave (and colonial) societies. Nonetheless, it is my contention that while slavery and colonization may have brought black peoples into modernity, black people, as the stories of messianic slave rebels in literature and history show, first have to attack the grounds of their existence in modernity as subordinate beings bound to live only as slaves do under masters.

G.W.F. HEGEL: LORDSHIP AND BONDAGE

Although this book is mainly about the meaning of slave rebellions in black writing, it is important that we should cast a quick glance at Hegel's allegory of Lordship and Bondage for two reasons: (1) recent thinking about slavery and black culture takes its fundamental assumptions about cultural and intellectual relations from this text; (2) a different way of making abstractions about the relationship of black cultures to slavery can also be derived from Hegel's story. Implied in varying degrees of explicitness in the positions staked out by Mbembe and Gilroy is the concern that theoreticians of modern black histories have not dealt adequately with the ramifications of Hegel's abstractions on the range of actions, physical or spiritual, available to the slave. It is possible to argue, for example, that the starting point of Gilroy's "primal history of modernity . . . reconstructed from the slaves' point of view" (55) is Hegel's allegory of Lordship and Bondage.[6] In the same vein, Mbembe, who says that "the 'slave' is the forename we must give to a man or woman whose body can be degraded, whose life can be mutilated, and whose work and resources can be squandered—with impunity" (234), clearly thinks of the fate of the colonized in terms analogous to Hegel's views on the condition of the bondsman.

As Hegel recounts it, the awareness a consciousness has of itself exists in the mind of the self-conscious as something that emerges and is known as such in relation to another self-present and self-aware consciousness. On its own, a self-consciousness discovers that there is at least one other self-consciousness that operates like it and desires everything it wants: "each sees the other do the same as itself; each itself does what it demands on the part of the other, and for that reason does what it does, only so far as the other does the same" (230). In this interaction of self-consciousnesses, "each is the mediating term to the other, through which each mediates and unites itself with itself" (231).

So long as this order of mutual recognition and definition prevails, no knowledge of independent *self-consciousness as self-consciousness* can be gathered from the interactions. That is, each party involved in mutual self-recognition "has not set aside the opposition it involves and left it there, but has made its account with it and become reconciled to it" (83) and cannot yet claim something Hegel calls "self-conscious freedom." In order for the self-conscious entities that mutually recognize each other to attain that state, each party will try to annihilate all competing others. Hegel captures the essence of this contest for independent "self-conscious freedom" in the proverbial summary that says, "It is solely by risking life that freedom is obtained" (233). This notion resembles, I cannot but note, the idea stated axiomatically in Yorùbá as "*ogun layé*" (existence is war).

The parties in the combat for self-conscious freedom duel so viciously that only one will "live"; the others will "die." The consciousness that "lives" retains life or "independence without absolute negativity," and the one that "dies" succumbs to "'negation' of consciousness, negation without independence" and is thus left without the significance of actual recognition (233). Having survived the battle for freedom, the victorious consciousness actuates its new status—a form of *pure* self-consciousness—by reducing its defeated (and "dead") adversary into an entity defined by material immediacy and the non-essential validation it is made to render. According to Hegel, "The one is independent, and its essential nature is to be for itself; the other is dependent, and its essence is life or existence for another. The former is the Master, or Lord, the latter the Bondsman" (234).

We must note that the free Lord or Master that now "exists *for itself*" (234) is not identical to the cognate entity that entered the battle of existence earlier. While the new form (the Master) still "mediated with itself through an other consciousness" (234), the after-battle mediator is a degraded and diminished entity not close in any way to the opponent that entered the battle earlier. This "dead" mediator—the slave and, according to Mbembe, the colonized—is content in "thinghood." After conquest (or surrender), determinate existence controls the Bondsman ("the immediate self-consciousness" whose "absolute object" is "the simple ego" [234]), and the Master alone promulgates the essential laws that govern the Bondsman. Being an arrested self-consciousness, the Bondsman loses the ability to do unto the Master what the Master can do unto it. As Hegel further tells the story, the continued domination of the "dead" by the "living" generates another series of problems in that the fallen thinghood that emanates from the slave's capitulation is now simultaneously the placeholder of the slave's own effete (in)dependence and the material form in which the master experiences his victory (236). An immitigable gap, as it were, separates mastery from its experience. Even so, the slave's consciousness remains "unessential" in that the master need not reckon with it.

Hegel notes further that in the Bondsman's "serving and toiling" (237) is carried out his "total dissolution" (238) of independent self-consciousness. However, the same motions of "work and labor" (238) that manifest his spiritual nothingness also alert him to the exact character of his existence: "In the master, the bondsman feels self-existence to be something external, an objective fact; in fear self-existence is present within himself; in fashioning the thing, self-existence comes to be felt explicitly as his own proper being, and he attains the consciousness that he himself exists in its own right and on its own account" (239). It is not clear from this description whether the experience of "independence" enabled by the relation of the slave to his labor—which also services the master's existence—shall ever rise to the level of that which the Master enjoys in relation to the slave. In other words, Hegel does not state explicitly if the "dead" and enslaved self-consciousness can ever truly regain "life."

Hegel's allegory describes an almost unbreachable phenomenological enclosure within which entities are defined completely by "*a continuous relation of elements within their unity*" (93; emphasis added). In this enclosure, the slave is really not the invention of the master but its consciousness opposite and the master is the systemic name of the consciousness that is not scared by the possibility of dying. But it is evident beyond the compelling logic of the story that Hegel does not view the slave and the master as moral equivalents. He speaks of the master as some entity that cannot be blamed for being what it cannot help and depicts the slave as something that falls into its nothingness because it lacks the moral courage to embrace death. As Hegel writes later, "If a man is a slave, his own will is responsible for his slavery, just as it is its will which is responsible if a people is subjugated. Hence the wrong of slavery lies at the door not simply of enslavers or conquerors but of the slaves and the conquered themselves" (quoted in Buck-Morss 849).

SLAVERY, SOCIAL DEATH, AND THE TRUTH OF BLACK EXISTENCE

Hegel's systemic characterization of subjectivity, in my view, is the basis of his appeal to new conceptualizations of modern black cultural and intellectual history. As it is now conceived, black subjectivity, being a function of modern slavery, cannot "cut loose from its containing circumference" and, to paraphrase Hegel, obtain an existence all its own, gain freedom and independence on its own account (93). Gilroy is very clear about Hegel's place in his conceptualization of black modern intellectual and cultural history. He says, "Hegel's allegory . . . correctly places slavery at the natal core of modern sociality" (63) and supports that view with an explication of Frederick Douglass's depiction of his transfigurative fight with Edward Covey, the slave breaker. According to Gilroy, the common tenor of Douglass's three versions of his duel with Covey indicates that the articulate militant slave may have been rewriting—"a supplement if not exactly a trans-coding" (60)[7]—Hegel's allegory from the vantage point of his experience. At the end of Douglass's famous fight, Gilroy says, "It is the slave rather than the master who emerges . . . possessed of 'consciousness that exists for itself,' while his master becomes the representative of a 'consciousness that is repressed within itself' " (60). As if the slave lived his life to show Hegel something, Gilroy says Douglass embraces literal death over an abbreviated existence and chooses the "moment of jubilee" over the "pursuit of utopia by rational means" (68).[8] Douglass's narration of his act of rebellion "underscored the complicity of civilisation and brutality while emphasising that the order of authority on which the slave plantation relied cannot be undone without recourse to the counter-violence of the oppressed" (63).

This interpretation of the slave's "counter-violence" yields to the resistance paradigm of writing about African American cultures. But, unlike traditional accounts of foundational opposition, Gilroy is not convinced that Douglass's privileging of militant representation derives from a "black" aesthetics that exists outside the "normative" imperatives of relations engendered by slavery. The survival of the *objectively* fittest narrative pursued by Douglass is a feature of the philosophical and cultural dominant of Douglass's immediate modern world. The militant slave constitutes his self-consciousness within the very condition of his struggles, like all modern men and women: in favor of manly calculations of risk and benefits, for example, Douglass rejects as irrational the "black magic" of herbs deemed capable of protecting the slave against the white master's lash. Like a perfectly modern person, Douglass also realizes after the fight that "to make a contented slave, it is necessary to make a *thoughtless* one. It is necessary to darken his moral and mental vision . . . to *annihilate the power of reason*" (*Narrative* 315; emphasis added).

The dominant motifs of spiritual nothingness, emptiness, and the completely encircling macabre conviviality that Achille Mbembe uses to characterize modern African reality indicate that his conception of Africa's historical subjugation is not unlike the conditions captured in Hegel's allegory. Africans became slaves literally and conceptually at the moment of conquest, and the gross distortions apparent in Africa's modern history manifest the fate of the defeated party in the battle of self-consciousness. As far as Mbembe is concerned, to the question " 'Who are you in the world?' the African of this century could say without qualification, 'I am an ex-slave' " (237).[9]

Orlando Patterson, whose main interest is not to make grand statements about the black condition in the modern world, also adopts Hegel for his conceptualization of the meaning of slavery in *Slavery and Social Death*. Slavery, Patterson says in a concise definition filled with echoes of Hegel, "is the permanent, violent domination of natally alienated and generally dishonored persons" (13). Patterson argues that slavery, as a form of exercising power, is not at all peculiar, illogical, or strange. Everywhere and across centuries, the slave is a dishonored and powerless person whose main mark is *not his exploitation* but his dehumanization, his "social death." He agrees with Ali Abd Elwahed that "'all the situations which created slavery were those which commonly would have resulted, either from natural or social laws, in the death of the individual'" (quoted on p. 5). To this way of thinking, violence, or the threat of it, is inherent to slavery. Slavery begins at the moment of capture in war when the victim's life is spared so that power can be continually exercised over the captive's body afterward. After the war, violence is still administered liberally on the slave's body and the specter of death preserved, usually in social rituals, to remind the slave of his withheld fate. Conceptually, the slave is an "interim" person kept alive literally but treated as if he were dead, mainly through exclusions "from all formal, legally enforceable ties of 'blood,' and from any attachment to groups or localities other than those chosen for him by the master" (7).[10] The social institutions from which Patterson says the slave is excluded are nothing more than symptoms of what Hegel may call the "living" Master's transcendence.[11]

Patterson, Gilroy, and Mbembe all take Hegel's allegory very seriously: Patterson's definition of the enslaved as the "socially" dead casts in sociological terms Hegel's allegorical notion that the slave's consciousness is a "dead" one; by depicting pervasive tyranny in postcolonial Africa as concrete evidence of the as yet unremedied loss of self-consciousness that occurred in the conquest of Africans, Mbembe endorses the Hegelian interpretation of the slave's condition as that of abject, possibly fatal, loss; Gilroy—like Patterson, who concludes that "the first men and women to struggle for freedom . . . were freedmen" (342)—finds a fruitful and comforting prospect for analysis in Douglass's inversion of Hegel. Of the three authors, only Gilroy considers the theoretical consequence of the possibility of the slave restarting the battle for self-consciousness and extracting freedom from slavery's barbarity: by fighting Edward Covey and writing about it later, Gilroy says, Frederick Douglass single-handedly liberates himself into a "self-conscious freedom." Other writers seem to agree with Hegel that the fight has been concluded at the moment of surrender. While Gilroy's reading is remarkably different from the other studies in this respect, it is surprising that he is still reluctant to query the supremacy of the "containing circumference" of slavery. Gilroy is not willing to admit, as Neil Lazarus puts it, that "the counter-culture of modernity" may not be "a theory of modernity," or that the goal of the slave's violence may be different from the master's. Douglass clearly doubts the rationality of believing that ordinary herbs can influence a master's disposition toward a belligerent slave, but he still carries the root on his body according to the conjure man's precise instructions.

Douglass, perhaps, did not win the battle of self-consciousness after his fight with Covey, in spite of what he writes to the contrary. If, as Patterson says, slavery is "the permanent, violent domination of natally alienated and generally dishonored persons" (13), Douglass did not cease to be a slave after the fight. In the 1845 account of the duel, Douglass says, "I now resolved that, however long I might remain a slave in form, the day had passed forever when I could be a slave in fact" (299). I take these words to mean that the slave has vowed to bring about his own literal death, if the need arises. Without committing suicide, however, literal death can only come by the grace of the masters, who are not positioned to give it. Edward Covey cannot desire Douglass's literal death because the slave breaker's interest can be well served only if Douglass is alive in slavery. When the psychologically and philosophically "free" Douglass is caught while trying to leave the slave territory some years later, his life is spared again; this time the masters lock him up.

According to Alexandre Kojève, the sentiment Douglass expresses in his freedom resolution amounts to no more than a "stoicism" with which "the slave [still living under bondage] tries to persuade himself that he is actually free simply by knowing that he is free—that is, by having the abstract idea of freedom" (61). If one were to agree with Kojève, then Douglass's elegant resolution, so long as it remains a mental act, "obliges him to be content with talking" (62). But, as Kojève says, the slave knows that "freedom is not an empty word, a simple abstract idea, an unrealizable ideal" (63).[12] Hence, the slave still has to negate the master literally and not just intellectually. The most remarkable element of Douglass's biography, therefore, is not the counter-violence that did not end his bondage but the "counter-violence" his running away inflicts on the master.

In theory, as Douglass's treatment after his fight with Covey shows, options for resolving the battle of "consciousness" are three (life, death, or captivity) and not two (life or death). Sane warriors do not ordinarily enter a battle to be captured or killed but actually risk their lives to survive first, then capture or kill their adversaries. If, unfortunately, they end up in captivity, the burden of sustaining the defeated's life falls on the captor desiring to enslave, and not kill, a sworn adversary. The warrior that enslaves thus brings upon himself the responsibility of managing a reluctantly living person. That is why in slaveholding societies, there is a permanent tension that frequently breaks into outright wars between the master and the slave. Slavery breeds permanent unrest because the slave is constantly attempting to be free of the "normative" circumference instituted when the initiative to die was taken away from him, and also because the master, knowing that the slave may not at all be grateful that his life is saved, issues draconian regulations to prevent the slave from fulfilling his "death wish." The master has to devise preoccupations, or instruments of "social death," that would prevent the slave from thinking about restarting the war of captivity. One could say, therefore, that *preventing the slave's literal death is the beginning of mastery.* Once the master is instituted, I believe, death—his and his slave's—becomes anathema to him. The master is not, as such, defined alone by the will to live, as Hegel's allegory suggests, but also by the will to prevent the defeated from dying, either by suicide or through a rebellious mutiny.

To claim, as I am doing here, that the slave survives the moment of capture because the master is fulfilling a desire should not be misconstrued as saying that the slave lacks the capacity to exercise subjective will. Within slavery, the subjected person continues to seek an opportunity to exercise the will to "die," or, to say the same thing, to be free. Slave rebellions, or the fear of them, are constant preoccupations in all slave societies because the slave's wish to literally die conflicts with the master's desires to live and also to prevent the slave from exercising his death wish. *The condition of being enslaved, I would suggest, is that of struggling to terminate, by fomenting either the slave's or the master's literal death, the sham "deferral" of death which the master believes he has earned the power to give and take when the slave is captured.* When C.L.R. James says that slavery is the cause of slave rebellion, we ought to believe that he is not just being curt; he is stating a phenomenological truth that Hegel did not analyze in Lordship and Bondage. The slave may be melancholic, as Hegel suggests. It may also be true that the slave's consciousness entails, as Gilroy says, an "extended act of mourning" (63). The source of the slave's sadness is the unending regret of the master's prevention of the slave's literal death. The motivation for the slave's self-liberation struggle, which almost always involves some effort to rebel physically, also emanates from the desire to snap, once and for all, out of the melancholy that arises from the master's prevention of the bondsman's literal death.

The alternative captivity milieu being presented here is meant in part to reaffirm the claims of the intellectual tradition that says the slave's existence inherently consists of battling against forces that stifle it. When Frantz Fanon, for instance, applies the Hegelian allegory to the black condition under chattel slavery, he finds that the master in the modern Atlantic world "laughs at the consciousness of the slave. What he wants from the slave is not recognition but work" (*Black Skin, White Masks* 220). Fanon insists that the slave cannot induce full recognition from the master as long as he remains a slave and the master remains a master.[13] This discussion is also intended to indicate that it may be a misinterpretation to presume that the slave's struggle can one day result in his becoming the master qua master. Within the captivity environment against which the slave fights, there can only be one master who, once deposed, cannot be replaced. Knowing this, the object of the right thinking slave's striving would be the elimination of the office of the master. That is why, I believe, leaders of slave insurrections often speak in millenarian and apocalyptic terms of a new earth and a new heaven. Indeed, when Hegel is not writing about slavery, he acknowledges that normativity, because of its dependence on boundaries, invites a phenomenological unrest:

> The circle, which is self-enclosed and at rest, and, qua substance, holds its own moments, is an immediate relation, the immediate, continuous relation of elements with their unity, and hence arouses no sense of wonderment. But that an accident as such, when cut loose from its containing circumference,—that what is bound and held by something else and actual only by being connected with it,—should obtain an existence all its own, gain freedom and independence on its own account—this is the portentous power of the negative; it is the energy of thought, of pure ego. Death, as we may call that unreality, is the most terrible thing, and to keep and hold fast what is dead demands the greatest force of all. (93; emphasis added)

The cataclysmic death Hegel speaks of in this passage as something "unreal" and terrible has been rethought in the question Judith Butler poses as: "If subordination is the condition of possibility for agency, how might agency be thought in opposition to the forces of subordination?" (10). Butler cautions that the conundrum inherent to this question cannot be left unaddressed or else a logical aporia may transpose into political inertia. As Butler argues it, there is no doubt that slavery's normativity "initiates" the determinant facets of a slave's acts: "to persist in one's being means to be given over from the start to social terms that are never fully one's own" (28). But the slave is that subject duty bound to "desire something other than its continued 'social existence'" (28) and to test the contingency of norms. Certainly, the venturesome slave who acts on this desire and refuses to persist in the position assigned him or her within the norm faces "some kind of death" or dissolution (as Hegel suggests above). But acknowledging this fact should not lead to the fatalistic conclusion that there is no outside to the subjecting enclosure's power and affirming indirectly the naturalness of the norm. To use Judith Butler's terms, the slave rebel's life shows that "agency exceeds the power by which it is enabled" (15).

If slavery is "social death," as Orlando Patterson argues, what is slave rebellion? A short and direct answer will be that it is a sure means to "literal death." But that response will be inadequate because death, as Patterson has shown, entails more than the cessation of breath. In literature and history, I would say, the slave's rebellion is a name given to the path to a revolution (the annihilation of master and slave alike) that has no model. Rebellions crystallize the struggle to break the "normativity" that constraints existence, either as chattel slavery or colonialism, racism, or sexism. The world sought by the slave rebel, fundamentally a realm without masters and slaves, is always different from the one against which the struggle is launched. Antebellum African American novels projected that realm as Emancipation; between Emancipation and 1965, historians and novelists believed that the future may come in the form of socialism; in late-twentieth-century Africa, decolonization was expected to usher in that masterless and slaveless future. Although in every instance the future never arrived exactly as envisaged, I hesitate to label the projections as futile strivings against "normativity." Butler makes a similar point more cogently in the following words: "Without a repetition that risks life—in its current organization—how might we begin to imagine the contingency of that organization, and performatively reconfigure the contours of the conditions of life?" (28–29).

Recent empirical studies of shipping records show that rebellions were frequent on slave ships and that the resisters did not act in vain. Mutinies or some other form of the slave's counter-violence occurred on about one in ten transatlantic slave voyages and constituted the largest single set of risk to slavers. Planning against mutinies forced ship owners to carry more personnel and equipment than they would otherwise. The extra cost imposed by anti-mutiny precautions reduced by no less than 10 percent the total number of slaves that would have been shipped across the Atlantic.[14] I see in these studies that the hopes for liberation which the writers studied below reposed in the historical slave rebel were not misplaced.

2

NAT TURNER AND PLOT MAKING IN EARLY AFRICAN AMERICAN FICTION

Eugene Genovese clinches his analysis of the relative insignificance of violent revolts—events he described as the only truly "political action" that could have "challenged the power of the [slaveholding] regime" (598)—in antebellum African American consciousness with the evidence observed from the general silence of slave autobiographies on such topics: "as the slave narratives suggest, southern slaves as a whole know little about the slave rebels" (597). The silence is considered a sure archival testimony to the absence in slave life and culture of a sustained need to rebel, and the possibility of it being a textual strategy is ignored. Like contemporary African American literary theorists who also rely on slave narratives for outlining the forms of the thought trends that animated antebellum black literature, Genovese translates into larger intellectual and political pathways the literary byways specific to slave autobiographers that take after Frederick Douglass.

The story of slave rebellions and antebellum black American literary and cultural consciousness is not as straightforward as it is portrayed in statements that equate the themes of slave autobiographies and general slave concerns. As shown in the opening section of this chapter, the story of the specific form in which Harriet Jacobs reports the repercussion of Nat Turner's revolt in her North Carolina locality demonstrates that the slave autobiographer's explicit textual statements are not the only fruitful means of understanding the complexities of antebellum African American thought and politics. Jacobs's story shows that factors of literary production not directly reflective of the slave's inner consciousness determined the contents of the slaves' autobiography.[1]

Let us first consider some details of Harriet Jacobs's rendering of the effect of Nat Turner's little insurrection on her hometown of Edenton, North Carolina. When the news of the "great commotion" (63) touched off by Nat Turner and his collaborators reached Jacobs's town, able-bodied white men quickly gathered a fully armed militia to terrorize the black community, harassing innocent black people, whipping them without mercy, some for as many as 500 lashes, and framing them for sundry violations. During the frenzy, some "searchers scatter[ed] powder and shot" in the belongings of slaves and then tipped off other patrol units to discover and use them as proofs of conspiracy to rebel. A black preacher who kept "a few parcels of shots" for his wife's weighing scales was arrested and tortured for violating ammunition laws. He would have been summarily executed had some members of "the better class of the community" not intervened. In Jacobs's household, the mob seized one of her letters on the suspicion that it might be a communication of conspiracy. The local black church was demolished and blacks were barred from congregating without a white person present. The slaves were so thoroughly intimidated that a man who "had not even heard the name of Nat Turner," but "had not the fortitude to endure scourging," confessed falsely to knowing about the revolt (67). The confusion subsided only when the slaveholding classes realized that their "property is not safe from the lawless rabble they have summoned to protect them" (67). Jacobs's experience agrees in almost every detail with other historical records of slaveholders' response to actual and rumored, "great" or minor, insurrections.[2]

While this story alone—especially given that similar episodes are not reported in other "great" slave narratives—may not be enough to make a case that enslaved Americans studied and internalized the import of their masters' fearsome reaction to insurrections, its narration of the mass terror they organized and supervised brings into view the masters' considerable anxiety over the possibility that their own local slaves may have harbored the kind of deadly thoughts that Turner and his men acted upon in Virginia. Jacobs's report seems specifically intended to attack the masters' paternalist assurances about their slaves. The narratorial introduction, for example, wonders in a mocking tone: "Strange that they should be alarmed, when their slaves were so 'contented and happy'!" (63). Bruce Mills has proposed that this "isolated and transitory" (257) report is most meaningful when read within Jacobs's larger abolitionist design and, perhaps, not as an index of a particularly militant outlook.

The story of how the Turner event gets into Jacobs's narrative, well told by Bruce Mills, says a great deal about the indirect relationship of conscious intent to what is published in slave-authored records of slave rebellions. Jacobs's original draft was to end with a chapter about John Brown's attack on Harper's Ferry, but her editor, Lydia Maria Child, advised her to replace that topic with the story of her grandmother's death because the fresh national uproar provoked by John Brown "does not naturally come" into the story and will dissipate the force of the narrative's revelation of the effects of the perverse structure of plantation sexual order on the slave woman's domestic life.[3] That Child's suggestion was followed is revealed in the last paragraph of Jacobs's narrative where the author fondly recollects her grandmother's protective affection: "It has been painful to me, in many ways, to recall the dreary years I passed in bondage. I would gladly forget them if I could. Yet the retrospection is not altogether without solace; for with those gloomy recollections come tender memories of my good old grandmother, like light, fleecy clouds floating over a dark troubled sea" (201). In the Civil War climes of the narrative's publication, Jacobs's imageries of gentle clouds counterbalancing the sea's stormy waves "calm more than agitate" (Mills 257).[4]

But Mrs. Child did not just ask that the potentially agitating narrative references to John Brown should be dropped; she also advised Jacobs to replace her discussions of the persecution suffered by blacks after the Brown campaign with her recollections "of the outrages committed on the colored people in Nat Turner's time" (Jacobs 244). At the time these suggestions were being made, the Brown incident was less than a year old and would have been fresher in the reader's memory than the Turner revolt which occurred twenty-eight years earlier, when Jacobs herself was just about eighteen. Child's advice that Jacobs should refer obliquely to the threat posed by slave rebellion to the nation's social well-being with an older event instead of the fresher John Brown incident fits the typical usage of the Turner event in abolitionist popular press, folklore, and fiction. Here in the slave narrative, and, as we shall see momentarily, in fiction, the black writer is being counseled by her editor (who is sincerely devoted to the abolitionist cause) to avoid referring to a fresh anti-slavery uprising.

The editor's urging Jacobs to recall the distant Turner revolt steers a middle course between totally excluding the slave rebel's story and fully endorsing violent actions. With this strategy, the text would sway readers "to be morally outraged" without "agitating" them. This middle course may also be reflecting the waning in the late 1850s—especially after the Dred Scott decision—of the long-standing resistance of many abolitionists to what was then called "violent means." (In 1836, for example, a member of the Philadelphia anti-slavery society left the organization because it supported a resolution affirming nonviolence. A totally different scenario prevailed in 1859 at a Massachusetts anti-slavery meeting where the motion was passed "'that resistance to slave holders and slave hunters is obedience to God, and a sacred duty to man . . . that it is the right and duty of the North . . . to instigate the slaves to insurrection'" [Demos 524].)[5]

The most pressing inference I would like to draw from the editorial exchanges between Lydia Maria Child and Harriet Jacobs is that the relative absence of specific references to slave rebellions in slave autobiographies might have arisen from the peculiar difficulties of depicting black political violence in texts addressed primarily to a largely pacifist abolitionist audience. Further evidence of the slaves' general relationship to emancipatory mass violence should be sought, I would add, in sources other than the literal claims of the archives generated under the auspices of abolitionism prior to 1850.[6]

I argue in this chapter that the prominence of slave insurrection plots in early African American fiction invites a reconsideration of some of the paradigmatic uses of the thematic features of the slave narrative in the writing of antebellum black American literary history. A considerable part of abolitionist African American fiction, it would be shown, took its distinctive form by extending the conventional closure of the typical fugitive slave's journey in Canada or a free state. In Frederick Douglass's *The Heroic Slave* (1853), William Wells Brown's *Clotel* (1853), and Martin Delany's *Blake* (1859), three of the earliest attempts at explicitly abolitionist fiction in antebellum African American writing, the runaway slave usually returns to, or remains in, the South until implicated in a planned or actual slave revolt. Between 1853 and the beginning of the Civil War, roughly the same era the abolitionist movement began to accept the moral logic of anti-slavery violence, the plot outlines of African American fiction about slavery foreground slave rebellions and slave rebels so prominently that they seem to be conscious attempts to correct for the exclusion of such topics in autobiographical narratives.

Placing escaped slaves in the South and embroiling them in revolts, I suggest, allows these abolitionist novelists to create a culture hero that is very different from the well-known writer-protagonist of the slave narrative. Nat Turner's brief rebellious career, as recorded in Thomas Gray's *Confessions,* is the unacknowledged source of this model of resistance, which was largely created by writers who themselves were highly successful producers of slave autobiographies. The first section discusses (1) the plot structure of black antebellum stories of rebellion, (2) the difficulties of representing Nat

Turner as a cultural hero, and (3) a close reading of the tortuous collaboration of Turner and Thomas Gray in *The Confessions.* The second part of the chapter describes how the jagged edges of the narrative structure of Martin Delany's *Blake,* the longest of these stories attempting to give a literary form to the slave insurrectionist's plot, can be evened out if the novel is viewed as an innovative fusion of the aborted fugitive slave's escape plot and the failed/suspended slave rebellion story. The chapter concludes with a discussion of how plot patterns in black antebellum fiction of slave rebellion can be integrated into main currents of African American literary history.

"A NOVEL ADVENTURE": PLOTTING SLAVE REBELLION

In *Clotel,* the title character, one of Thomas Jefferson's two black children, successfully escapes from Mississippi, passing as a Spanish gentleman. After traveling as far north as Ohio, she parts ways with a fellow fugitive who has been passing as her body servant. While her companion flees to Canada, Clotel heads for Virginia, driven by what the narrator describes as "that over-willingness of woman to carry out the prompting of the finer feelings of her heart" (251). When she arrives at Richmond, the Nat Turner "disturbance" has just been quelled and the entire state, much like in Jacobs's South Carolina, is in the middle of its panic response to the bloody revolt. One of the vigilante groups roaming the state searches Clotel and finds women's apparel in her suitcase. After further investigation gives away Clotel's cover, she is arrested and locked up in a Washington cell from which she escapes again. With the jailers closing in on her, she stops running and dives into the Potomac, killing herself at some point between the White House and the Capitol. Thus, the story that starts out as a traditional fugitive slave tale detours into a peculiar tragic mulatto narrative complicated by the Turner insurrection.

Clotel's plot introduces some innovations to the conventions of narrating black antebellum experience in fiction: the protagonist's traveling as far north as Ohio before veering back south tropes upon the course of the typical slave narrative and, more important, the direct linkage of the tragic mulatta's fate to the slaveholders' fierce response to the Turner rebellion fuses a slave narrative and a "failed" rebellion in the life of one character. This innovative amalgamation could not have thrived in the traditional abolitionist cultural work that generally shunned "violent means" and endorsed only truthful narratives. Although Clotel's act repeats the tragic mulatta's textually obligatory act of self-destruction, the causative role of the state's reaction to the larger violence designed and executed by Turner in the events leading to the suicide constitutes a politically novel way of formulating the tragic fate of a freedom-seeking black person.

The most notable aspects of Frederick Douglas's *The Heroic Slave,* like *Clotel* published in 1853, are also connected to a violent rebellion. Madison Washington, the namesake of a historical Washington who led a successful revolt aboard the slaving brig *Creole* in 1841,[7] flees from Virginia to Canada, after a five-year sojourn in a maroon camp. Believing that his freedom is incomplete with his wife still in bondage, Washington gets pulled back south, like Clotel, by family concerns. The strong filial attachment Brown calls a peculiarly feminine attribute, we now see, overpowers the chivalrous Washington,[8] who, after failing to raise enough funds to buy his wife's liberty, reverses the slave narrative plot and returns to his old master's plantation to smuggle her out. Like Clotel, he is discovered and chased. Unlike Clotel, however, he is captured and his beloved wife killed. On his journey to New Orleans after being sold down south, Washington and eighteen other slaves take over the slave vessel and force the crew to steer them to the free British colony of Grenada.

Washington's giving up his freedom in Canada, his returning to Virginia, and his daring struggles both on shore and on the sea countervail the usually amicable ending of the runaway tale. Here, the same Frederick Douglass whose autobiography perfects the form of the slave narrative extends and supplants the fugitive slave plot with that of a dissatisfied runaway. Douglass's revision indicates that in the decade leading to the Civil War black, abolitionist yearnings may have outgrown the classical runaway tales that end in the free North.

Martin Delany's *Blake,* like the other two stories, revises the fugitive slave's plot. Blake, the leader of a band of runaway slaves, reaches Canada like Douglass's Madison Washington. He too abandons Canada for a "southward" journey, this time to Cuba, where he finds his wife and gets to free her under Cuba's complex slave laws. Perhaps self-consciously, Delany titles the chapter in which Blake begins his southward journey "A *Novel* Adventure" (157; emphasis added). Blake's story, like that of Washington and Clotel, gets entangled in armed insurrectionist plots. Blake joins the underground Cuban resistance movement before traveling on a slave ship, in a reverse Middle Passage itinerary, to Dahomey. "Dressed as a native" (219), he infiltrates King Gaza's security cordon and spreads anti-slavery messages. On the return journey, Blake plots a slave ship mutiny that never breaks out. Landing in Cuba again, his ship barely escaping British anti-slavery gunboat patrols, he is elected commander of the resistance forces. The story closes with the conspirators postponing all actions until a "proper" time because their plans have been betrayed to the Spanish authorities.

The narrative plots summarized here rewrite the well-known self-centered quests of the slave autobiography by depicting the escape model of resistance to slavery as one road to freedom that even successful runaways find unfulfilling. By extending the established runaway plot, reworking the details of historical revolts, inventing others, and even broaching the possibility of a transatlantic rebellious solidarity of the slaving classes, the texts project a resistance model that emphasizes the slaves' awareness of the norm-breaking potential of violent rebellions.

PLOTTING BLACK REBELLION: WHITHER NAT TURNER?

The first of these novels was published more than half a century after Gabriel Prosser nearly pulled off an insurrection in Virginia in 1800, thirty-one years after the betrayal of Denmark Vesey's plot, and twenty-two years after the Nat Turner incident.[9] Among the historical plots, only Turner's got off the ground. Turner's tale was never written in his own hands—I will discuss below how he insinuates himself into the Gray pamphlet—and neither Prosser nor Vesey left any memoirs. Given the lack of participant accounts of the rebel plotters' thoughts and deeds, that Douglass, Brown, Jacobs, and Delany make heroes of rebellious slaves is noteworthy. That these fictional portraits appeared in the decade preceding the Civil War signals a concert of efforts to draw attention to the full range of political and cultural alternatives available for prosecuting the slave's quest for freedom.

As innovative as these stories are, the problem of historical plausibility as dictated by conditions in the United States limits imagination. None, for instance, involves a successful rebellion on U.S. soil. Douglass's *The Heroic Slave* follows history in the expatriation of Madison Washington's success to Granada.[10] As it is in history, the named principal insurrectionists in *Clotel* kill only a few planters before they are caught. Among the rebel leaders not drawn directly from history, only the fair-skinned Horatio Green is given an opportunity to verbalize his thoughts on liberty, and the motivation ascribed to him repeats the miscegenation theory of blood incompatibility: "Aware of their blood connection with their owners, these mulattoes labour under the sense of their personal and social injuries; and tolerate, if they do not encourage in themselves, low and vindictive passions" (252). Nothing hitherto unknown is said about Turner. *The Heroic Slave* too does not waiver noticeably from historical facts.

Of the three stories being used for illustration here, *Blake* displays the most militant tendencies. The novel's dark hero has a cogent understanding of the philosophy of slavery and a grand plan for subverting it. During his travels all over the South to mobilize fellow slaves for rebellion, Blake speaks with the conviction that slavery is an inherently violent institution that can only be successfully destroyed with commensurate organized violence. His journeys take him to a maroon hideout of Nat Turner and Denmark Vesey's confederates, where he is consecrated as "a priest of the order of High Conjurors" (114). By becoming a "seven finger High-glister" (115), he inherits the political legacy of Turner and Vesey. A similar initiation into the masonry of black rebellion is repeated in Cuba when the Conspiracy elects him a commander. Its self-conscious radical intent notwithstanding, no insurrection breaks out in the novel, although events are moved offshore to Cuba. For black abolitionist novelists, the license of fiction appears not to be strong enough to enable the creation of a native heroic slave rebellion.

Black novelists were not the only writers for whom the literary representation of the Turner model of slave emancipation was a great difficulty. A few weeks after the Turner revolt, the 17 September 1831 issue of *The Liberator* carried a "folk" account of black heroism dealing with Gabriel Prosser's 1800 insurrection plot. In the story, culled from the *Albany Evening Journal* and titled "Gabriel's Defeat," three black men are spotted riding their master's horses without his authority. The slaveholding community, which already suspects that some "colored people" are planning "to spread slaughter and devastation among the whites," arrests the slaves and compels them to confess to treason. To catch the leader of the plot, the state governor and some unnamed gentlemen put forward a $10,000 bounty that is doubled within a few days. After Gabriel's arrest the narrative flips into a flashback—a literary device not commonly found in folk narratives—about his life before the insurrection plot. Gabriel is revealed to be an exceptional slave who manumitted himself for the exorbitant price of $500. At his trial, the defiant Gabriel tells his accusers that "he had traveled expressly through the Southern States by night, riding down man and horses, in preparing the Africans for his measures—and that he had formed in caves and remote places, depots of arms." (All of the first section of Delany's novel expands upon the broad outlines of a similar undertaking by Henry Blake.) At his sentencing, Gabriel relates to the court, in words that are very similar to the ones spoken by Douglass's Madison Washington, that slaves "'have as good a right to be free from your oppression, as you had to be free from the tyranny of the king of England.'" He also predicts that his "example will raise up a Gabriel, who will, Washington-like, lead on the Africans to freedom.'" Gabriel's execution is gruesome: he is torn to pieces by horses attached to each of his four limbs.[11] Parts of this narrative clearly resemble some aspects of the stories of the heroic rebels discussed above: unflagging courage, ability to read, willingness to lead selflessly, speaking to white interlocutors on the justness of slave revolts, and so on.

Probably because they suspected that Gabriel's adventure is a panegyric for the contemporary Nat Turner, the pro-slavery editors of the *Richmond*

Enquirer promptly repudiated what they called the "falsities" of the story. They snickered that Gabriel is neither a Pole nor a Greek but a Bandit, renamed the story "a silly romance from beginning to end," and accused "the man who penned it" of deliberately dressing up "the Bandit Gabriel as a Hero—and for that purpose has not hesitated to forge statements to suit his case." In short, they sought to replace the Gabriel "romance" with truthful history and journalism. In Richmond at that time, it seems, a black insurrectionist cannot rightly be a literary hero.[12]

But history and journalism did not successfully destroy fiction. When John Brown attacked Harper's Ferry about three decades later, the same story resurfaced. According to Thomas Higginson, the Philadelphia press "resuscitated" it and other publications copied it extensively (344). Although Higginson believes the story to be false in every respect, he commends its being "fresh, spirited, and full of graphic and interesting details" (344). Higginson also says that the substance of the "romance" was condensed into a folk song.[13]

To commemorate Turner in 1831, the "romancers" exhumed the memory of the long dead Gabriel. To remark on the 1859 exploits of John Brown, another militant abolitionist, popular imagination went back again to 1800. At the brink of the Civil War in 1861, Lydia Maria Child, as noted earlier, advised Harriet Jacobs to substitute a recollection of the thirty-year-old Turner revolt for an account of John Brown's very fresh actions. Nat Turner's exploits seem to be especially unapproachable directly in folk "romance," the slave narrative, and even black abolitionist fiction.[14]

THE CONFESSIONS OF NAT TURNER

A first person quasi-autobiographical story about Turner exists in Thomas Gray's *Confessions of Nat Turner*. For my purpose here, the most intriguing aspect of this pamphlet is not the veracity of its details about Turner's life but the striking similarities of its plot structure to antebellum black fiction of slave rebellion and the folkloric "Gabriel's Defeat." Gray's little book crosses, like the works of fiction discussed above, the "aborted" fugitive slave narrative and the "failed" rebellion. The *Confessions* reads partly like what Robert Stepto has called an "eclectic" slave narrative in which authenticating devices are assembled, unsubordinated to the control of a single authorial experience. The book is prefaced with markers of juridical truth like the copyright issued by Edmund J. Lee in the District Court in the District of Columbia, a statement of attestation signed by members of the court that convicted Turner, and another attestation confirming the identity of the Court members. The string of authentication continues at the end of the pamphlet with a reproduction of the charge sheet and summary of court proceedings, a list of the victims of the rebellion, and a table of the accused and their various sentences. These authentication moves attest to Gray's "slave narrative" design.

The slave narrative intent continues in the opening sentence that "quotes" Turner on his motivation for leading a rebellion: "Sir,—You have asked me to give a history of the motives which induced me to undertake the late insurrection, as you call it—To do so I must go back to the days of my infancy, and even before *I was born*" (44; emphasis added). The italicized clause points to the slave narrative striving of the story.[15] Turner is also reported as saying that his unusual childhood prepared him for the work he is going to do later in life: like the hero of "Gabriel's Defeat," he says, "I was intended for some great purpose" (44).

Speaking further like a fugitive slave narrator, Turner relates the process by which he becomes literate: "I acquired it with the most perfect ease, so much so, that I have no recollection whatever of learning the alphabet—but to the astonishment of the family, one day, when a book was shown me to keep me from crying, I began spelling the names of different objects" (45). He also emphasizes the life-changing impact of literacy on him: "When I got large enough to go to work, while employed, I was reflecting on many things that would present themselves to my imagination, and whenever an opportunity occurred of looking at a book, when the school children were getting their lessons, I would find many things that the fertility of my own imagination had depicted to me before" (45).

After becoming literate, it seems as if the ability to decipher divine signs provokes in Turner an unbounded desire for freeing the masses of slaves. Now, he can *read* divine injunctions that direct him to lead an insurrectionist plot which will end slavery and reconstruct the world. He says, "These revelations being made known to me, I began to direct my attention to this great object, to fulfill the purpose for which, by this time, I felt assured I was intended" (46). In this quotation, as in several other statements, Turner joins the acquisition of literacy to decoding "the language of prophecy"[16] that foretells the violent destruction of slavery. The "great day of judgment" (47) and the "fight against the serpent" (48), as described in the book of Revelation, meant for Turner a call to plot a bloody end to the evil of slavery.

But before giving a detailed account of the bloody events he engineered to carry out the spiritual directives against slavery, the narrative takes a little detour to include the story of how Turner abandoned the chance to run away. After he has reached a full understanding of his life goal, namely to seek freedom for all, his first impulse is to pursue the fugitive slave's course like his father: "I was placed under an overseer, from whom I ran away—and after remaining in the woods thirty days, I *returned* to the astonishment of the Negroes on the plantation, who thought I had made my escape to some other part of the country, as my father had done before" (46; emphasis added). Had Turner taken this path to freedom, he would have joined the great company of runaways in typical slave narratives. His rejecting this conventional route leads him back to rebellion. Turner's path to insurrection is the model later followed by the rebellious protagonists created by Brown, Delany, and Douglass.

Questions that have developed about the text, mainly in the debates that greeted the publication of William Styron's *The Confessions of Nat Turner,* include: Is this book really a confession? Could Gray's motive be altruistic when it is clear that he is under severe financial pressures at the time of the Turner revolt? Could Gray have been harboring a secret (or perverse) admiration for Turner? Could the patently intelligent Turner willingly have made himself the demented figure *Confessions* portrays him to be? There are no unambiguous responses to any of these questions.[17] I argue here that if read very closely, the text, regardless of Thomas Gray's motives and political schemes, reflects, perhaps unwittingly, Turner's undoubtedly active contribution to the form of the narrative. Because, as William Andrews concludes in *To Tell a Free Story,* "Turner needs Gray as much as Gray needs Turner" (76), I am willing to attribute literary influence to this story in spite of the controversy of authorship and the immanently racist politics of representation that surrounds it.

At the most basic level, the text nudges the reader in at least two directions, one controlled by Turner (the ostensible speaker and subject of the narrative) and the other by Gray (the interrogating listener-writer). Turner's voice gives an account of exoneration and the story of how things came to be, but the writer's, for the most part, attempts to rework that perspective into a narrative of maniacal delusion and guilt. In effect, one narrator seeks a "confession," and the other recounts a *history* of motives. That it is possible for a reader to separate the voice that tells the history of motives from the one that speaks of guilt, as the discussion below insists, suggests that Turner may have succeeded in making Gray a collaborator[18] and, consequently, *Confessions* into a very influential text in nineteenth-century African American narrative, as attested by the central plot line of stories that morph the itinerary of the fugitive slave into slave revolts.

In parts where Turner's experience is the primary focus, events are represented as inevitable acts. So, Turner depicts himself as not being in a position to either disobey God and his parents, or disappoint the larger community that tells him he is destined to devise great events. His followers, he also shows, are convinced of his deep and sincere spirituality, free of "conjuring and such like tricks" (46).

But the eyewitness of great deeds is not in full charge of the narrative. His narrative partner, the writer, often superimposes a rhetoric of guilt on the story of inevitability and converts into delusions what the eyewitness presents as bare facts of spirituality and obedience to divine instructions. The preface, for example, says that the pamphlet "is a faithful record" of Turner's "frankly acknowledged . . . full participation in all the *guilt* of the transaction" (41). However, in the authenticating court records, he "pleaded not guilty; saying to his counsel, that he did not feel so" (56). This plea is corroborated in the "confession" proper where Turner, taking care to show that he is never a slacker, at no point admits to any wrongdoing.

Narrative authorities contrast further in the parts that catalogue the extent of "terror and devastation" (50) perpetrated by the Turner band. On one hand, Turner continues the inevitability story, representing his deeds as acts of war, his confederates as soldiers, and his ultimate goal as an inspired military crusade. On the other hand, the voice I have been calling the writer's reports murderous mayhem. In the list of victims, whenever a woman, a child, or an entire family is killed, it is often reported as murder: the Turner family was murdered, and so were Mrs. Reese, Mrs. Turner, Mrs. Newsom, Mrs. Walker and children, and the families of Jacob Williams and Mrs. Vaughan. Grown men, in contrast, are typically reported as having fallen to the insurgents' "*work of death.*" Those taken in the "work of death" include Messrs. Bryant, Francis, and Peter Edwards. Mrs. Reese's son fell into "the sleep of death" (49). This difference in diction appears to be a further manifestation of authorial dissonance between Turner, the participant, and Gray, the writer. The implication of guilt and criminal malice inherent in "murder" and "untimely death," terms reserved almost exclusively for describing female victims, seems to agree with the confession intent advertised in the title. Turner and his followers, however, seem to have approached their killings as the outcome of a righteous call to arms. Killing, for them, is "*work.*" It should be considered significant that in the textual "epilogue" where Gray editorializes on the "confession" trope, he parodies what looks like Turner's choice of words: "Few indeed, were those who escaped *their* work of death" (56; emphasis added). This unmarked quotation is clearly intended to mock Turner; but it also helps the close reader to attribute words to him, since it is only to Turner and his men that killing is "work."

That Turner views his actions in strictly depersonalized terms is further clarified in the military language he uses to describe the movements of his followers. During the encounters, he acts like a commanding general, giving orders to his men to "mount and march" and to "halt and form" (50–51).

After invading the house of Mrs. Travis, the second on their itinerary, the rebels regroup like true soldiers: "I formed them in a line of soldiers, and after carrying them through all the maneuvers I was master of, marched them off" (49). Turner also describes the end of his short-lived campaign as a "defeat," his initial withdrawal as a "retreat," his sending of men to spy on the attacking white men as a reconnaissance (52), and his effort to boost his shrinking ranks as a recruitment drive.

In the section that catalogues the killings, Turner is reported as admitting, without remorse, that he spilled "the first blood" (49). He is also reported to have said, "On my way back . . . the white families having fled, we found no more victims to *gratify our thirst for blood,* we stopped at Majr. Ridley's quarter for the night" (52; emphasis added). The words attributed to Turner here imply impenitent wrongdoing, if not outright depravity. But in narrative parts that deal with events that could have been experienced by Turner only, blood is strictly associated with divine revelations about freedom and salvation. Turner says, for example, that

> while laboring in the field, I discovered drops of *blood* on the corn as though it were dew from heaven—and I communicated it to many, both white and black, in the neighborhood—and I then found on leaves in the woods hieroglyphic characters, and numbers, with the forms of men in different attitudes, portrayed in *blood,* and representing the figures I had seen before in the heavens. And now the Holy Ghost had revealed itself to me, and made plain the miracles it had shown me—For as the *blood* of Christ had been shed on this earth, and had ascended to heaven for the salvation of sinners, and was now returning to earth again in the form of dew—and as the leaves on the trees bore the impression of the figures I had seen in the heavens, it was plain to me that the Saviour was about to lay down the yoke he had borne for the sins of me, and the great day of judgment was at hand. (47; emphasis added)

In this passage, blood is consistently linked, as in Turner's main inspiration, the Book of Revelation, to regeneration and not gratuitous killing. Gray's editorializing in the "epilogue" gives away the possible source of the culturally emotive terms used in passages that insinuate Turner's admission of guilt. For example, the writer says Turner's calm composure has a blood-chilling effect on him: "The calm, deliberate composure with which he spoke of his late deeds and intentions, the expression of his fiend-like face when excited by enthusiasm, still bearing the stains of the blood of helpless innocence about him; clothed with rags and covered with chains; yet daring to raise his manacled hands to heaven, with a spirit soaring above the attributes of man; I looked on him and my *blood curdled* in my veins" (55; emphasis added). This passage, I suggest, reveals Gray to be the source of the words that speak of Turner's revolt as depraved bloodletting. It is Gray who views the killing of slaveholders as a wanton spilling of "the blood of helpless innocence." To Turner, none of the victims is killed out of sheer malice.

The interpretation proposed here is not to exonerate Nat Turner, whom the text shows, in my view, to have ably defended his cause. It is also not intended to discredit Thomas Gray. All I am after is a useful way to recover Turner's participation in the tortuous collaboration that produced *Confessions* for literary history, and to show that the fusion of the aborted slave narrative and the failed rebellion in the plot lines of abolitionist African American novels of slave insurrection are derived from the details of Turner's life. In Gray's story, the writer and his protagonist do not share one political goal: the writer wants to create a villain out of a slave rebel who believes his acts are heroic. When Douglass, Brown, and Delany returned to the slave rebellion theme in the years leading to the Civil War, they reshaped the outline of Gray's story by harmonizing the writer's abolitionist aim with that of the heroic rebel.

LENDING FORM TO AN INSURRECTION THAT HAS NO MODEL: MARTIN DELANY'S *BLAKE*

Blake's lumbering plot and the narrative difficulties critics have associated with it encapsulate the practical problems involved in converting the literary plot-making patterns outlined above into artful narratives. In this novel, insurrectionist plotting constitutes the central narrative preoccupation, and the normal course of a rebellion—planning, mobilizing, execution, the emotional fluctuations that accompany failure and success, and so on—takes up greater space than in similar stories. Clotel walks into a rebellion that is not of her making, and Madison Washington springs into a mutiny only as a last ditch effort to save his life. In either case, the conventional escape itinerary of the slave narrative predominates until unforeseen circumstances force the protagonist into something else. Henry Blake, in contrast, originally intends to rouse all slaves who will follow his secret "plan for a general insurrection" (39) to fight for freedom. Precisely because it is driven by a rebellion plot, the novel exhibits fully both the problems and prospects of novels of its kind. My main goal in this section is to read critical concerns about the story as symptoms of the problems that are specific to the creation of militant abolitionist fiction in the antebellum United States. What narrative obstacles confront the black novelist who wants to give a fictional form to an idea that has no model—a successful land-based slave rebellion in the United States—is the key question.

Most readers of *Blake* consider its radical politics to be its main contribution to antebellum African American literary history. Focusing on how the story digests for abolitionist thought the political implications of (1) the Cuban slave uprisings of the 1840s, (2) the debate over American plans to annex Cuba in the 1850s, (3) the Fugitive Slave Law of 1853, and (4) the Dred Scott decision of 1857, Eric Sundquist praises the novel for its "compelling portrait of a revolutionary ethos" in the actions of a protagonist who combines "the vision of Nat Turner" and "the commanding intelligence and authority of Toussaint" (*To Wake the Nations* 183–84). Against the U.S. national dream of a hemispheric slave economy, Sundquist notes, the novel proposes "the vision of a modern black state that unites the splintered [freedom] aspirations of the peoples of the African diaspora" (188). Except for believing that Delany's aims are not that altruistic, Robert Levine agrees with Sundquist on almost every point regarding Delany's novelistic intervention in the discussion of the future of slavery in the United States in the 1850s. Delany, Levine suggests, wrote *Blake* to argue for the superiority of his own racial nationalist politics over competing ideas supported by Frederick Douglass. The "intelligent, 'full-blooded' black leader" (180) portrayed in Blake is a thinly concealed attempt at self-fashioning on the part of his creator (177).

On the way to pointing out the virtues of the novel's radical abolitionist politics and the author's rather precocious transnationalism, critics almost never fail to enumerate its countless artistic flaws. "The novel's multiple and conflicting sources, purposes, and audiences, and also its truncated ending," Levine points out, recommend that readers should be skeptical of formulating a "'coherent' formalist reading" of the story (179). The story's "interesting formal devices," Sundquist says, are "rather awkwardly crafted" and "more often resemble a manifesto or a political anatomy of slave culture" (183). Roger Hite believes that the book will reward mainly "those less interested in judging the artistic and aesthetic merits of a work, and more intent upon understanding the rhetorical design of art as social protest" (192). Germain Binvennu suspects that the novel's "serious stylistic flaws" may be partly responsible for its long critical neglect (406). John Ernest too is unable to place the novel structurally. He says "the relation between the first half of the novel (set mainly in the United States) and the second half (set mainly in Cuba and Africa) still is not entirely clear and remains unsolved" (111).

The main source of critical displeasure with the story remains a sprawling plot that seems to lack one overriding motivation and is riddled with sudden changes. *Blake*'s narrative structure commands an almost unanimous negative critical judgment because it combines virtually all the major narrative genres that have been devised for writing about the black experience in the antebellum New World—the fugitive slave narrative, "spiritual" conversion, maroon resistance, Middle Passage horrors, and so on—without seeming to be able integrate them.

JOURNEYS OF REBELLION

The story's first conflict arises when Maggie, Blake's wife, is sold, against all earlier assurances made by her master, who is also her father. Blake, imprisoned after impudently protesting his wife's sale, escapes from a holding pen and foils his master's plan to sell him too. Instead of getting out of the slave belt, Blake travels, in the story's first extended adventure, all over the South preaching revolt. The rebellion plan is later suspended abruptly after he has successfully inspired insurrectionist cells all over the slave states. Without any apparent cause, Blake abandons rebellion and launches an escape run to Canada. This second journey ends in the North like the typical fugitive slave plot. After witnessing three marital unions of his runaway companions, Blake renews his search for his wife and begins a third journey that will take him to Cuba. He swears, "'By the instincts of a husband, I'll have her if living! If dead, by impulses of a Heaven-inspired soul, I'll avenge her loss unto death!'" (157). When this new journey begins for real in New York, Blake sails as an attendant on a clipper, the *Merchantman,* that will be refitted in Havana as a slaver in which his old master and some others in Cuba and the United States are heavily invested. In Cuba, Blake redeems his wife in no time and takes up again, now within an already well-organized resistance movement, the rebellion plot he left uncompleted in the United States. This plan, like the earlier one in the United States, is suspended when Blake takes off on another trip, to Dahomey, intending to provoke a slave ship mutiny on the now-refitted clipper that brought him to Cuba. Blake returns to Havana to resume a mass-slave insurrection.

The purpose, destination, and character of each of Blake's journeys are different: mobilizing for insurrection in slave states, leading runaway slaves to Canada, and taking over a slave ship on the Atlantic. The conventions adopted for reporting each adventure varies according to the purpose and destination. The aura of secrecy necessary for spreading words of rebellion is manifest in the many textual silences and gaps of the report of the first journey. While the novel foregrounds events that highlight the evil effects of the Fugitive Slave Acts in free states, the escape to Canada follows the North Star as convention dictates. The trip to Cuba is uneventful and very short. The journey to and from Dahomey is full of the thrill of an anticipated slave ship mutiny.

Carla Peterson (575) agrees with Robert Levine (191) that the very thin narrative thread that joins all these journeys is to be found in the brief details of the illicit transactions that launch the *Merchantman.* The deal is in the works at the beginning of the story when Maggie is transferred to the new owner who will take her to Cuba and sell her there, and the whole enterprise is about to set sail when Blake joins the crew in New York en route to Havana. Blake travels to and from Dahomey on the same vessel, now outfitted as a slave ship. In the reading that takes the *Merchantman* to be the fulcrum of the narrative, it is considered significant that the factors that put the ship to work are responsible for selling Maggie, Blake's wife, and also for indirectly setting Blake on the path of rebellion. Although this attempt to find artistic merit in *Blake* shows a great advancement in the reception of the novel, some further revision is called for because it still does not account for the textual value of the novel's central task: overcoming the difficulties of constructing a land-based mass slave rebellion in the United States. The inability of critics to account for revolts in the reading terms applied to black antebellum stories like *Blake* lends support to John Ernest's observation that contemporary literary criticism is inadequately educated in the "history and culture" of how nineteenth-century African Americans tried to invent "a world that doesn't yet exist" (112), that is, a world without masters. Given the main tendencies in *Blake* interpretation, it may be said that the antebellum black fiction writers' calls for a masterless world in stories of slave rebellion are the least understood.

The main task Delany tries to accomplish in *Blake* involves joining in fairly realist forms the well-known fugitive slave story line to a relatively novel way of speaking about the alternative liberation plot embodied in Nat Turner's exploits. But this critical aspect is seldom appreciated because it is hardly ever read in tandem with similar stories of rebellion. Thus it is usually noted that the novel's "geographical compass" has "outgrown the boundaries of North America," as Paul Gilroy says (27), but only a very scanty attention is given to how the achievements and failings of its narrative structure derive from developments within the trials and errors of African American stories of rebellion. Reading the rebellion plot as an integral part of the narrative helps to explain the story's bumpy focus shifts. At every point that the plot shifts into a different journey and narrative register, it is always because a slave insurrection has to be postponed for a more auspicious time.

WEAVING THE STORY OF AN INSURRECTION

The overriding story in *Blake* is the depiction, in a passably truthful form,[19] of the determination (and failure) of a black hero to fight slavery with violent means on a grand scale. For good reasons, historians say, this feat was not achieved in the United States because the interplay of sociology, geography, ideology, and economy made physical planning for a large-scale revolt unprofitable. According to Genovese, the impersonal master-servant relationship that bred and nurtured violent revolts in South America and the Caribbean was absent in the United States partly because the settler planters installed a successful paternalist hegemony. Even for those who might have seen through the sham of paternalism, Genovese says, rebellion was still going to be a very tough project to accomplish because the particular form of slavery instituted in the United States created tactical and logistic obstacles against mass mobilization. Unlike in the Caribbean and Brazil, where the average plantation had 200 slaves and few white managers, U.S. plantations, which were usually located far apart, averaged only 20 slaves. Genovese further shows that slave-owning interests in the United States had no deep internal political divisions—like the ideological discord the French Revolution created among Haitian planters—that rebellious slaves could have pressed for tactical advantages in a large scale war of independence. Slaves in the United States, unlike their compatriots further south, did not develop one unifying ideological apparatus—*vodun* worship in Haiti, for example—that could have eased some of the tactical problems of mass mobilization.[20] To be sure, Genovese says slave revolts faced bleak prospects of success anywhere in the Americas. In the United States, where inconducive physical and political circumstances reduced the chances of success from minimal to zero, only madmen could have dared to raise an army of revolting slaves.[21]

Delany's Blake is very sane, and if his plot is to have a reasonable chance of succeeding, he will have to overcome the geographical and ideological obstacles enumerated above. But even in fiction, doing so, in the abolitionist environment dominated by an overwhelming predilection for truthful presentation, would be difficult. However, because there already exists a "proto-tradition" founded in 1853 by Douglass and Brown, Delany did not need to invent a fantasy, and his plans to make his protagonist create a land-based mass insurrection (like the historical Denmark Vesey) ought to be read as manipulations of this tradition.

The project Delany devises for Blake requires that he should be able to travel around the slave states to mobilize bondsmen and women. This also means that he has to overcome the tactical and ideological obstacles that stand in the way of making this happen. Douglass's Madison Washington and Brown's Clotel, who start their journeys as fugitive slaves, do not face these problems because the insurrections they confront are forced on them or take place within the confines of a ship. Historically, runaway slaves have little to say about violent rebellions while still in the South, and slave rebels, except for the case of few actors in the betrayed Vesey plot, do not travel extensively as Blake does. Delany is probably self-consciously alluding to the historical uniqueness of his protagonist's travails in Blake's words to his closest confidantes to the effect that he will stay in the South to agitate for mass agitation: "No one has ever originated or given us anything of the kind, I suppose I may venture" (38).

In order for Blake's plans to be successfully implemented without upsetting the conventions established by Douglass and Brown, he moves around like a fugitive slave and inspires followers like Nat Turner. He travels in the slave states like a conventional runaway slave, using his literacy skills to augment his "shrewdness and discretion" (68) as he passes through plantations. He deduces the identity of plantation owners from each settlement's names and recounts these as quick answers to patrollers that stop and question him (68). Like a slave on the run, Blake relies on the "underground" communication relays furnished by trustworthy contacts that are either prearranged or that he himself develops. At every stop, he appoints a few dependable and intelligent leaders—the first quality he fathoms through a typically long interrogation and the second from the recommendation of other slaves (78–79, 83–85)—to whom he discloses the grand plan for a general insurrection, with the instruction that they should "impart it to some other next to them" while they wait for further directions from him. Because he usually holds only one "seclusion" at each stop, Blake's (and the novel's) "progress was very rapid, in whatever direction he went" (83). In effect, the journey through the slave states, which takes up more than a full third of the narrative, serves as an attempt to unite isolated plantations and to indicate ways of overcoming definite obstacles to mobilizing tactically for an insurrection. When Blake discovers that slaves on remote plantations are already aware of his activities at earlier stops, he asks, "'Can you get word from each other so far apart, that easy?'" (89). This question is without doubt a self-reflexive comment on the positive result of the novel's plotting strategies. It also demonstrates that the distance between far-flung plantations is not permanently unbridgeable.

During this first journey, Blake also speaks like a Nat Turner whose model of liberation is not the New Testament angel of the apocalypse but the Old Testament Moses leading the enslaved people of Israel out of Egypt: "From plantation to plantation did he go, sowing the seeds of future devastation and ruin to the master and redemption to the slave, an antecedent more terrible in its anticipation than the warning voice of the destroying Angel in commanding the slaughter of the firstborn of Egypt" (83). To speak of the necessity of constructing a future that has no exact earthly (i.e., national) model, the story invests Blake with a prophetic persona delivering a long-awaited message to eager believers. At his first stop, the first person Blake meets tells him, "'Dis many day, I heahn on yeh!'" (70). In Mississippi, he discovers "people looking for a promised redemption" (74). Aunt Rachel in Arkansas tells him, "'We long been waitin' foh some sich like you to come 'mong us'" (89). In South Carolina, an acquaintance of Denmark Vesey says, "'Dis many a day I been prayin' dat de Laud sen' a nudder Denmark 'mong us!'" (112). Blake further encourages the yearning slaves to intensify in the interim acts that historians have documented as "everyday" resistance, or, to use Genovese's term, "prepolitical" actions—such as pilfering, lying, deception, property wastage, work slowdown, occasional murder, and, in the extreme, suicide—so long as they do not jeopardize the grand plan. As if readers are potential betrayers of the text's confidence, very little narrative space is given to the specific details of this grand plot.[22]

The story's first major narrative wrinkle develops when Blake abruptly ends his travels and, seemingly without motive, returns to a traditional northward escape quest. He tells his colleagues:

> A slave has no just conception of his own wrongs. Had I dealt with Franks as he deserved, for doing that for which he would have taken the life of any man had it been his case—tearing my wife from my bosom!—the most I could take courage directly to do, was to leave him, and take as many from him as I could induce to go. But maturer reflection drove me to the expedient of avenging the general wrongs of our people, by inducing the slave, in his might, to scatter red ruin throughout the region of the South. But still I cannot find it in my heart to injure an individual, except in personal conflict. (128)

This turn of events is surprising because Blake's audiences have been very receptive to his plans, and none of his followers has betrayed his secrets. A few lines before asking his friends to "get ready immediately to leave [their] oppressors tonight!'" (128), Blake thanks God for giving him the opportunity to teach the slave "'to strike for Liberty.'" His rationalization that the Canadian route to freedom is the most a slave could "take courage *directly* to do" sounds rather bizarre because Blake cannot just be discovering that his own moral constitution does not permit the kind of insurrectional killings he has been propagating. His pacifist rationale, "'I cannot find it in my heart to injure an individual, except in *personal* conflict,'" rings untrue and negates the message of rebellion he has been teaching others.

However, excessive flogging of narrative inconsistencies like this in *Blake* contributes very little to the critical understanding of the radical symbolic aesthetics that black writers were trying to create in the years leading to the Civil War. Blake's contradictions and Delany's narrative failing can be better assessed if the story as a whole is compared to others of its kind. Here Delany, clearly a self-conscious visionary and agitator struggling not to allow historical limitations and established conventions of writing about the grim prospects of black rebellion to deter his protagonist's will, seems to be groping for a way to join Blake's experience to existing patterns of fictionalizing the slave's insurrection. At the time Blake suspends the rebellion for the first time, his wife has not been recovered. Given the direction taken by the rebels in Douglass's and Brown's stories, Blake's insurrection cannot be expected to start until efforts to reconstitute the protagonist's family are finalized. As noted above, conventions of antebellum stories of slave rebellion dictate that it is the search for a family member that should lead the protagonist directly into rebellion. Maggie, whose sale awoke Blake's murderous fury against slavery, is not yet recovered and cannot be recovered in the South, since she is in Cuba. Although the story is different from *The Heroic Slave* and *Clotel* in that it begins earnestly as a straightforward rebellion narrative, the twist introduced with the trip to Canada shows that the convention started by Douglass has a strong influence on Delany.

Reading the novel as a story driven largely by Blake's efforts to keep his family intact while he forms a massive insurrectionist coalition that can defeat slavery permanently makes the novel's northern turn at the end of the southern immersion journey less whimsical. The trip to Canada provides a needed physical respite for Blake and a narrative intermission for the rebellion plot. His rapid, utterly conventional—the fugitives follow the North Star at night and rest during the day—and uneventful journey from Mississippi to Canada further shows that its main purpose is to quickly return the narrative to the suspended family reunion and mass rebellion plot which will be taken up again in Cuba. The transitional character of the Canada trip is also shown in Blake's very brief stay there. The main goal, it seems, is to transport the protagonist to his wife in Cuba with little delay.[23] When he gets there, it does not take Blake a long time to discover his wife and buy her freedom. He also quickly arranges for his son and some others he left in Canada to join him in Havana.

But family reunion makes up only one half of his reasons for leaving Mississippi in the first place. The postponed struggle for mass liberation still needs to be carried out. Blake once tells his uncle, Placido, "'I have come to Cuba to help to free my race; and that which I desire here to do, I've done in another place'" (195). Readers are now informed, without previous preparation, that Blake is originally Cuban and another narrative wrinkle develops. However, while it could be justifiably argued that making Blake a Cuban so abruptly demonstrates the author's inattention to details—we cannot forget that Delany serialized the story in a magazine—Placido's reaction indicates that Delany himself may be aware of the suddenness of this new fact that will take the story in an unanticipated direction: "'Who would have believed it!'" (194), the poet exclaimed. Of greater importance, I think, is that Blake's resuming the insurrection plan after freeing his wife puts the story squarely in the tradition of black American antebellum stories of rebellion. Structurally, therefore, Cuba should be viewed as a variation of the southern United States and the Havana episodes a continuation of the insurrection left hanging in Mississippi. Considered in this light, Cuba is a variation of the slave brig *Creole* (the theater of Madison Washington's rebellion) and of Virginia (where Clotel's journey became complicated by Nat Turner's rebellion).

In the United States, Henry Blake, regardless of his lofty intentions, remains an escaped plantation slave subject to being recaptured at any moment; his grand rebellion plot is necessarily rural and will be difficult to pull off; most of his followers are illiterate, and his recruits are far-flung. The metropolitan setting of Havana removes all these tactical problems and the prospects of relating a believable land-based revolt suddenly improve dramatically. The Havana conspiracy, made up of mainly "bourgeois" elements, has an ample cover for its meetings and that crucial difference is reflected in the considerable narrative space devoted to the plotters' deliberations. Whereas the slave-owning class in the southern United States suffers from no internal divisions, in Cuba an ongoing contention about how to check the potential for insurrection separates American expatriate planters (who believe that a successful revolt may lead to black domination) from Spanish colonists (who deliberately encourage the domination fear to counteract America's annexation plans for Cuba). However, in spite of moving the plot to a more conducive environment, the insurrection still does not take place. What then is achieved with the Cuban part of the story?

We cannot answer this question without first considering the composition of the black high command set up to steer the revolution. The conspiracy consists mainly of "comfortable" leaders whose material interests are at odds with those of the slaves they seek to lead to freedom. Under the U.S. slave system, all slaves, regardless of their assignments—preacher, overseer, field hand, or house help—are all substantially deprived of social life. Their free counterparts are not much better off. The apparently well educated and well traveled Blake that speaks in this environment sounds superior and condescending. After returning "home," the Cuban Blake, "the son of a wealthy black tobacco, cigar, and snuff manufacturer" (193), finds himself in the midst of other "bourgeois" revolutionaries that include Placido, the poet laureate to the colonial governor, and Montego and Ricardo, two notable gentlemen. The group also includes persons of "great fortune" and women of means like Cordora and Ambrosina, "the wife and daughter of a deceased wealthy mulatto merchant," and Cordelia Barbosa, "a wealthy young quadroon widow" (249). Also included in the leadership group are subalterns "of note but humble pretensions," like Abyssa and Mendi, the two Africans, and Gondolier, the governor's chef.

The incipient transnationalism of this assembly of black notables and their helpers has stimulated great critical interest and some very compelling interpretations. The story's transatlantic "geographical compass," at whose center is Cuba, confirms for Paul Gilroy that leading black thinkers and writers of the nineteenth century like Delany conceived the problems—and solutions—of black existence hemispherically. Delany's imagination, according to Gilroy, has "outgrown the boundaries of North America" (27). Blake's travels to Dahomey, his enslavement in the United States, his flight to Canada, and his planned revolt in Cuba depict an "explicitly anti-ethnic" vision that transcends "narrow African-American exceptionalism" (27). The political solidarity that spearheads Blake's Cuban exploits "makes blackness a matter of politics rather than a common cultural condition" (27). In the Cuban setting, Gilroy says, Delany's rebel plotters install "a new basis for community, mutuality, and reciprocity" (29) so that they can overcome ethnic differences that camouflage as theological disagreements.[24]

I would like to think that the meaning of this black international assembly, which, by the way, does not include a truly American representative, is more complex than being a "Masonic, Pan-African vision of a regenerated and redeemed black community" (Levine 200). The Cuban high command consists of men and women of means who, but for racial slavery and prejudices, are entitled to the best living conditions in any nation. Their affluence belies the ostensibly natural incapacities that recommend blacks for unjust treatment. In the United States this class of black achievers lived not in the slave states but in urban centers of the free states where blacks in sundry professions and trades suffered the indignities of race prejudice. Delany himself was a prominent member of this black high society. Delany "exports" this class to Cuba, I suggest, because the political and social geographies of the United States could not at that time "truthfully" support blacks of achievement leading their people to freedom through an insurrection. In the United States, many obstacles stood between slaves and black people of means working together to form a racialized anti-slavery militant force. As the next chapter shows, the ramifications of the historical incapacity of black leadership to mobilize a fighting force extend to the Reconstruction period when black people of means, with no practical training in race mobilization, are caught off-guard by white supremacists. The point I am making is that the Cuban setting offsets the practical problems faced by free blacks in the United States.

Although Delany uses the Cuban setting to overcome American limitations, the honesty he applies to the depiction of the failings of the high command shows that the thematic purpose of creating the assembly of black notables is not simply to expose American political inadequacies but also to criticize the black petty bourgeoisie. The majority of the men and women of the high command are not really interested in cultivating any deep connections with the masses of slaves that are looking up to them for leadership. The insurrection they support is not intended to bring about a world in which there will be no servants or masters but one in which individuals of any race can exercise the freedom to rule others. In other words, they do not seek a genuinely "new heaven and a new earth." Their deliberations are rather elaborate for a political conspiracy: they debate most of the time not tactical plans but ideological matters such as the place of Christianity in their proposed dispensation and the epithet that will properly incorporate all shades of the black complexion. Also, these comfortable men and women are willing to move only when they are sure that their leadership in the proposed black order of things is not in doubt. Objectively, it seems, this group cannot really support a general slave insurrection, as we see at their very last meeting, when all that Blake proposes is a contingent declaration of war: "'In the name of God, I now declare war against our oppressors, provided Spain does not redress *our* grievances!'" (292; emphasis added). At this stage in the novel, it is not clear whether the referents of Blake's collective pronoun are all slaves or their black privileged leaders.

The distance between the enslaved black masses and the self-appointed leaders is most apparent in the reactions of representatives of the two groups to the provocative assault launched by American planters against Placido. The attending surgeon says, "'This is certainly a serious state of affairs; and that too without a medium of redress'" (309). Gondolier, the very indignant subaltern, speaking like the Blake of Mississippi, believes that a massive black retaliation will be an appropriate redress: "'We ought to by this time be able to redress our grievances'" (309). Montego, the conspiracy's Minister of War and Navy, admonishes the subaltern to abandon such disorderly thoughts: "'This is your failing, Gondolier . . . and one good reason why you should not hold command. I want no better under-officer, as orders received would be strictly executed'" (309). At the end of it all, the order passed down to the restless and ready slave soldiers is that the right time for mass retaliatory and liberating actions will be determined and disclosed later. The narration says, "Though the people generally despaired, their leaders were firm" (310). When Gondolier, again like the Mississippi Blake, swears against God on hearing the indignities suffered by Ambrosina Cordora at the hands of a white shopkeeper, Madame Montego, Ambrosina's mother, admonishes him not to blaspheme God, "'upon whom we depend for aid'" (312).

In the end, the rebellion plot does not break out. Although the unusual circumstances of the novel's serialization suggest that some chapters may be missing, divisions between the leadership and the masses that end the version we have now do not augur a unified eruption of slave insurrection. Large-scale slave rebellions did not thrive in North America, the novel seems to be saying, not just because detrimental political and tactical obstacles stood in the way or that slaves lacked the will to fight. The Turner model of agitation failed to spread because people with the intellectual and material means to galvanize the masses did not rise to the occasion. The ending criticizes the political short-sightedness of black American people of material means and technical know-how who were not willing to jeopardize their own positions, weak as these were, for general racial emancipation. Land-based rebellions stalled in the United States because black people of means could not identify with the slaves. Delany's story uncannily anticipates class divisions that will develop—for example, in Harper's *Iola Leroy* and Chesnutt's *Marrow of Tradition*—when propertied and educated black people refuse to repudiate their own objective class positions for the purpose of seeking universal freedom for all.

The preceding discussion of narrative somersaults in *Blake* is intended to describe antebellum black writers' efforts to construct an artful narrative of the slave's war against the master. Delany, Douglass, and Brown try consistently to breach, at the level of plot making, the cultural, ideological, and symbolic obstacles put in the way of the slave's rebellion by the master's preferred world. Delany's Blake, in particular, takes the ambitious gamble of seeking a land-based rebellion but fails. Delany also tries to commandeer free black people of means into the mass insurrection course, but that attempt too flounders. In these failures, however, Delany, as well as other writers, defines the truly heroic slave as one who seeks the master's literal death. The heroic slave relaunches the battle for freedom which the master wrongly thinks is already settled. In *The Heroic Slave, Clotel,* and *Blake,* the master, as Delany's narrator puts it, lives in a permanent limbo: "A sleeping wake or waking sleep, a living death or tormented life" (305). The cause of the master's "living death" is nothing other than the demonstrated readiness of the slave to die literally in the course of a rebellion.

To close this chapter, I would like to relate my reading of antebellum black novels of slave rebellion to two influential explanations of early African American literary history. Robert Stepto reads the best of the slave narratives as not merely the writers' testimonies of their freedom quest but manifestations of how "literacy initiates freedom" (*From Behind the Veil* x). The writer and the ex-slave realize freedom "when a questing figure gains both the ability to be variously literate and the opportunity to be so" (xi). Textually, glimpses of technical mastery gained in the process of acquiring and exercising literacy inflect the gradual expansion of the slave/narrator's humanistic aspiration for freedom. The slave narratives thus tend to celebrate the writer's mastery of writing more profoundly than physical freedom. In my reading of Stepto, sole authorship, artistry, or the marvel of the freedom to create and manipulate the material letter, rather than the writer's agonistic ideological engagements, determine the structure of the narratives. That reason, in Stepto's argument, accounts for why the most accomplished slave narrators invent many strategies to control "the intrusions of competing self-identities and the other Others—listeners, observers, and readers of many guises" (xi). The slave narrator establishes independence by appropriating the voices of valuable helpers that threaten to encroach upon the writer's narrative inventions. In this conception of black authorship and authority, the writer is a stable, unified creator to whom slavery primarily represents a lack of creativity.

Stepto translates the slave narrator's self-conscious preoccupation—taken to be the first of its kind in black American writing—into a major statement about black literature by defining the "pre-generic myth" of African American writing as "the quest for freedom and literacy." As African American writing grows, the pre-generic myth takes on three types of plot movements: ascent (the call), immersion, and hibernation (the response). Ascent plot patterns, best exemplified in the upward (and northward) movement of slave narratives, dominated the first phase of African American literary history up to Reconstruction. By the beginning of the twentieth century, some writers began to turn the ascent story on its head in narratives that typically end in an exploration of what makes the South hostile to blacks. The immersion stories, so named because the narration engages the South directly, launch a response to the call of the ascent stories. The life of the immersion story was cut short with the publication of James Weldon Johnson's *The Autobiography of an Ex-Colored Man* (1912), when the protagonist discovers the utter meaninglessness of black life to white southerners. The Ex-Colored Man's aborted immersion stagnates and transforms into a hibernation best exemplified by Ralph Ellison's *Invisible Man* (1952), a story whose plot culminates in a literal underground and not just a cartographic nether region.

Because Stepto writes about the evolution of the structure of the well-formed text, the not-so-well-formed antebellum black fiction of the South does not find a place in his historiography. Stepto dismisses *Clotel*, for example, as a "pseudo-novel" (44) because it does not handle well the already perfected techniques of "objective" and "integrated" slave narratives. Indeed, between 1853 and 1901, the year Booker T. Washington's *Up from Slavery* was published, Stepto's theory does not recognize texts that "create generic and, by extension, historical space for themselves" (32). In that barren half a century, no text succeeded in either "manipulating" or "sophisticating" the achievements of the slave narrative's ascent plot.

The ascent, immersion, and hibernation directions apparent in fictional plot patterns discussed above do not agree with Stepto's formulation. The expressed aspiration of each slave protagonist, to whom manifest control of self-representation is not the most pressing concern, differs from the individualism emphasized in the well-formed slave narratives Stepto relies on for his analysis. Each rebellious protagonist either escapes to the North successfully, or abandons the chance to do so. In either case, the hero heads south and immerses himself or herself, either by choice or force of circumstance, in a violent freedom struggle. If their efforts fail, they do not hibernate: Madison Washington fights his way to freedom in Grenada; Henry Blake, having become the General Commander of the rebellious forces in Cuba, postpones his revolutionary plan, waiting for the next opportunity; Clotel chooses suicide over captivity. Clotel's "ascent" is aborted in a suicide, and Madison Washington's "immersion" ends in the troubled waters of mutiny. Blake's immersion takes him far to Dahomey. All the stories turn the typical ascent slave narrative of freedom and literacy into a radical vision of liberating violent immersion.

As these stories show, literacy is not the only weapon of liberation denied the slave; firearms were too. (C.L.R. James says that a slave "does not need education or encouragement to cherish a dream of freedom" [*Black Jacobins* 18].) The slave rebels of the stories discussed above seek to acquire forbidden means other than literacy to free themselves and *others*. The central textual struggle of the stories is not "between the author and guarantor" (45), between artist and authenticator (editor, publisher, guarantor, patron), between the ex-slave and those who want to imprison the literary voice. Instead, the writers wrestle with how to convert historical bloody slave revolts into fictive narratives that will be acceptable to typically "nonviolent" abolitionist readers.

In his article "The Novelization of Voice in Early African American Narrative," William Andrews suggests that the fictive voice gradually evolved in antebellum black writing through the creation of a third-person narrative voice that authenticates historically recognizable tales with simulated "natural utterances" (26) like letters, political proclamations, and newspaper articles. The writers "launch[ed] their narrators on the seas of fiction while trying to moor them to the shores of fact" (25), and the texts created a closeness to truthfulness while separating the author's corporeal body from the narrator's claims. Novelizing the narrative voice this way redirects creative energies from strategies of proving the veracity of the claims made about people, places, and events to deploying what Douglass calls "'marks, traces, possibles, and probabilities'" (26) in *The Heroic Slave.* Thus, Andrews theorizes, "the authority of fictive discourse in African American narrative depends on a sabotaging of the pressure of authoritative plenitude of history as 'natural' discourse so that the right of the fictive to supplement (that is, to subvert) 'history' can be declared and then exploited" (30). In other words, early African American writers won their right to fictive imagination by substituting simulated "history" for truthful autobiography.

Besides recognizing the omniscient voice as the basis of fiction in these texts, Andrews finds little difference between early black novels and the slave narratives they are trying to supplant. He says, for example, "*The Heroic Slave* reads in some ways like a historical novel pared down to the basic plot of the slave narrative, the quest for freedom" (27). This claim relies on the historiographic paradigm that says antebellum African American writers could only create stories that were true to the contemporary experience sanctioned by the "peaceful" abolitionists. But as demonstrated above, fiction writers consistently exposed the limitations of the type of agitation exemplified in the hero of the slave autobiography. Andrews himself submits that by the 1850s the most important African American writers considered the narrative limits imposed by abolitionist politics rather stultifying: "Writers like Douglass and William Wells Brown knew that without a new and expanded awareness of black voice and the possibilities of black storytelling, the traditional medium of black narrative would continue to restrict, if not distort, its message" (24).

It has been the argument of this chapter that the "new and expanded awareness" freed up for circulation in the plot of the early novels is the alternative model of freedom embodied in the leader of a violent slave rebellion. It has also been my contention that the historical character that best exemplifies that ideal is Nat Turner. If freedom and literacy are the pre-generic myths of African American writing in general, plotting to bring about freedom through the slave's counter-violence is the original thematic preoccupation in fiction.

3

REVERSE ABOLITIONISM AND BLACK POPULAR RESISTANCE

The Marrow of Tradition

Nikki Giovanni describes Charles Chesnutt as "the zero" figure in African American fiction because his novel *The Marrow of Tradition* repudiates popular conventions of representing black characters in nineteenth-century American writing. Some of the leading characters gently defy attempts to subordinate them without a legitimate warrant. A few others are outright belligerent in their protest. Giovanni, herself an accomplished poet and maker of symbolic images, measures the literary significance of Chesnutt's novel by the daring actions of these characters: "The old mammy dies in the [race] riot. The Black folks fight back. The crackers are milling around smoking their cigars, deciding which Black folks will have to die, while we are preparing for a siege" (104). Chesnutt, Giovanni believes, paid a very steep price for his audacity because the vicious backlash provoked by his innovative characterization snuffed out his fledgling fame. Of course, things are not as straightforward as Giovanni's reading suggests: not all victims of the "race" riot morally deserve suffering or dying, and the plot resolution raises conundrums rather than state a clear stance on racial nationalist militancy. Nonetheless, Giovanni's spirited endorsement of the novel reflects the just satisfaction a sympathetic reader can derive from the willful counter-violence of the slaving classes against their tormentors.

Chesnutt's story demonstrates that after Emancipation the character of the relationship between the slaving class and the master class takes on radically new guises, at least in theory. In the American Reconstruction context of the story, the new "master" class includes descendants of slaves who have taken advantage of the political and economic advancement avenues opened up by Emancipation. In this milieu, because older definitions of "slavery" and "mastery" fail to apply exactly, they become materials for metaphor making. In *Marrow,* white supremacists cast themselves as "slaves."

The consequence of the steady ideological and socioeconomic changes going on in the American southern Reconstruction society is marked most visibly in *Marrow* in the defeat of the Democratic Party in statewide elections by the Fusion alliance consisting of Republicans, Populists, and the black voting bloc. To regain power, leaders of the Democratic Party invent an *abolitionist* discourse to mobilize white racialist sentiments against the ruling alliance. Using the fear-inducing slogan of "nigger domination," this discourse portrays white people as victims of a racial social structure that must be razed so as to make room for the reemergence of the natural order of things. Chesnutt's main plot narrates the tragic consequences of the inabilities of the emergent black bourgeoisie in Wellington, a fictional North Carolina town clearly modeled on Wilmington, to formulate an adequate response to the black inferiority (which is also a white supremacy) campaign.

To many literary critics, the referential parallels between key events in the novel and the 1898 Wilmington race riot make the story a historical fiction.[1] I want to locate the significance of Chesnutt's observations not in the relationship of the content of the story to actualities contemporary to the time the novel was published but in the way its reinterpretation of the values of subaltern protests reflects the fundamental sociopolitical changes going on in the country as a whole. In historical slave societies, Chesnutt shows, post-Emancipation developments complicate the meaning of identities inherited from the old relations of slave and master. Since political struggles in this era of "universal" freedom are not aimed at bringing about a new "heaven" and a new "earth," terms based on the relations of "Lordship" and "Bondage" function mainly as metaphors.

Marrow is different from American antebellum stories of political rebellion in the crucial respect that the revolt occurs onshore. But that is not even the most striking feature of the story. Compared to the novels discussed in the last chapter, the oddest feature of this novel is that bourgeois white supremacists mobilize support for their cause by speaking and acting like black antebellum abolitionists seeking to free themselves from bondage. In their war of "liberation" (against black Emancipation), well-placed white men plot, without any self-conscious sense of irony, to free their city by destroying black professionals and by compelling working-class blacks to end their unbecoming arrogance. The reversals are seen in black people, too. Divided by objective economic and political affiliations, they cannot marshal a unified response to the white "slaves" striving to be "masters" again. Black domestic servants of white people do not trust the political judgment of industrial workers, and the latter group does not defer to white people the way domestic workers do. In addition, the upwardly mobile black middle class of doctors, lawyers, and political appointees cannot identify with the cause of either the industrial or domestic working classes. The black bourgeoisie believes that signs of "blackness"—illiteracy, speaking in dialects, excessive religiosity, exaggerated deference to white people, subscribing to folkways inherited from slavery, and so on—ought to be jettisoned because they block the path to social advancement. When blacks fight white "abolitionists" at the end of the novel, the point that everything is upside down cannot be missed. The indecisions witnessed in Delany's black high command are extended manyfold in *Marrow.*

WHITE "SLAVES" AND REVERSE ABOLITIONISM: JOUSTING FOR POWER AFTER EMANCIPATION

Lurking in the background of events in *Marrow* are the post-Reconstruction constitutional realities that forced white politicians to reckon with black voters. Within that world, the major political parties either have to court black voters or ensure that their rivals do not get black votes. In Wellington, the Fusion alliance of Republicans and Populists has taken over control of the local administration. To regain power, the Democrats invent a drama of racial gallantry in which they cast themselves as "Anglo-Saxons" fighting the "nigger domination" embarrassment they say is disguised as the Fusion Party. (A black servant eavesdropping on Democratic Party leaders thinks they are calling themselves "angry-Saxons" fighting for "nigger damnation" [38]). The Democratic Party, it is obvious, does not know how to win black votes and will see to it that this bloc of ballots, which seems to have made Fusion victory possible, is not cast again.

In the reverse abolitionism plot formulated to effect the plan, Democratic Party leaders, acting as spokesmen of an enslaved race, construct a discourse of necessary violence without which the dignity of natural laws that are ostensibly being violated in the unbridled upward mobility of black people cannot be restored. The success of black professionals and the appointment of blacks to political offices violate divine laws, they say, because these occurrences deny white people their natural rights to rule and to prosper. The class that considers itself "natural" rulers (or "masters") now speaks as if Reconstruction has artificially forced it into slavery: "'Wellington is in the hands of negroes and scalawags. What better time to rescue it'" (183).

To denote the historical lineage of the moral outrage being mouthed by the Democratic Party leaders, Chesnutt recalls slave owners who used to justify slavery with explanations that allowed them to go to bed and not be haunted by their real fear of the bondsmen and women they had under leash:

> In the olden time the white South labored under the constant fear of negro insurrections. Knowing that they themselves, if in the negroes' place, would have risen in the effort to throw off the yoke, all their reiterated theories of negro subordination and inferiority could not remove that lurking fear, founded upon the obscure consciousness that the slaves ought to have risen. (276)

The white supremacy campaign, Chesnutt says further, is a "curious illustration" of how the "curse" of slavery abides "long after the actual physical bondage had terminated" (276). By harking back to slavery to place the new white supremacy historically, Chesnutt demonstrates that the white resistance ideology is being formulated by remnants of the plantation class—the "broken down aristocracy"—for whom unfree black labor used to be a source of sustenance. For this class, free black labor and black political and economic prosperity are crises of nature that must be settled swiftly. To restore normalcy, the "broken down aristocracy" invents a crisis called black domination, borrowing strategies anachronistically from the anti-slavery movement.

Clearly, the inheritors of the old plantation system are becoming less relevant in socio-economic matters. Industries are expanding, out-of-state trading and manufacturing interests are moving in, and the "multiracial" Fusion alliance is in power.[2] The voice of Old Mr. Delamere, the aged plantation farmer, is no longer deemed important in the community. Chesnutt symbolizes the moral and social degeneration, as well as the political decline, of the plantation system in the behaviors of Tom Delamere. Tom is an incautious alcoholic and a chronically insolvent gambler. He steals a servant's suit and puts on black face to perform in a cakewalk. To get money to settle some of his debts, Tom, in black face and wearing his uncle's servant's suit, kills his aunt, Mrs. Ochiltree, knowing that the black face will be attached to the owner of the suit when the murder investigation is conducted. While Tom Delamere's literal "self-negrification" (and self-denigration) depicts the extent of the aristocracy's social decline, its inability to lynch Sandy Campbell, the black owner of the suit worn during the murder, dramatizes its loss of power. Contrary to what would have occurred in the past, merely exposing Tom Delamere to be a killer shuts down the plan to lynch a black man. The paternal old Delamere himself dies soon after the criminal in the family is caught.

Phillip Carteret's work, home, and leisure routines give the best clues to the critical changes occurring in the society. Primary among the determinants of social achievement for Carteret are gender and race: men are naturally superior to women, and whites to blacks. He believes, like Judge Bullard in *Blake,* that "the darker race, docile by instinct, humble by training, patiently waiting upon its as yet uncertain destiny, was an incubus, a corpse chained to the body politic, and that the negro vote was a source of danger to the state, no matter how cast or by whom directed" (80).[3] His newspaper, the *Morning Chronicle,* relentlessly preaches "the unfitness of the negro to participate in government" (31) and attributes that disability to the black person's "limited education, his lack of experience, his criminal tendencies, and more especially to his hopeless mental and physical inferiority to the white race" (31). The paper teaches "that the white and black races could never attain social and political harmony by commingling their blood" and that "no two unassimilable races could ever live together except in the relation of superior and inferior" (31). For the cause, "statistics of crime, ingeniously manipulated, were made to present a fearful showing against the negro. Vital statistics were made to prove that he had degenerated from an imaginary standard of physical excellence which had existed under the benign influence of slavery" (238). Not convinced that an electoral victory for the Democratic Party will lead to a clean removal of the black political and economic "incubus," Carteret tacitly endorses the deployment of a militia of white men to occupy the streets and carry out virtual "abolitionist" violence against black franchise, bringing to mind the reign of terror that usually followed episodes of slave revolt in antebellum times.

In a clear reversal of antebellum order, a local black newspaper, the *Afro-American Banner,* "the first local effort of a struggling people to make public expression of [black] life and aspirations" (84), becomes the defender of the political status quo, speaking against the "radical" abolitionism of Carteret's *Chronicle.*[4] The *Banner*'s editorials condemn the constitutional overreaching that the Democratic Party is conducting under the guise of white abolitionism/supremacy, and, in a complete turnaround of antebellum proslavery rhetoric, accuse defenders of the "broken down aristocracy" of crass immorality. Although Chesnutt does not give narrative prominence to examples of the *Banner*'s content, the only reported editorial from it—picked up by Carteret in a wastebasket—summarizes all the terms of white abolitionism and the black reaction to it:

> The article was a frank and somewhat bold discussion of lynching and its causes. It denied that most lynchings were for the offense most generally charged as their justification, and declared that, even of those seemingly traced to this cause, many were not for crimes at all, but for voluntary acts which might naturally be expected to follow from the miscegenation laws by which it was sought, in all the Southern States, to destroy liberty of contract, and, for the purpose of maintaining a fanciful purity of race, to make crimes of marriages to which neither nature nor religion nor the laws of other states interposed any insurmountable barrier. (85)[5]

When Carteret reprints the article many months after its original publication, he presents it as another evidence of black plans for the domination of white men and interprets its defense of "*liberty of contract*" very liberally to mean nothing other than a call for interracial marriage. Although it is very obvious that Carteret's statewide canvassing for the restraining of black political rights (239–40) is meant to bail the decline of the plantation aristocracy—for example, to protect McBane's profits from prison gang labor and to improve the deteriorating fortunes of Belmont's law firm—the agitation is disseminated in (abolitionist) terms that make white people practical slaves suffering unjust, ungodly, and unnatural restrictions.

FIGHTING THE "ANGRY-SAXONS"

As noted in the last chapter, antebellum black novelists did not have vast narrative options for fighting slavery. Whenever the aim pursued by the lonely, eloquent, and literate autobiographical protagonist involves physically challenging either a plantation operative or a patroller, it is usually done in defense of individual rights. With the exception of *Blake,* resorting to violence arises in fiction as a desperate measure taken by the protagonist whose freedom quest will be aborted otherwise. In *Marrow,* the upwardly mobile individualist typified in the antebellum autobiographer and the rebellious collectivist found in the fictional protagonist coexist and talk to one another, as different entities, in the communal response to the physical aggression of white supremacists. Dr. Miller, one of Wellington's leading medical practitioners, embodies the individualist, upwardly mobile character, and Josh Green, a stevedore, represents the tradition of the militant collectivist. In *Marrow,* the truculent militant and the man of deliberate defiance meet for the first time.

But the textual cohabitation of these two forms of black resistance energy fails to thrive because they have different life pursuits. Josh Green could not convince either Dr. Miller or Mr. Watson, the black attorney, to lead an armed resistance to racist aggression. This was the case, we should recall, even in

Blake's antebellum setting, where the black petty bourgeoisie sought to dictate the time the masses of slaves should strike for freedom. In *Marrow*'s Reconstruction, the masses seek, to no avail, the leadership of black people of means and technical know-how. In antebellum times the consequence of not acting is continued slavery for all. During Reconstruction, the militant subaltern stands a greater chance of dying: Green, who raises a small posse of poorly equipped blacks to halt the white militia's unprovoked and indiscriminate destruction of black lives and property, gets killed.

Critical responses to *Marrow* show that deciding the appropriate terms of articulating black militant political action is a major concern in the age of Chesnutt. Critics usually read the plot resolution that kills Green and spares Miller as a clue to the author's view on the evolution of a plausible alliance between members of the "better" classes of the two races. Reading the novel in conjunction with some of the author's letters leads Charles Hackenberry to suggest, for instance, that the novelist and his Dr. Miller are both political "moderates" who reject violence and staunchly support "the vote and equality before the law" (195). Although Hackenberry says the narrative does not render the choice between Miller and Green simplistically, he notes that Miller's survival endorses the "viewpoint of the pragmatic positivist" (196) against Green's deadly forcing of things. Miller's survival signals the author's anticipation of a time, Hackenberry says, "when blacks could take their rightful place in American society through the process of elevation of the individual by means of education, culture (as it is popularly conceived), and hard work" (196). Marjorie George and Richard Pressman believe, like Hackenberry, that the story "makes violence non-viable as a political tool for either blacks or whites" (288). Miller, they believe, "carries Chesnutt's rational message of cooperatism and non-violence—the one he intended consciously—while Green and especially Janet [Miller's wife] carry the strong underlying, unconscious message of resistance and independence. With Green's anger dead and Janet's purged, the two tendencies would seem to be reconciled within the more rational, cooperatist ideology" (298). Stephen Knadler, whose reading is well informed by more recent identity theories, says: "While Josh Green's black pride serves as a rebuttal to Dr. Miller's accommodationism, Chesnutt pictures this [Green's] nationalist model of black identity as repeating the history of racial violence, severing class and racial alliances among people of color" (442). In Knadler's view, Green's militancy sounds too much like Carteret's; hence Chesnutt rejects it.[6]

The novel's subplot of a multiracial family (and nation) divided by an unbecoming racist prejudice[7] that must be overturned makes very plausible and morally feasible Dr. Miller's calm acceptance of the death of his son as a necessary sacrifice. Janet Miller is the half-sister of Carteret's wife, Olivia. Janet, borne by a slave woman after the death of Olivia's mother, is maneuvered out of her inheritance from her father's estate by Olivia's maternal aunt and later Olivia herself. After the anti-black riot masterminded by her husband, Olivia acknowledges her blood ties to Janet Miller—"You are my sister" (327)—who then permits her husband to go save the life of Carteret's son. In the traditional Chesnutt hermeneutic, the mutual recognition of the two sisters allegorizes the novelist's preferred race relations, and Mrs. Carteret's confession of kinship points at the future reconciliation of the national interracial family. Wolkomir, for example, says that "tradition disintegrates" after the emotional meeting of the two women (255).

Except in criticisms sympathetic to black nationalism, Josh Green's death in the white "abolitionist" riot is often read as a clear sign of the novel's rejection of the militant political action embodied in his character. Green's death is also often viewed as Chesnutt's endorsement of Dr. Miller's pacifism. Emancipation seems to have nullified the effectiveness of subaltern political violence. Because neither character completely eschews militant defense of constitutional rights, I am not convinced that the choice embodied in the difference between Miller and Green is the moral necessity, or otherwise, of political violence. To say that the two characters symbolize the incompatibility of pragmatist and retaliatory response to politically motivated racial threats is to think of Miller and Green as complying with and functioning within the theory of undifferentiated blackness constructed by the white "abolitionists." Chesnutt's main achievement in the depiction of the disagreement between Miller and Green is that he shows the profound social and ideological stratification that developed within the black population after Emancipation. The story's radical rejection of instinctive black solidarity in the pathetic inactions of Miller and Watson indicates that the material relations that obtained within and between the races in the antebellum era are different from those that prevailed in the post-Reconstruction world of *Marrow.* In this epoch, ending "black superiority" is the goal of white "abolitionist" politics.

Miller's petit-bourgeois class is new in black southern society and fiction. Miller is an entrepreneurial physician highly regarded in society, for different reasons, by both the white supremacists and black masses. Belmont thinks of him as a "very good sort of a negro, [who] doesn't meddle with politics, nor tread on any one else's toes" (251–52). He is unlike the "New Negroes," who are not "respectful, humble, obedient, and content with the face and place assigned [them] by nature." To black folks, the proprietor of a hospital, who owns his own buggy and wears a diamond ring (251), is definitely a "new" Negro. Whenever any social crisis arises, he is the first person they call upon for leadership.

Miller's in-between social situation reflects the predicament of the black bourgeoisie on matters relating to militant racial/class struggles. The material position of the black bourgeoisie makes them practically "white": they take whiteness, as it is practiced in Wellington, to mean formulating and pursuing the *ideology* of the freedom to participate (or to aspire to do so) at all levels in market-oriented economic activities and instituting a sociopolitical program that guarantees the stated economic aspiration. Miller, for instance, speaks and thinks most of the time like his white counterparts in virtually everything social and political. He believes that vengeance is a base emotion; he thinks that calm rationalization is superior to physical expression of disgust; he accepts the interpretation given the Scriptures by the contented class. However, because the society's racialism refuses to reckon with the profound changes brought about by Emancipation, and blackness is still viewed by many as something synonymous with economic and intellectual poverty, Miller, perhaps unbeknownst to him, is "lost" to both his black admirers and the white supremacists willing to accommodate him. Hence he is simultaneously an "old" and a "new" Negro to both groups.

Miller acts meek, weak, and is therefore "good," as Belmont says, because his class is incapacitated by its undiscriminating acceptance of the ideology of reason and the universal goodness promised in bourgeois social ideals. After suffering the indignity of ejection from a "white" railroad car for which he has fully paid, Miller eases himself into a long rumination on the fate of "Negroes" and comforts himself with a verse from the Beatitudes: "'Blessed are the meek . . . for they shall inherit the earth.' If this be true, the negro may yet come into his estate, for meekness seems to be set apart as his portion" (62). To the extent that Miller is meek, as the Bible advises, he is a "good" Negro. But to live meekly all the time under Wellington's virulent racialism is to refuse to claim the full gains of Emancipation and unwittingly endorse white supremacy's reverse abolitionism. White supremacy is not meek, and it wants to inherit all of the earth.

When Green visits Miller's clinic for the treatment of a fracture he sustained during a scuffle with a fellow dockworker, the doctor advises him to be gentler in his ways: "'These are bad times for bad Negroes. You'll get into a quarrel with a white man, and at the end of it there'll be a lynching, or a funeral. You'd better be peaceable and endure a little injustice, rather than run the risk of a sudden and violent death'" (110). Here we have a complete revision of the views of slave insurrectionists who would not trade life for injustice. Miller's words, which imply that badness and goodness are politically neutral terms, are identical to Belmont's characterization of the "good Negro" as discussed earlier. But Green's political response to the doctor's advice exposes their actual discursivity and reaffirms the racially different meanings given to the juxtapositions "old/good" and "new/bad" in the description of black people: "Ef a nigger wants ter git down on marrow-bones, an' eat dirt, an *call 'em 'marster,'* he's a good nigger, dere's room fer him. But I ain' no w'ite folks' nigger, I ain'. *I don' call no man 'marster'*" (113–14; emphasis added). To Green's *political* definition of good and bad, Miller gives a *medical* retort: "'You're feverish, and don't know what you're talking about'" (114).

The successful riot staged by the white supremacists thoroughly repudiates Miller's philosophies of universal good judgment and idealistic Christianity. Overrating the good sense of white "abolitionists," Miller turns down Green's call for help to form a black militia that can defend black property, including Miller's hospital: "'They'll not burn the schoolhouses, nor the hospital—they are not such fools, for they benefit the community; and they'll only kill the colored people who resist them'" (295). As Green suspects, the hospital is razed. He and other leaders of the black militia actually die in the inferno as they try to defend the buildings.

The heavy toll paid by Green's militia cannot be rightly described as an endorsement of pacifism, as some commentaries discussed above suggest. The deaths of the militants result from the political naiveté of a black bourgeoisie that cannot respond to the sinister "abolitionist" plot of the white supremacists. Physician Miller, attorney Watson, and stevedore Green constitute the black opposite of the white troika of editor Carteret, lawyer-politician Belmont, and prison gang leader McBane, all Civil War veterans. That McBane is a necessary inconvenience in the white supremacy is remarked all over the novel. His clothes, manner of speech, and reasoning lack the poetry of the traditional aristocracy. Belmont and Carteret include him in their plans because he intercedes between the conspiracy and the white masses. Virtually all that is known about McBane comes through his interaction with his social superiors. Green, whose biographical background is filtered through Miller's thoughts, is similar to McBane in this respect. However, while the white vanguard comes together, probably because they have had a good experience in racial solidarity in the Confederate army, the "universal" black alliance never convenes. The white troika creates a social problem it calls "negro domination" and against which it organizes an abolitionist plot. Within the black troika, Miller and Watson, the two people equipped by education and material means to hammer out an answer to white supremacy, disable themselves with paralyzing reason and condemn Green and his militant cohorts as "bad" Negroes. The black leaders, in effect, naively translate the material distinction between them and the masses into an unbridgeable political chasm.

At every political turn, the black masses make earnest solidarity gestures to the middle class. In one instance, when white men attempt to use their suspicion of Sandy Campbell to reiterate their long-held views about "black" brutishness and inherent animality (181–82), Miller and, most surprising, Watson the attorney throw up their hands, even after Josh Green volunteers an alibi (188)! Miller proposes that black leaders should appeal "to the principal white people of the town" (189), namely Old Mr. Delamere, to prevail upon the crowd set on lynching. Watson does not entertain any doubt that Mrs. Ochiltree's killer may not be a black person, as alleged, despite Green's words that he was with Campbell at the time he is supposed to have murdered Mrs. Ochiltree. Watson says, "'It seems that some colored man attacked Mrs. Ochiltree,—and he was a murderous villain, whoever he may be'" (189). Watson believes that Green's many infractions with the law will discredit any evidence he may provide in court, despite the fact that Green has "'never harmed any one but himself'" (189). An apparently exasperated Miller is even more damning in his words: "'The whole thing is profoundly discouraging. . . . Try as we may to build up the race in the essentials of good citizenship and win the good opinion of the best people, some black scoundrel comes along, and by a single criminal act, committed in the twinkling of an eye, neutralizes the effect of a whole year's work'" (190). Miller's "best people" are the remnants of the paternalistic plantation patriarchs who ruled with a racialist sense of noblesse oblige. It takes Green's folksiness to stop Miller's moralism and Watson's pragmatism: "'It's mighty easy to neut'alize, er whatever you call it'" (190). He also reminds them that the immediate political question is not how to deal with black scoundrels but how to repel a blatantly murderous racism. Green, confident that something could be made of the numerical strength of black people in Wellington, tells the educated men that he is willing to raise a group to guard the jail before Jenkins's arraignment: "'Dere's two niggers ter one white man in dis town, an' I'm sho' I kin fin' fifty of 'em w'at 'll fight, ef dey kin fin' anybody ter lead 'em'" (189). But Miller and Watson see no strength in the folks.

The resolution of the "race riot" with the simultaneous deaths, in front of Miller's burnt down hospital, of McBane, the "working" class member of the white conspiracy, and Green, the aggressive working member of black resistance, seems to endorse the self-preservation tactics of Miller and Watson. McBane fires a pistol at Green as he plunges "a huge bowie knife, a relic of the civil war," into McBane's heart. The narratorial comment that follows says, sounding like Miller, "One of the two men died as the fool dieth. Which was it, or was it both? 'Vengeance is mine,' saith the Lord, and it had not been left to him" (309). Green seems to be the avenging fool who does not allow God to deal with McBane for killing Green's father. But the narrator also adds: "They that do violence must expect to suffer violence. McBane's death was merciful, compared with the nameless horrors he had heaped upon the hundreds of helpless mortals who had fallen into his hands during his career as a contractor of convict labor" (309–10). This comment can be said to be implying that McBane received his just deserts and that his death is the poetic punishment for his murderous activities in the Klan. It is clear in the commentary, however, that the moral proof that his death is timely comes from his harsh treatment of convict labor. Surprisingly, conventions of Chesnutt criticism view the moral intention of the story as a condemnation of bloody vengeance. According to Jay Delmar, for example, "The unlettered, primal Green hates his white oppressors and lives for the day when he can return violence for violence" (269). There is ample evidence in the story that refined education, wealth, and social respectability, in themselves, do not purge from individuals the capacity for vengeful and self-serving political violence. Also, illiteracy does not in itself increase racial animosity in blacks. The uneducated Jerry Letlow is killed by the white mob in spite of his outward expression of love toward the white people.

I am not able to think that Chesnutt wants to reject, with McBane's and Green's deaths, McBane's violent racism and Green's violent anti-racism, as if they were moral equivalents. To pursue that interpretation is to omit crucial facts about the plot resolution. Neither Green nor McBane commits any moral infraction that is more heinous than those perpetrated or sanctioned by Carteret, Belmont, and Tom Delamere. Carteret organizes a political riot that he knows might result in many deaths; Belmont masterminds a violent takeover of legitimate civil authorities; and Tom Delamere kills his old aunt in the process of robbing her. But at the end of the story, Carteret goes home to his family, Belmont's *coup d'état* succeeds, and Delamere is merely eased out of town. To interpret Green's and McBane's death as Chesnutt's allegorical rejection of their political and moral infractions means we should infer that the success of Belmont and Carteret signifies the novelist's endorsement of white supremacy's murderous rioting. If that is the case, then the moral direction of the tale is against neither bloodshed nor vengeance.

The story, I would suggest, illustrates the political abilities of the white bourgeois class that emerged after Reconstruction to claim for itself the right to continue the exploitative racialism that prevailed during slavery. The novel also illustrates the abject weakness of their black counterparts. *Marrow* draws up a complex political allegory of the internecine war going on within the post-Emancipation southern bourgeoisie, which has expanded to include nontraditional members like Miller, Watson, and Barber. The rise of the black bourgeoisie has eroded the clout of those whites who used to profit from the coercion of *all* black people into servitude. Because black members of the new bourgeoisie are flustered by the exploitative racism of the white supremacists—a mode of thinking that disagrees with the meritocratic capitalism propagated by the larger society—Watson and Miller do not know how to counteract the "negro domination" slogan and the abolitionist plot directed at black people generally.

Joyce Pettis says the story demonstrates "the profound absurdity of class and political interests, of assumptions about racial superiority and inferiority, and of racially motivated negation of human and blood kinship" (46). This aseptic view of social harmony denies significant elements of the story. White supremacy/abolitionism wins a clear victory at the expense of poor whites and black masses. Stephen Knadler applies more patently theoretical terms to the plot dynamics Pettis calls absurd. The novel, Knadler says, cancels out both the accommodation symbolized in Miller's behaviors and the naturalist nationalism symbolized by most of Carteret's actions and some of Green's words: "Chesnutt viewed both black and white identities as contingent historical constructs that had, within the logic of capitalist exchange, been reified as biological facts" (244). Knadler demonstrates here a common tendency of contemporary criticism to conflate causation and contingency. In Knadler, as in most of cultural studies today, history happens for reasons that are not necessarily causes because historicizable events take place within discursive parameters. As *Marrow* shows, racialism, even when constructed and contingent, as seen in the efforts of the white troika and the resistance of Green and his friends, is driven by material interests that will not hesitate to destroy the disposable classes. It is true that only a few texts can parallel the novel's demonstration of the constructedness of historical events. Equally true, however, is the novel's insistence on the causative effect of constructed political movements on the lives and careers of their acolytes and victims.

At the end of the story, virtually all the prominent members of the black underclass perish. The Mammy (Jenny Letlow) and her grandson (Jerry), both of whom work for the Carteret family, die. Their loyalty to the aristocracy could not save them. The narration of Jerry Letlow's death is instructive. While he is running out of Miller's hospital, which has been set ablaze by the white gang, he catches a glimpse of Carteret leaving the horrific site, disgusted by the crass barbarity being displayed by his followers. Letlow hails his employer: "'Majah Carteret—Oh majah! It's me, Jerry, suh! In did n' go in dere myse'f, suh,—In wuz drag' in dere! In would n' do nothin' 'g'inst de w'ite folks, suh,—no, 'deed, I would n', suh!'" (307). But his voice is drowned out in the fiery din. Letlow falls, his "flag of truce, his explanations, his reliance upon his white friends, all failed him in the moment of supreme need." He dies, like other workingmen and women drawn into the race riots.

In contrast, the story ensures the survival, at a relatively minimal cost, of the bourgeois class regardless of its moral infractions. Belmont and Carteret, ruthless politicians who are no less morally repugnant than either McBane or the sycophantic Letlows, survive. So also does the black attorney, Watson, who is more cowardly than Jerry Letlow. Shortly before his conscription into the black militia, the narrator characterizes Jerry Letlow as one who is afraid for his life: "He valued his life for his own sake, and not for any altruistic theory that it might be of service to others. In other words, Jerry was something of a coward" (300). Earlier in the day, Watson tells Miller that he is going to comply with the quit-town order given him by the white supremacists because, among other things, he is "worth too much" to his family "to dream of ever attempting to live here again" (279). When Green and his gang offer him physical protection, he declines: "I have a wife and children. It is my duty to live for them. If I died, I should get no glory and no reward, and my family would be reduced to beggary" (281). (In Hegelian terms, both Watson and Letlow are "slaves.") Dr. Miller—"a very good sort of Negro" (252), just like Jerry Letlow, "a very good Negro" (84)—also survives, although his son is killed.

The most coherent lesson that can be inferred from the pattern of deaths is that the weaker classes die so that the stronger ones can collaborate. At the very end of the story, after Olivia Carteret has successfully used moral blackmail on her "half-sister," normalcy returns. The hitherto broken-down aristocracy makes itself relevant to the social and political order again. In the process, it spares among the nascent black bourgeoisie the lives of those that are likely to know their place and keep to it; the troublesome working peoples are all sacrificed. We see, as Carteret turns his back on the dying Jerry Letlow, that the "aristocratic" class is abandoning paternalism. And as Miller goes to heal Dodie Carteret, the aristocratic class is shown to have successfully coerced the cooperation of the compliant black bourgeoisie.

The story's clearing out of the militant unwashed in the "abolitionist" riot concludes logically what is obvious in the novel's depiction of the lower classes of both races. In descriptions of McBane, the Letlows, and Green the narrator uses naturalist idioms that are hardly different from the ones Carteret uses to refer to blacks generally. The narrator usually depicts Letlow's speeches, Green's comportment, and McBane's behaviors as outward manifestations of some inner weaknesses. For these workingmen of both races, the narrator establishes a strong correlation between socioeconomic standing and natural gifts. McBane carries a body made for labor and hard work: "His broad shoulders, burly form, square jaw, and heavy chin betokened energy, and unscrupulousness" (32). His constantly sloppy appearance reinforces the idea of his natural roughness. So do his severe handling of prisoners and murderous acts in the Klan. Natural gifts "are not impartially distributed among even the most [socially] favored race," says the narrator. While there are no obvious "natural" markers of the working class in him, Jerry Letlow is seldom discussed by either the narrator or his white employers without a reference to his natural racial limitations. Letlow would "hear the words 'vote,' 'franchise' . . . and other expressions . . . he could not follow . . . partly because he could not hear everything distinctly, and partly because of certain limitations which nature had placed in the way of Jerry's understanding anything difficult or abstruse" (80).

In contrast, the working classes do not use naturalist language. McBane uses the language of natural whiteness and superiority only when he is with members of the "broken down aristocracy." He also does not speak in the idioms of social superiority Belmont is fond of using. For McBane, the white supremacy campaign is a means of returning the Democratic Party to power so that he will get more business from convict labor (34–35).

The racialist dimensions of the American manifestation of the master/slave dialectic breaks down in the Reconstruction era of *Marrow* because the traditional class of "masters" has been compelled to include and recognize black men like Dr. Miller and Attorney Watson and also to change its method of extracting profit from forced labor to wage payment. In the new dispensation, the character of putting others to work and subjecting them to authority has changed radically. When Josh Green, a member of the historically slaving race, says, "'I don' call no man 'marster'" (114), he means he is not a slave in the antebellum sense and that whites are no longer masters in the way they used to be. Black professionals like Miller and Watson feel exactly like Green, but, because they do not belong to the slaving class any more, cannot understand his advocating counter-violence against the white supremacy campaign. Miller and Watson fail to grasp the abstract quality of Green's quest for justice under the banner of race, and the meaning of his willingness to die eludes them: "'You'd better be peaceable and endure a little injustice, rather than run the risk of a sudden and violent death,'" Miller advises Green (110). In essence, he is asking Green to stay content with being a "slave," although not exactly in the antebellum sense. We see, however, that the class analogous to antebellum slaves, the working people, will win the chance to live as it desires within the new order only if it demonstrates a readiness to fight the class of new masters to death. The living descendants of the old class of masters (the broken-down aristocracy) hold on to the race tack in their intra-class fight against other masters (the emergent black bourgeoisie) and win because the rising blacks are still new to the political gamesmanship of masters. In the white supremacists' success, Chesnutt shows that the colloquial relationship of "lordship" to "bondage," of power to subjection, did not end with constitutional Emancipation and legalistic declarations of equality. The moral conundrums that close *Marrow* demonstrate very well that the antagonism has mutated into baffling forms. The straightforward antebellum confidence in the usefulness of social rebellion as a tool for defining black self-definition reaches an impasse. That confidence would not return until the Great Depression.

4

SLAVE REBELLION, THE GREAT DEPRESSION, AND THE "TURBULENCE TO COME" FOR CAPITALISM

Black Thunder

> The "now" of reading and writing history at once determines the readability of historical images and is determined by them, as they are always already written. The "truth" of such history is neither timeless, nor arbitrarily associated with the temporality of a historical consciousness, but rather is inscribed within the temporality of the rhetorical structure functioning in any given present.
>
> —TIMOTHY BAHTI, *"History as Rhetorical Enactment"*

When Arna Bontemps's *Black Thunder* revisited the meaning of subaltern revolt in the form of a historical slave rebellion, the intellectual fine points of racial and class solidarity that baffled Chesnutt's post-Emancipation milieu were being rendered insignificant by the gritty deprivations and cruelties of the Great Depression era. To individuals who cannot fulfill basic needs, the most pressing social problem was not the harmony of white and black bourgeoisie but figuring a way to overcome the material and spiritual lack threatening to overwhelm the society, particularly the working classes. Nineteenth-century slave rebellions gave Arna Bontemps the historical precedence and intellectual confidence to deliberate on the possible heroic actions oppressed peoples might undertake to free themselves and take a decisive charge of the course of events.

Upon its release in 1936, *Black Thunder* earned the author, in his words, "no more than its advance" (xxix), promptly going out of print and not reissued until 1968, amidst the civil rights maelstrom. On the two occasions it was released, great political and cultural changes trailed the novel. In 1936, the cultural renaissance centered at Harlem had long waned, and many of its leaders, including Bontemps, had moved out of New York. Also, the long legal saga of the Scottsboro Trials that began in 1931 was reaching one of its many contested resolutions. The latter event brought to international attention the Jim Crow cruelties that had been exacerbated by the widespread deprivations brought about by the Great Depression.[1]

Certainly, similarities between the impatient political mood of 1968 and the general apprehensiveness of the mid-1930s justified the novel's second release. But that is not the subject of discussion here. This chapter puts forth the view that the novel's use of a historical slave rebellion to contemplate the ability of slaving workers to strive for their freedom commemorates less the specific heroism of nineteenth-century African Americans and concentrates more on the meaning of the slaves' rebellion for how to anticipate the range of actions open to working peoples in a depressed capitalist economy. The main significance of the novel, it is suggested, is in its use of a historical slave rebellion to draw attention to the general struggles of the downtrodden in desperate economic circumstances. The fictional recreation of rebelling slaves in 1800 Richmond, Virginia, is an allusion to what workers laboring under the severe economic climate of the Great Depression, but creatively managing their own nationalist (historical) materialism, might be pushed to do.[2]

There are three parts to the chapter. The first section relates the rebellion theme to the dominant tendencies of early-twentieth-century African American writing and remarks how the theme introduces to black American fiction an early version of what Richard Wright called "radical perspective" in his essay "Blueprint for Negro Writing." The two other sections analyze Bontemps's interpretation of the slaves' material and expressive cultures as structures of working-class transcendence. Presenting the slaves' "folk" culture as a discourse of transcendence, it would be suggested, constitutes the very means the novelist uses to denote the relevance of the historical slave rebellion to the novel's contemporary society.

SLAVE REBELLION AND THE BLUEPRINT FOR BLACK WRITING

Bontemps remarks in the retrospective preface to the 1968 edition of his novel that the revolutionary heroism exhibited by nineteenth-century slave rebels captures for him the essence of the response which the repressive atmosphere of the 1930s will eventually provoke among the oppressed. The "self-emancipation" efforts of nineteenth-century rebellions, Bontemps writes, are "a possible metaphor of turbulence to come." The writer discovers after moving out of Harlem that chattel slaves who had next to little chance of success once rose against their owners, and that fact encouraged him to believe that the drudgery of scrounging for an existence does not exhaust in humans the will to strive for spiritual freedom. Bontemps also indicates in the retrospective essay that a deep-seated antipathy toward black heroism prevented the American interwar reading public from accepting the novel's "theme of self-assertion by black men whose endurance was strained to the breaking point" (xxix), despite the timeliness of its subject. Although this explanation came many decades after the fact, its tenor is not different from the ones proposed half a century earlier about factors militating against black writers' determination to change popular conceptions of black people through literary heroic types. Using the example of slave rebels specifically, James Weldon Johnson, in "The Dilemma of the Negro Author," bemoans the fact that the white American reading public's notions of literary heroism, a crucial factor all American writers had to consider seriously, completely exclude black people:

> It would be proof of little less than supreme genius in a Negro poet for him to take one of the tragic characters in American Negro history—Crispus Attucks or Nat Turner or Denmark Vesey—put a heroic language in his mouth and have white America accept the work as authentic. American Negroes as heroes form no part of white America's concept of the race. . . . The Aframerican poet might take an African chief or warrior, set him forth in heroic couplets or blank verse and present him to white America with infinitely greater chance of having his work accepted. (479)[3]

It is possible, I would say, that the initially poor sales of *Black Thunder* were not caused solely by the trained racialism of white American readers. Rather, it may be that the dominant tendencies of early-twentieth-century black fiction and criticism, particularly as they were propagated in the Harlem Renaissance, have abandoned slavery as a formative aspect of African American consciousness and have conditioned white and black reading publics not to look for practical heroism in the experience of slavery. According to Darwin Turner, for instance, a general reticence toward slavery is a defining feature of twentieth-century black fiction until the 1960s. Turner suggests that three factors may have been responsible for this disinclination: (1) elite black writers, who seem to have accepted uncritically the mainstream American doxa that social success is guaranteed "for all but the lazy," were embarrassed "that their ancestors remained slaves for two centuries"; (2) early-twentieth-century writers, aiming to hasten racial harmony, probably believed that a general silence about black experience in slavery might make their southern white counterparts remember less their own hardships during the Civil War and Reconstruction; and (3) publishers simply detested such stories (111).

Critical statements made by participants in the Harlem movement confirm parts of Turner's arguments. Bontemps himself said in a 1973 interview that his interest in the American past of black peoples was not a common tendency early in the twentieth century: "Unlike most black writers I yearned for something in my past because I had something there that I could look upon with a certain amount of longing. A great many writers whom I have known have wanted to forget their pasts" (14). Alain Locke's "The New Negro," virtually the manifesto of the Harlem revival, apologized that the movement's ethnocentricism was not a means of projecting an inherent black nationalism but of channeling "balked social feelings" into useful expressions that highlight representative deeds of the "advance-guard of the African peoples in their contact with twentieth-century civilization," and of championing the restoration of black "prestige" that has been lost, due largely to "the fate and conditions of slavery" (30). Read in light of Turner's views, Locke is suggesting that slavery, notwithstanding its moments of unalloyed heroism and the vast materials it has produced for myth-making, belongs to a past that early-twentieth-century advanced black thinkers and writers would rather not commemorate. Ameliorating the spiritual degradation suffered under slavery and restoring racial "loss of prestige" cannot be well served by recalling the primal scene of shame itself. As it happened, early-twentieth-century writers who followed this view of the African American past skipped slavery and celebrated Africa, an Africa which the best known of the writings spoke about in ambivalent terms.[4]

When *Black Thunder* appeared in 1936, an aesthetics that would replace the one defined by Alain Locke had not been formulated. Between 1929—to retain the common periodization of the end of the Harlem movement with the beginning of the Great Depression—and the publication of Richard Wright's "Blueprint for Negro Writing" in 1937, some kind of interregnum in formal African American cultural programming was in place. (I do not mean to say that those years were barren. Zora Neale Hurston continued her unapologetic celebration of black rural southern folk life. In her novels, the connection to the slave past was not unduly isolated for celebration or commentary, but descendants of slaves to whom the memory of bondage is not too distant continue to organize their world with their received traditions.[5] This period also witnessed the emergence of Richard Wright's "engaged" existential realism that will later dominate the black literary landscape in the 1940s.) The fluid environment of the black literary 1930s allowed various visions, among which stands out Bontemps's historical examination of the revolutionary elements of black folk life. In some ways, Bontemps's slave insurrection plot reflects the spirit of Hurston's expositions on the life and lore of ordinary blacks and foreshadows the engaged realism of the Richard Wright "school."[6]

Richard Wright wrote two texts that are directly relevant to determining the pertinence of Bontemps's novel of slave insurrection to the evolution of twentieth-century black American radical fiction. Wright's April 1936 review of Bontemps's book for *Partisan Review and Anvil* praises the story in terms that anticipate the recommendations of "Blueprint for Negro Writing" published the following year. The review praises *Black Thunder*'s "forthright" portrayal of the "historical and revolutionary traditions of the Negro people" and its filling "a yawning gap" (31) in the "barren field" of African American fiction. About Bontemps's protagonist, Wright says, "There is in his attitude *something which transcends the limits of immediate consciousness.* He is buoyed in his hope and courage by an optimism which takes no account of the appalling difficulties confronting him" (31; emphasis added). That radical transcendence, Wright believes, "sounds a *new note* in Negro fiction" (31; emphasis added). Gabriel impresses Richard Wright this much because his stubborn belief that the patent goodness of his cause is sufficient to sustain the insurrectionist is uncommon. That Bontemps made Gabriel's single-minded pursuit of freedom the main factor of plot development, Wright believes, renders the novel a compelling and honest artistic whole.

The "Blueprint" essay shows later that Wright praised *Black Thunder* because the narrative defies the general trends of early-twentieth-century black fiction. Unlike texts preoccupied with social decorum, *Black Thunder,* in contradiction of Alain Locke's program, positively makes a heroic tale out of the representative "needs," "sufferings," and "aspirations" (54) of black folks from a perspective that depicts the slaves' insurrectionist plot as an example of courageous black nationalism. Black fiction up till 1937, Wright says, has suffered from the influence of its middle-class provenance both in terms of thematic preferences and artistic direction. Narrative content, in particular, has served as either a "sign" of middle-class achievement or a means of "pleading with white America for justice" (53). Its form too has refused to draw from the expressions of the masses, the fountainhead of genuine black nationalism and "the emotional expression of group feeling" (58). Lacking a serious theoretical view of the society they were beseeching for accommodation, early-twentieth-century black novelists were misdirected in their search for a "simple literary realism" (59).

Wright's cure for these ideological and literary ills includes the cultivation of a "social consciousness" that can simultaneously bear the weight of the writer's sense of how the world is structured and his or her projection of the historical course it may follow in the future. A consciousness that is up to this task will manifest the writer's perspective of patterns in the history of the nation and of the forces that have shaped their development: "Perspective for Negro writers will come when they have looked and brooded so hard and long upon the harsh lot of their race and compared it with the hopes and struggles of minority peoples everywhere that the cold facts have begun to tell them something" (62).[7]

Wright was not the only writer who saw in *Black Thunder* the promise of a new direction for black writing. Dorothy Peterson observed in her review that its depiction of "the slaves' *self-initiated* fight for freedom, although a failure, represents more clearly than we have had brought to our attention in other stories of slave days the power and daring of the slaves and the real fear that such a display of power inspired in their masters" (46; emphasis added). In the same issue of *New Challenge* in which "Blueprint" was first published, Eugene Holmes referred to the novel as an example of the direction black writing should follow (71–72). Earlier in the spring issue, Marian Minus too singled out *Black Thunder* for praise because its use of black history challenges the tradition of representing black people: "The provinces of folk prose and poetry, dialectical refinements, and phases of Negro ideology as it has been colored by centuries of oppression are still to be exhausted. The 'great Negro novel' has not been written because these fields have been too meagerly explored. Arna Bontemps' *Black Thunder* approaches the incorporation of these elements more completely than any other novel" (10). To these commentators, *Black Thunder* is the first "great" black novel.

Bontemps's 1968 retrospective preface confirms the extent to which his novel anticipated Wright's ideas about effective cultural and materialist black nationalism. Bontemps says he selected the Gabriel Prosser incident over other instances of American slave insurrection plots because Gabriel's approach to self-emancipation is driven by a native (Peterson calls it "self-directed") materialist ethos. Unlike Nat Turner, who had "'visions' and 'dreams,'" and Denmark Vesey, who overreached himself with a plot that was too extensive to succeed, Gabriel did not rely on religion, magic, or other "mumbo-jumbo" (xxvii) to rationalize his plot. Instead, he used sensible calculations and deductions to win over fellow slaves. Bontemps also admires Gabriel because his methods of strategic planning and of evoking loyalty turn mainly on objective criteria. Bontemps believes that Gabriel's plot is so reasonably crafted that historical records, made up mainly by Gabriel's "prospective victims," acknowledge that his strategy would have succeeded had inclement weather not foiled it. Gabriel is, in short, a man of "science" who, exercising reason under the most improbable environment, can look into the future and work actively to make it conform to his own aspiration.

RELOCATING 1800 TO 1936

The narrative flows in two directions in *Black Thunder.* One stream follows a realistic portrayal of the slaves' drive to rebel against their masters.

Here, slaves compare the price they may pay for the risk of rebellion to the nonguaranteed benefits they may enjoy after the battle. In the other stream, which assumes a symbolic dimension, we see slaves striving to construe the larger spiritual meaning of their contemplated actions. In these continuous streams, the novel relocates 1800 to 1936 with both the realistic descriptions of the forbidding circumstances in which blacks, like modern industrial workers groaning under the Great Depression, slaved for meager recompense, and the slaves' methodical ruminations on what they may gain materially and "spiritually" by moving against their tormentors. Two watershed events would suffice for illustration: (1) Mr. Prosser murders his slave, Bundy, because the old man has taken to drinking and can no longer contribute meaningfully to the plantation revenue; (2) other slaves, seeing their own fate in Bundy's death, use the occasion of his funeral to bring into the open their hitherto clandestine schedule for an insurrection they envision would end their being treated like Bundy. By making Bundy's murder and the uprising continuous sets of events, the novel connects the slave's experience of the master's cruelty to the collective effort needed to remedy it.

The slaves' collective response to Bundy's shabby fate is the main link between the novel's "literal" subject matter, the 1800 slave rebellion, and the dominant political questions of the Great Depression era in which the story was published. Clearly, 1936 is not 1800 and industrial laborers are not literal chattel slaves. However, the ill usage that leads to Bundy's death is not unrelated to the social conditions of slaving workers in the "depths of Depression," a time when, as Bontemps says, "even conservative people could understand why certain writers could be taking positions that were quite radical" (Interview 11). To his master, Bundy is "a worthless old scavenger. . . . Too old for hard work, too trifling and unreliable for lighter responsibilities. Not worth his keep. No better'n a lame mule" (14). These words, uttered just before Prosser inflicts the fatal punishment, plainly indicate that the total worth of the slaving worker's life is measured by the class that puts it to work mainly by the profit-making potential it promises. Bundy's only material crime in this instance is that he cannot any longer help his owner make more wealth and has become, more or less, a broken piece of machinery whose maintenance exceeds the gain it may ever deliver.

The persistence of the desperate downtrodden to resist their oppression comes out in Bundy's unexpected lashing back at his master after he is first struck in the head. Although drunk and down, he manages to seize the bridle of his master's horse. The startled Prosser wonders for a moment, asking himself: "Was Bundy trying to resist?" (14). Bundy's feeble and ineffective symbolic resistance morphs into the general insurrection plan that Gabriel and other leaders of the revolt introduced after the funeral obsequies.

Bontemps's fighting slaves act not simply because they want to avenge personal wrongs, although that is no less important as a motivation, but because the spirit of freedom that fills the political air moves them too. Gabriel catches that spirit one day after eavesdropping on some white men speculating about what might be the case if the French Revolution were to be repeated in the United States. At some point in the conversation, an American radical, Alexander Biddenhurst, says to his French interlocutors: "'You had the filthy nobles in France. Here we have the planter aristocrats. We have the merchants, the poor whites, the free blacks, the slaves—classes, classes, classes . . . the whole world must know that these are not natural distinctions but artificial ones. Liberty, equality and fraternity will have to be won for the poor and the weak everywhere if your own revolution is to be permanent" (21). One of the Frenchmen responds that germs of revolutionary thought native to America exist already in Thomas Jefferson's *Notes on Virginia* and Judge Tucker's *Dissertation on Slavery*, referring obliquely to the internal debate among Virginian intellectuals early in the nineteenth century about the place of slavery in a free republic. This conversation speaks of the French Revolution and a potential general American slave insurrection in a language of class conflict that is closer to the leftist activism of the 1930s than to 1800. Biddenhurst's socialist views on the materialist foundation of race and class formations may also be alluding to the crisis of theory and practice for early-twentieth-century American communists struggling to reconcile the historically understandable ethnic nationalism of American working blacks to the tenets of "raceless" class-consciousness promoted by the CPUSA.[8]

The illicit conversation Gabriel overhears about classes and equality is crucial to the narrative development of his character. The white Jacobins give him "words for things that he didn't know had names" (21). Biddenhurst's juxtaposing revolution, classes, liberty, equality, and fraternity concretizes for Gabriel the perspective he has long sought about the political rumblings around Richmond. The seditious words also open up a large framework for him to think about the meaning of the clandestine meetings he has been holding with like-minded slaves. In short, the conversation educates Gabriel in how to give *thought* to *things* and make them transcendent. Indeed, his psyche is completely transformed after the experience: "he felt less wretched than he had felt earlier" (23), and his body develops a strange ability to absorb physical punishment without feeling any pain.[9]

In the Great Depression context of the novel's publication, Gabriel's drawing inspiration from the Jacobins could also be said to be speaking directly to some of the unformed questions of working peoples. The French Revolution may, for example, be alluding to the European socialist revolutions of the early twentieth century, whose promise of a "miraculous" means of restoring "pride" to the working weary, as Arnold Rampersad has said, found favor among many concerned American intellectuals. That is to say, Bontemps may have been using the ideology of his white Jacobins to refer to the revolutionary alternatives available for the slaving workers of the 1930s. This reading is recommended by the similarity between some of the terms used by the 1800 slave owners to characterize the French Revolution and vulgar anti-communist propaganda. Like twentieth-century anti-communists, slave owners in the novel teach the poor white public that the French Revolution perpetrates ungodly "distribution of wealth, snatching private property, elevation of blacks, equality, immediate and compulsory miscegenation" (65), and they stereotype a Jacobin as "an abandoned, villainous person with a foreign accent and a soiled shirt" (38). Bontemps's readers, eavesdroppers on Gabriel's historic deeds, are being called upon, through Gabriel's enthusiastic acceptance of the Richmond radicals, to reconsider these cliché portrayals of revolutionaries.

In the introduction to the 1992 edition of the novel, Arnold Rampersad cautioned against making Bontemps a socialist of any stripe because "revolution and radical socialism had held little appeal for him during the 1920s" (xi). Bontemps himself has maintained that his sensibilities detest doctrinaire political theories. Unlike his contemporaries—Richard Wright and Ralph Ellison, for instance—who struggled unsuccessfully against it early in their writing careers, he says, "party-line communism" was not attractive to him: "I always avoided it because, having grown up in an environment where my father had been a preacher, I was turned off by denominational, doctrinal infighting" (11). But in the same interview, Bontemps admits that "in the depths of the Depression" radical solutions to social and economic difficulties tantalized even conservatives. For him, who was not a conservative, I would say that the attraction of a working class revolt should not be ruled out completely.

At any rate, the most pertinent consideration for understanding the repositioning of black fiction that Bontemps's novel helped to bring about is not really the exact character of the author's personal commitment to socialism but his subscription to the general idea that capitalism was in crisis and that interpreting history in a certain way shows that slaving workers would very likely take charge of events. The main concern Bontemps expressed about this view of history is that doctrinaire materialist thought, in which the movement of history is akin to a river lunging irreversibly toward a sure end, may not be able to account for the participation of black people in world historical events. To revise that notion such that it could accommodate the historic deeds of black slaving workers, Bontemps proposes the idea that "time is a pendulum" moving back and forth (perhaps dialectically).

REVOLUTIONARY NATIONALISM IN THE SOUL OF SLAVE FOLKS

Bontemps swings the pendulum of history to the emblematic full participation of black slave workers in the shaping of the "Age of Revolution" by grounding the particulars of Gabriel's insurrection in typical elements of slave folk culture.[10] Slaves fought because their material conditions dictated that they do so. But the struggle played out as recorded because the slaves' culture gave them the structures of transcendence with which they ascribed meaning to gross everyday events. As Eric Sundquist says, the novel's strategic use of slave culture is Bontemps's main achievement: "His extensive use of folk beliefs is a means to put the languages of the masters and the language of the slaves on a continuum and to discover in the coded discourse of vernacular an equivalent to the philosophical language of the Rights of Man." Alongside Gabriel's Enlightened reason, "the whispering, singing, humming, and silent language of the slaves runs in a remarkable undercurrent throughout the entire text, giving a special voice to those whose testimony, in court and in history, had been accorded no legal or official historical meaning" (*Hammers of Creation* 100).[11]

But Bontemps's depiction of black folk life signifies more than merely revealing the slaves' concealment of their idea of freedom. The masters do not have that much trouble with the slaves' peculiar culture (or secret language)—which they know exists but treat with benign neglect—so long as it is not used for a systematic subversion of the plantation order. Gabriel's owner allows slaves to worship in a supervised setting and gives them the chance to bury their dead and carry out other rituals of daily living according to their native wisdom. For him and other masters, slave culture is like a poor person's eloquence that, as a Nigerian proverb says, means no more than a cutlass good only for bush clearing. Gabriel and his fellow rebels choose to fight to cancel the peculiar conception of freedom that authorizes masters to restrict the slaves' true articulations to a secret language. Gabriel knows that the slaves' secret language epitomized in "conjure" may actually be serving the master's universe of lies, if all it does is help slaves endure daily drudgeries.

What Bontemps's use of folk life highlights vividly, I would say, is the slaves' articulation of the will to overstep the discursive limits set by the master. The critical cultural question for the rebels is not the richness of the slaves' language but how it could be deployed to communicate rebellion, or, to rework the Nigerian saying, how the poor person's eloquence could be made to signify more than a readiness for bush clearing. In political praxis, doing this requires not just subversive inflections of the speeches of the powerful in the vernacular, as Sundquist suggests, but also devising means of reversing the order responsible for the master's position in the first place. In short, Bontemps's use of slave culture to further the slaves' rebellion produces a model of ethnic nationalism that does not contradict forward-looking politics. As Wright says in "Blueprint,"

> The Negro writer who seeks to function within his race as a purposeful agent has a serious responsibility. In order to do justice to his subject matter, in order to depict Negro life in all of its manifold intricate relationships, a deep, informed, and complex consciousness is necessary; a consciousness which draws for its strength upon the fluid lore of a great people, and moulds this lore with the concepts that move and direct the forces of history today. (59)

I would discuss a few emblematic instances of the slaves' self-conscious selection of elements of their culture to further the rebellion. The first reported meeting of the insurrection leaders is virtually a Christian fellowship trying to understand the extent of God's distaste for the oppression of the poor and to ascertain the level of his willingness to support a group seeking to throw off its earthly yoke. As Gabriel and others read it, the Bible prescribes death for stealers of men, prohibits wickedness towards strangers, and endorses a universal proclamation of liberty. The good Lord also promises to "spoil the soul" of the oppressors of the poor, especially those who deny them fair compensation for their labor. Those that violate this covenant, God promises to deliver "into the hand of their enemies, and into the hand of them that seek their life; and their dead bodies shall be for meat unto the fowls of heaven, and to the beasts of the earth" (45). The narrative later speaks of Gabriel as that person chosen by God to wedge the gap (47) that separates the oppressed from the fulfillment of God's freedom covenant. This interpretation of the slave community's "shared" scriptural "code" offered by the conspiracy's avant-garde is clearly *discontinuous* with the view of the master class. The insurrection leaders do not invent new symbols; instead, they recode existing texts to carry the burden of their subversive aspirations.[12]

The story also reflects the stress that elements of compliant slave culture can exert on mobilizing for a rebellion. Ben Sheppard, for example, is repulsed by the "desecrating, sinful thing" (62) he imagines that rebellious "black slaves coming suddenly through . . . windows, pikes and cutlasses in their hands, their eyes burning with murderous passion" would be. The contrasting Christianity of the rebel leaders and Sheppard reveals the diversity of views among the slaves and also shows that subversion did not come to Gabriel and his comrades intuitively.

The function of cultural signs in the revolutionary process is further examined in the conspiracy's discussion of what sign to use to announce the beginning of the revolt. Gabriel picks a signal derived from biblical descriptions of the apocalypse: "This going to be the sign: When you see somebody riding that black colt Araby, galloping him for all he's worth in the big road, wearing a pair of Marse Prosser's shiny riding boots, you can know that the time's come. You going to know yo' captains, and that's going to be the sign to report" (55). This signal barely conceals the connection between the emergence of a new existence foretold in the book of Revelation and the liberating violence being plotted by the slaves. At the beginning of the end of the inherently corrupt order of things, according to the book of Revelation, God will send seven seals to the faithful. The seals will contain horses of different colors, some of which shall be let loose on earth to launch the beginning of Christ's second coming. The third seal contains a black horse upon which is mounted a rider with "a pair of balances in his hand" (Rev: 6:5). The rider of the black steed is explicitly instructed as to how to measure and reward *labor* justly: "A quart of wheat for a day's wages, and three quarts of barley for a day's wages" (Rev. 6:6).[13] Out of the remaining seals come great forces that will unleash massive destruction on "the kings of the earth, and the great men, and the rich men, and the chief captains, and the mighty men, and every bondman, and every free man" (Rev: 6:15).

That Gabriel's choice of a messenger of rebellion is fashioned after an episode from the biblical apocalypse speaks to Bontemps's view of the telos of the struggles of the downtrodden in the nineteenth century—and, by extension, victims of twentieth-century industrial capitalism—as the hastening of the coming to pass of a "new heaven and a new earth." In other words, Bontemps figures Gabriel's plot as the expression of a desire to establish a new set of material and ideological (spiritual) relations.

We can step back to consider the rebels' use of mundane culture. The narrative first broaches the conspiracy idea when a drunken Bundy invites Ben Woofolk, Tom Sheppard's old servant, to join a local unit of black Freemasons. Woofolk, being a devout Christian, promptly rejects the invitation, calling masonry a "'chillun's foolishness'" (12). This view is not in itself reactionary in the black antebellum world. (Frederick Douglass once dismissed black masonry as an institution "swallowing up the best energies of many of our best men, contenting them with the glittering follies of artificial display" [quoted in Levine 8].) In this instance, however, the said masonry is a cultural cover used by the conspiracy to hide its secret plot. Masonry, as a cultural and political tool, was common in free states where blacks, excluded from white institutions, formed and used their lodges "as an oppositional response to white racism, one that provided disempowered blacks with a fraternal base on which black community and black leadership could be built"

(Levine 8). Because black masonry is not known to have existed extensively in the antebellum south, it would be right to assume that Bontemps uses the term as a metaphor for the exclusive mobilization institution devised by the rebels. Ben Woofolk's quick rejection of Bundy's invitation may, in this light, be signifying the pious Christian's fear of what an independent cultural institution might induce its members to think.

For narrative purposes, it should also be said, the self-selecting masonry is an appropriate forum for managing the insurrection as it pertains to the recruitment of participants and clandestine planning. However, this pinnacle institution cannot facilitate a rebellion without admitting a mass of noninitiates. The contradictory demands of this structure are revealed partially at Bundy's funeral when the "masons," normally guided by written testaments like the Bible, try to make "folk" recruitment appeals to their largely illiterate community of slaves. To accommodate this situation, members of the inner conspiracy put new recruits under obligation by making them swear with "the Book," a "pot of blood," and a "black cat bone" (54). They do not read letters of encouragement from Haiti and do not quote the example of the French Jacobins.

Moving further back to individual slave rebels, we can see that each person reconciles himself to his position in the struggle with elements drawn from "folk" culture. The story, for instance, reiterates Gabriel's "folk" radical materialist nationalism with his "signature" aphorism: "'A wild bird what's in a cage will die anyhow, sooner or later. . . . He'll pine hisself to death. He just is well to break his neck trying to get out" (69). This proverb rhetorically turns the desperation of a slave's life into an act of necessary revolt. Other times Gabriel will say that "everything what's equal to a ground hog want to be free," "anything what's equal to a gray squirrel want to be free," "I feel sort of like a caged thing that needs the open," or "there ain't nothing but hard times waiting when a man get to studying about freedom." These sayings, which only Gabriel uses, are repeated so frequently that the imagery of the caged bird dying to be free becomes a dominant narrative motif.

WHAT IS THE MEANING OF A SLAVE REBELLION IN 1936?

As noted earlier in the case of antebellum novels, giving meaning to a slave rebellion in light of "the turbulence to come," to use Bontemps's phrasing, involves goose-stepping around historical facts. Sundquist identifies this problem in *Black Thunder* with his suggestion that "the spiritual truth of the rebellion lies in the conspiracy itself rather than in the revolt that never comes to pass" (*Hammers of Creation* 101). He goes on to fix the terms of the novel's "spiritual truth" around a critique of the legal endorsement of Jim Crow cruelties in the famous Scottsboro trials: "Scottsboro appeared to prove that little had changed through the Civil War, Reconstruction, and rise of Jim Crow. The thwarted black rebellion more than one hundred years past thus became the means for Bontemps to examine the depressing spectacle of the Scottsboro trial through the deflecting screen of historical research and imagination" (96). Sundquist believes that to speak against the Scottsboro travesties, Bontemps uses Gabriel's exploits to restate black people's capacity to "desire freedom and equality on their own, organize and act on their own, and draw philosophical support from the fundamental ideology of American democracy—in essence be governed by the same principles of natural rights and liberty" (95). In other words, Gabriel's plot refutes the racist orthodoxy that views the intervention of Communist International in the defense of those accused in the Scottsboro case as an indication of black incapacity for autonomous thought and action. Blacks, Bontemps seems to have been saying, do not need communists to teach them about their "own revolutionary significance in America" (Cruse 184).

In *Radical Representations,* Barbara Foley argues the opposite line, calling the story a "Marxist reenactment" of Gabriel's insurrection (370). To make a counter-proposition stick, she says, one would have to turn a blind eye to the white Jacobins who play critical roles in Gabriel's development as a hero. At the deeper structural level, she adds, there is a "didactic connection" between the slaves' struggle and Jacobinism, between Gabriel's fate and a white Jacobin's cruel death: "Bontemps connects the Rights of Man movement with the Prosser rebellion by juxtaposing Gabriel's hanging with the death by stoning of M. Creuzot's servant Laurent, who is branded a 'Jacobin' by a mob of reactionary whites" (381). Those who killed the two men are motivated by their concern for a social totality they believed Laurent and Gabriel threatened to undermine. The "leftist" (382) social totality framework of the novel "establishes the relevance of Gabriel's rebellion for the world of the present—where, presumably, black rebels need no longer hesitate to reach out to their white allies, and white radicals need no longer feel powerless to act in solidarity with their black compeers" (370).

Notwithstanding the eminent sense made in both Foley's and Sundquist's reading, I would suggest that the focus of the novel's closure, and by implication its lasting meaning, is how to overcome the dispiriting effect of the collapse of the insurrection. The "spiritual truth" (Sundquist's phrase) that the novel explores is not the meaning of Gabriel's death but his defiance of historical impediments. In colloquial history, Bontemps failed. Being a "historical" novel, Bontemps's work retains the bare outline of the tragic ends of the historical rebellion and its leaders. But the main theme of the story is the working peoples' will to defy the handed-down order of things and to desire a new regime that can accommodate their own social objectives.

The importance of defying old history and making new ones comes out fully in the story's internal debates on the meaning of a failed rebellion. These arguments begin on the day appointed for the insurrection. That morning, one woman and eleven hundred men, many of whom have consulted Catfish Primus for charms and amulets that will give them extra armor against the enemy, set out to explode "black thunder" on their masters. The heavens, however, surprise them with a torrential rain that breaks out at the moment the sole female warrior, Juba, signals the beginning of troop movement: "There it was now—thunder. Yes, and rain too. There it was, a sudden spray in her face, a few big broken drops" (81). The meaning of the rain becomes a subject of discussion and distraction for the troops, who wonder whether it is a sign of divine blessing or ill will, whether it means that the attack plan should be revised.

Everyone, including Gabriel, believes that the rain is a "sign" of something, but they are all unable to agree on what that is. One of Gabriel's lieutenants, like many other commanders and troops, thinks that the rain manifests a "bad hand or something like that" (84). Others think the rain is not natural, and that it signifies the displeasure of the stars (103, 113, 149). Gabriel snaps back that the rain can only signify a blessing: "'Whoever heard tell about rain being a sign of a bad hand against you?'" (84). He also admonishes his comrades: "A little rain won't hurt none" (83). At one point, he uncharitably accuses them of hiding their fear of proceeding under their interpretation of the weather's omen (103). In reality, however, the downpour has kept about two-thirds of the troops from advancing: creeks have become too deep to cross (85), troops and commanders could not get to Richmond (88), bridges have been washed off (93), key commanders could not report punctually, wagons are stuck in the road, and horses struggle in the muddy roads already strewn with fallen trees. The rain, in short, makes the chosen time an unfit "night to break free" (97). Even so, Gabriel, not persuaded that the heavy rainfall should mean the postponement of the struggle, leads four hundred reluctant men and one woman into a battle that he soon discovers cannot be won by sheer courage alone. He realizes rather too late that "'it's more dangerouser than going frontwise'" (109).

According to Hazel Carby, novels of slavery conventionally close with the protagonist's "escape, emancipation, or death" (139). Options available to American novelists of historical rebellion are even slimmer because there are no successful insurrections to emulate. Events preceding Gabriel's execution indicate that Bontemps wants to move beyond history, without tampering with its known outlines, and preserve a sense of the slaves' history-defying will to freedom. On the morning after the aborted insurrection, the community notices amid the devastation wreaked by the previous day's storm "a scrawny red rooster, looking very tall and awkward on a small raft, drifted steadily downstream. He had not lost his *strut,* but his feathers were wet and he seemed, in his predicament, as dismayed as an old beau" (110; emphasis added). Like the rooster, Gabriel and his followers have been beaten to near despair by the rain. Like Gabriel and his troops, the rooster maintains its inborn pride in spite of the strong water currents that have taken over control of the directions of its movements.

The narrative further defrays the dispiriting effect of the rebellion's tragic failure with an imagined confrontation between Gabriel and his prosecutors. Baited with a promise of a lenient sentence if he would reveal the names of which Jacobins "planted the damnable seeds" of rebellion in him, Gabriel replies with utter disdain: "Might just as well to hang" (210). The interrogator warns him, "Don't *strut,* nigger" (211). Gabriel speaks with even more defiance: "No, suh, no *strutting.* But I been free this last four-five weeks. On'erstand? I been a gen'l, and I been ready to die since first time I hooked on a sword. The others too—they been ready. We all knowed it was one thing or the other. The stars was against us, though; that's all" (211). I take Gabriel's words to be a self-critique and not some indignation at an unmerciful constellation offended by the insurrectionist plot. Slaves in Gabriel's community look up to the "stars" for guidance on how and when to make critical human judgments in ways that the conspiracy leadership failed to consider well enough. Gabriel and his fellow "masons" committed a tactical error by their inattentiveness to the beliefs of their followers. As Juba learns from one old medicine woman she consults about possible help for Gabriel while he is trying to escape after the whole plan had gone awry, Gabriel is too alienated from non-Christian wisdom: "Too much listening to Mingo read a white man's book. They ain't paid attention to the signs" (166). The woman tells Juba that by disregarding non-Christian fortification, Gabriel's adoption of Toussaint L'Ouverture's tactics is done only halfway because Toussaint and his followers also "kilt a hog in the woods. Drank the blood" (166). "'Maybe we should paid attention to the signs,'" Gabriel says on his last day in court (214). He insists till the very end that the slave owners would have had no chance against them had the rebel plans been realized.

The only reason a historical novelist would manifestly try to overlay an optimistic interpretation on a tragic historical fact, the way Bontemps does here, is to encourage readers to consume history actively and not digest handed-down traditions as passive events. Readers who may find inspiration in the events, and not the long dead historical subjects, are the ones being served by the novelist's positive interpretation. *Black Thunder*'s story of "the stricken slave's will to freedom" is meant to light up a corner of "the darkening Depression settling all around" the national landscape in the mid-1930s.

Stories of rebellion always mark the possibility of new beginnings, whether it is emancipation from slavery, freedom from racist restrictions, or from unconscionable economic exploitation. Besides its symbolic celebration of the slaves' will to resist their subjugation, *Black Thunder,* as remarked by several of the commentators cited above, also demarcates the beginning of a new way of commenting on the black experience. To conclude this chapter, I assess the novel's significance in black American literary history with a brief comparison to Richard Wright's *Native Son.* When Wright says in his review of Bontemps's novel that Gabriel's "mind is a confused mixture of superstition, naive cunning, idealism, and a high courage born partly of his deep ignorance and partly an amazing ability to forget his personal safety" (31), he could, with little modifications, have been writing about his own Bigger Thomas, who is a sort of "black thunder" waiting to explode. Bigger may not be superstitious (and Wright obviously exaggerates that aspect of Gabriel's story) or idealistic, but he is sometimes courageous, if only waywardly, and clearly ignorant and cunning, although not in Gabriel's positive manner.

Another similarity is that both characters are tried for capital offenses, the report of which each author uses to close his story. At Bigger Thomas's trial, the prosecution speaks of his victim's parents as great philanthropists: "He was welcomed there with lavish kindness. He was given a room; and he was told that he would receive extra money for himself, over and above his weekly wages. He was fed. He was asked if he wanted to go back to school and learn a trade. But he refused. His mind and heart—if this beast can be said to have a mind and heart!—were not set upon such goals" (375). These pieces of information are meant to show the aggravating circumstances of Bigger Thomas's crime and to portray him as a conscienceless creature that viciously bites the proverbial fingers that feed him. An almost exact tactic is used in Gabriel's trial. "Were you not treated well?" (210), an interrogator asks to establish the absence of a clean motive to rebel for a favored slave like Gabriel. A state witness also expresses his moral indignation at Gabriel's ungratefulness to a benevolent master: "Mad dogs—that's what you are. The audacity! It's inconceivable that well-treated servants like—" (212). To characterize Bigger Thomas as someone beyond human help and compassion, his prosecutor calls him "this mad dog who sits here today" (374). In both novels, the protagonists are set for execution as bourgeois justice fails them.

The apparent environmental determinism theme commonly advanced in interpretations of *Native Son* may also be traced to Bontemps's Gabriel.

Wright's novel, for example, opens with Bigger's killing the rat that attacks him in desperation after it has been chased into a corner. The rat's condition, clearly foreshadowing the analogous situation that will arise later for Bigger when he is run into a corner by policemen, brings to mind Gabriel's proverb of freedom: "'A wild bird what's in a cage will die anyhow, sooner or later. . . . He'll pine hisself to death. He just is well to break his neck trying to get out" (69). Bigger, the rat, and Gabriel all break their necks in the struggle against daunting social forces.

The features highlighted above indicate that the narrative tendencies heralded in novels such as *Native Son,* stories in which realistically portrayed black characters unsuccessfully navigate overwhelming social environments that eventually engulf them in spite of their best efforts, could be said to have started in *Black Thunder.* The nature of the obstacles faced by the protagonists is determined by the historical difference between Gabriel's antebellum slave society and the barren opportunities for upward advancement confronted by Bigger Thomas, and even Lutie Johnson in Ann Petry's *The Street,* in pre–World War II urban industrial cities. Many of the protagonists that came after Gabriel isolate themselves from large political communities and battle their alienation alone. In that, they may not be said to share Gabriel's firm conviction about the collective power to hasten the certain arrival of a just "new world and new heaven."

Partly because Bontemps's temperament is perhaps more optimistic than Wright's, and partly because the actions of the historical subjects he writes about suggest they have an unflappable confidence that their actions could influence the coming of a new heaven and a new earth, he jettisons realism for symbolism and makes the defeated rebels strut their optimism. "The Negroes remembered Africa in 1800" (52), Bontemps's narrator observes about the impressive funeral fellow slaves give Bundy. As I have discussed, the Richmond insurrectionists are not recalling Africa just for its own sake but to construct an elaborate cover for their work on a pending war of independence. The same could be said of Bontemps in 1936: he commemorated the slaves' 1800 remembrance of Africa with the intent to foreshadow the coming of another war of (workers') independence.

5

DISTILLING PROVERBS OF HISTORY FROM THE HAITIAN WAR OF INDEPENDENCE

The Black Jacobins

> One must begin somewhere
> Begin what?
> The only thing in the world worth beginning:
> The End of the world of course.
>
> —AIMÉ CÉSAIRE, *Notebook of a Return to the Native Land*

Intellectuals in other parts of the black world were also preoccupied with deciphering the meaning of slavery's past for the future of their contemporary societies. Within négritude, arguably the best known strain of anti-colonial rethinking of world politics to emerge in this era, black writers all over embraced the past of their people, in the words of Aimé Césaire, "totally, without reservation" (39). In the acclaimed classic of the movement, *Notebook of a Return to My Native Land,* Césaire declares that the origin of the movement is in Haiti, "where négritude arose for the first time" (15). Césaire's poem also claims for négritude the passion of the grand slave rebel, Toussaint L'Ouverture:

> What is mine also: a little cell in the Jura,
> a little cell, the snow lines it with white bars
> the snow is a jailer mounting the guard before a prison
>
> What is mine
> a lone man imprisoned in whiteness
> a lone man defying the white screams of white death

(TOUSSAINT, TOUSSAINT L'OUVERTURE)
a man who mesmerizes the white sparrow hawk of white death
a man alone in the sterile sea of white sand

In this excerpt that pits Toussaint's defiant blackness against the false aggrandizement of elemental whiteness, the black will to live triumphs. This chapter is not about négritude. It analyzes C.L.R. James's inauguration of black anti-colonial "realistic historicism" in his interpretation of the Haitian War of Independence. I open with these remarks about négritude and Césaire to reiterate black writers' common use of historical slave rebellions in the 1930s and to introduce new directions in their understanding of their societies and the world in general. There was something compelling about slave rebellions and the political climate of the 1930s that drew writers of diverse ideological temperaments to revisit the Haitian War of Independence. Arna Bontemps, whose other novel of slave rebellion was discussed in the last chapter, wrote about Haiti in *Drums at Dusk.* Two other texts of the Haitian struggle, Carpentier's *The Kingdom of This World* and James's *The Black Jacobins,* are the subjects of this chapter and the next.

We can begin to develop an idea of the impact of C.L.R. James's study on its readers by examining the grammar of the title of George Lamming's long review of the book. In that piece, titled "Caliban Orders History," the novelist commends James's interpretation of the audacious intervention of Haitian slaves in the shaping of the history of the colony. The declarative syntax of Lamming's title places Shakespeare's archetypal colonial servant in the subject position in an attempt to replicate grammatically the intellectual feat James's book is believed to have accomplished. Lamming, not a stranger to the power of felicitous symbols, recommends that the book should be "Bible-reading for every boy" (119) so that they can feel the miracle of how a community of "languageless and deformed slaves" transformed themselves into speaking beings. *The Black Jacobins* stirs this high level of inspiration not so much for its factual accuracy[1]—which Lamming does not evaluate—but for its symbolic reconfiguration of the slaves' will to freedom. In Lamming's view, James's portrait of the slaves contradicts the best-known literary record in the English language and shows "Caliban as Prospero had never known him" (119). In Toussaint L'Ouverture, James transforms Caliban into "a great soldier in battle, an incomparable administrator in public affairs; full of paradox but never without compassion, a humane leader of men" (119).

Lamming is not alone in reading the book as a revolutionary account of black people's full-fledged participation in the world historical acts of the age of revolution. Robin Kelley notes that the book "ultimately re-wrote the history of the modern world" (112) because it challenged traditional explanations of the role of black peoples in the French Revolution. James refutes "established fictions" (112) by demonstrating the dependency of the French bourgeoisie on the profits generated from slave labor and also by showing that "the slaves themselves forced French Revolutionaries to debate the meaning of freedom and liberty as the natural right of man" (112). Because James's interpretation of the archives privileges the slaves' motivation and drive, *The Black Jacobins* "dramatically *revised the way history was written*" by recharacterizing the nature of the movers of the spirit of modern history to include "*all* who labor" (112; emphasis added).[2]

The main point of adulation for both Kelley and Lamming is James's refutation of many untruths about the subjective capacity of black people to *experience* and to *make* history. The reading proposed in this chapter deals with the theory of history, "realistic historicism," that James uses to interpret the past heroic deeds of one black people as a reliable index to the future of not only all black people but of colonialist capitalism as a whole. The truly revolutionary aspect of James's work that should be celebrated, I suggest, is not his coaxing facts of black revolutionary traditions out of colonialist archives but his making *historical* heroes out of slaves.

REALISTIC HISTORICISM AND THE DECOLONIZATION OF THOUGHT

What is historical? How is the historical moment to be recognized? Is history self-constituted by the event? Or is it done after the fact by the writer? If it is done by the writer, isn't history then determined by narrative? These are some of the large questions posed consistently by Hayden White, who, as far back as 1966, has been proposing textualist models of history writing as his own way of instigating contemporary historians to rethink the nature of their discipline. White's two main lines of metahistorical inquiry concern the role of interpretation in the study of archives and the determinant function of writing in the production of historical knowledge. Histories, according to White, do not simply explain the facts recorded in the archives in the way they happened in real lives. If events could plainly reveal their own logic as written histories present them, there would be no controversies at all about the past. That controversies exist among historians about how different authors depict a set of events they all agree happened implies that their representations involve some processes that unwittingly obfuscate facts. A crucial element of those processes, says White, is the ordering faculty that historians deploy to filter and present—that is, rewrite—what archives reveal. This faculty of interpretation is not a mere product of the author's sensibility. Historical interpretation and writing involves some extra-factual choices among which the selection of a narrative strategy, or "culturally provided *mythoi*" (60), is very significant. However, because true histories are not simply fictions, the investigator has to explain the relationship of the facts that allow the story to cohere as a culturally recognizable *form of knowing*. The historian, unlike the "ordinary" aesthete and/or philosopher, usually portrays archival facts as indices of some underlying patterns of which the present instance being studied is a variant.

White warns that his own literary view that makes historiography seemingly unscientific would be wrongly construed if it were taken to imply that "there are as many types of interpretation in history as there are historians of manifest genius practicing the craft" (70). The broad types of narrative, explanatory, and ethical choices available to the historian are rather limited: "The analysis of plot structures yields four types: Romance, Comedy, Tragedy, and Satire. That of explanatory strategies has produced four paradigms: idiographic, organicist, mechanistic, and contextualist. And the theory of ideology has produced four possibilities: anarchism, conservatism, radicalism, and liberalism" (70). Whatever the ideology, the plotting strategy, or the form of explanation chosen, historians, at least since 1850, see "the historical imagination as a faculty which, beginning in man's impulse to clothe the chaos of the phenomenal world in stable images—that is, in an aesthetic impulse—discharged itself in a tragic reaffirmation of the fundamental fact of change and process, providing thereby a ground for the celebration of man's responsibility to his own fate" (48). Hayden White names as "realistic historicism" this paradigm of history within which the "the task of the historian was less to remind men of their obligation to the past than to force upon them an awareness of how the past could be used to effect an ethically responsible transition from present to future" (49). History, in essence, is not merely what happened, or got recorded, or the simple corrections that must be made in the archives.

C.L.R. James's radical retelling of the Haitian War of Independence is fully invested in conceiving modern black realistic historicism. He uses the historical narrative, according to Paget Henry, as a "modern ontological" mode of inquiry for discovering and describing the inexorable laws that circumscribe events as "human self-formation." From his earliest fiction and social commentary to his last writing on sports and Pan-Africanism, Henry notes, James conceives of history as "an arena of continuous becoming in which growth was fueled by the conflicts between thesis and antithesis, between projects of group formation and the opposition generated by their internal contradictions" (52).[3]

The Black Jacobins, for example, constantly draws parallels between eighteenth-century Haiti and early-twentieth-century colonized Caribbean and Africa. Haitian slave women poisoned their white rivals to retain the attention of white admirers in the way colonized Kenyan women did to the British (15); some of the tactics used by Haitian planters to subdue their slaves are very similar to the ones being used in colonial Kenya (24); Haitian colonists tried to eradicate indigenous religious practices in the same ways that colonial officers were doing in Africa (18); "well meaning" people spoke against slavery the way some were doing against colonialism (51); Abbé Gregoire, who in 1789 suggested that Haitian mulattoes be granted equality immediately and that the rest of the nonwhite population be gradually freed, was roundly denounced in the same way as anyone who advised the apartheid regime of South Africa to grant equality to the black middle class and to gradually repeal pass laws for the rest of the black population (141).

James also draws parallels between the tactics of black leaders in Haiti and those of African anti-colonial fighters: Haitian slaves "watched their masters destroy one another, as Africans watched them in 1914–1918, and will watch them again before long" (82). The final pages of the book are even more emphatic on how the eventual attainment of independence in Haiti foretells what would happen in Africa:

> While if today one were to suggest to any white colonial potentate that among those blacks whom they rule are men so infinitely their superior in ability, energy, range of vision, and tenacity of purpose that in a hundred years' time these whites would be remembered only because of their contact with the blacks, one would get some idea of what the Counts, Marquises, and other colonial magnates of the day thought of Jean-Francois, Toussaint, and Rigaud when the revolt first began. (376)

The theme of this passage is that the slave shall rebel, come what may. The book's last paragraph projects that in the African future the rebellion will be socialist: "International socialism will need the products of a free Africa far more than the French bourgeoisie needed slavery and the slave-trade. . . . The African faces a long and difficult road and he will need guidance. But he will tread it fast because he will walk upright" (377). In these paragraphs, the Haitian slave insurrection functions as a figurative juncture where the past and the future shake hands.

It is possible to simply stop here and say that *The Black Jacobins* is establishing black historicism on the terms laid down by Hegel, Balzac, and Tocqueville and not really differentiating the "spiritual" specificity of anti-colonial struggles. Another way this objection could be expressed would be to say that James's historicism is a normatively preprogrammed response within the structures of colonialist capitalism itself. Skeptics would like to know if James's historicism merely repeats the master's discourse in the colonies or whether there is a truly "native" ground upon which to stand to criticize Europe and, in the process, invent the colonized's subjectively independent history. The very sense of reordering that Lamming praised in *The Black Jacobins* can now be seen rather dubiously: everyone knows that "Shakespeare was great" but "we cannot merely continue to act out the part of Caliban" (Spivak 37). In readings that favor this line of critique, classical texts of anti-colonial thought like *The Black Jacobins* are said to be "anchored in the 'deep structures,' codes or grammars of imperial discourses" they claim to be criticizing.[4]

Those who want to preserve James's sincerely anti-hegemonic and decisively anti-imperialist intentions wave away these critiques.[5] James's partisans advise that while his historicist vision (or that of any other colonized historian, say Nigeria's Kenneth Dike)[6] may resemble that of Hegel, Balzac, or Tocqueville, the colonized historian could not have been saying that black people are Europeans. Nationalist historians from the colonies work from a great disadvantage because their profession excludes, *a priori,* the past of colonized communities from those concerns that are believed to be responsible for the movement of history, that faculty of ordering which Lamming's laconic title praises James for giving to Caliban. The inauguration of realistic historicism in nineteenth-century European philosophical discourse also witnessed, it could be pointed out, a simultaneous exclusion of Africa and Africans from that subject, as in Hegel's infamous claim in *The Philosophy of History* that the moving Spirit of history failed to stop in Africa, it being "the unhistorical continent, with no movement or development to exhibit." Excluding Africa from the conclave of history, we should also note, was not a harmless intellectual rumination. In 1854, the vice president of the American Colonization Society, U. S. Navy Commander Andrew Foote, who may or may not have read Hegel, told his organization, "'If all that negroes of all generations have ever done were to be obliterated from recollection for ever the world would lose no great truth, no profitable art, no exemplary form of life. The loss of all that is African would offer no memorable deductions from anything but the earth's black catalogue of crimes'" (quoted in Nwaubani 238). As late as 1951, Margery Perham, who probably has read Hegel but not James, was presenting to readers of *Foreign Affairs* the Hegelian notion that Africa presents the lamentable fact that it is the "largest area of primitive poverty enduring into the modern age" (quoted in Dike 177). This anthropological evidence, for Perham, reveals that Africa is a place "without history."[7]

In classical conception, the realistic historicist is given the "moral charge to free *men* from the burden of history" (White 49). When a native historian from the colonies deployed this discovery axiom in the first half of the twentieth century, he had to first create "men" out of materials totally alien to the discipline. To refer to Lamming again, the native historian had to transform Caliban into a man of logic and reason. Kenneth Dike, for example, argued back at Margery Perham that interpreting the lack of large political "unities" in Africa as evidence of the absence of history indicates a willed failure of reason. Were it not the case that statements about Africa are traditionally written with little regard for reason,[8] Dike argues, the existence of the "Negro empires of Western Sudan" obviously refutes the generalized thesis of inherent "multi-cellular tissue of tribalism" which Perham says plagues Africa. It is not reasonable, he adds, to expect large political formations in the densely forested regions of Africa.

In the sections of *Black Jacobins* where James reports positively the little that was then known about African societies, the sense of historicism he deploys stresses the fact that although the contact with Europe may have introduced Africans to modernity, it does not, by any stretch of imagination, initiate them into a hitherto unknown sense of "being-human," which is also to say being reasonably historical. Since racist historicism is in James's view irremediably ideological, he, unlike Dike, spends little time—beyond the intermittent ribbing of the "impertinent follies" (14) of the defenders of property interests—refuting the errors of European chroniclers. Instead he looks, to borrow the formulation Achille Mbembe uses for another occasion, for "what [Haitian] agents accept as *reasons for acting*, what their claim to *act in the light of reason* implies (as a general claim to be right . . .), what makes their action intelligible to themselves" (7).

WHAT IS HISTORY?

But even after acknowledging, as persistent James scholars have suggested, that texts such as *The Black Jacobins* aimed to capture the essence of the confrontation between the colonized and the colonizer and not the bloodless *textual* and "semio-linguistic" (Henry and Buhle, "Caliban as Deconstructionist" 130) concerns that deconstructive historicism may find in them, it would still not be imprudent to read beyond James's facts and study how his book makes "men" out of rebellious slaves. Since there is no reasonable doubt that the insurrection took place at a particular time in a particular society, the proper focus of gauging the significance of James's achievement should be on the sense of metahistory he uses to reciprocate intellectually the heroic deeds of Haitian slaves. According to Hayden White, "Every proper history presupposes a metahistory which is nothing but the web of commitments which the historian makes in the course of his interpretation on the aesthetic, cognitive, and ethical levels" (71). James's work is radical, conceived with a Marxist framework, and favors the search for determinative factors within social dialectics. *The Black Jacobins* shows that besides these obvious allegiances James is deeply interested in the "science," "art," and "purpose" of history *writing*.

In the preface to the book's first edition, James describes the world historical significance of the Haitian insurrection and War of Independence in superlatives that facts will probably never refute: "The transformation of slaves, trembling in hundreds before a single white, into a people able to organise themselves and defeat the most powerful European nations of their day is one of the *epics* of revolutionary struggle and achievement" (ix). In this curious construction, the historian uses the same term to describe both the literary form of incredible deeds and the literal great achievements they represent. Later in the narrative, when Toussaint L'Ouverture's fall is named a tragedy, it becomes clearer that the initial literary description of the insurrection may not be a slip of thought after all: "The defeat of Toussaint in the War of Independence and his imprisonment and death in Europe are universally looked upon as a tragedy" (289). Normally, historians "'liken' the events reported" (White 91) in their texts to literary and cultural forms and thereby conceal their own narrative (inventive) discretions. Historians take stories to be tangential to their main enterprise because events, the primary subjects of history, are not "written" like creative literature that typically follows generic prompts. Because events have no preset grammar, or genre, to which they answer, neither historians, nor the historical actors they study, can manipulate the subject the way a creative writer does. Any patterns revealed in historical narratives are believed to have been formed beforehand in the events and not from the willful creation of the historian.

James's latching of history to literature, and vice-versa, is precociously "postmodernist." Even Hayden White seems to be more restrained than James. White, who has said in many ways that "the form" is the only "nonnegatable element" in a properly conceived history, because that factor alone makes possible the transcoding of scattered events into an understandable whole, cautions that "we do not *live* stories, even if we give our lives meaning by retrospectively casting them in the form of stories" (90). White, in short, retains the traditional order that puts events ahead of the historian's plotting. In contrast, the implication of James's literary terms quoted above is that "narrative" choices are made by the historical subjects' manipulation of event variables, as if they were constructing a "social text." If James's overview of his work is read in a certain way, he is suggesting that modeling historical actions with rhetorical and literary categories can enable the formation of a historiography capacious enough to make men of slaves. It is this trust in the *poeisis of events,* I will propose, that enables James to represent Haitian slaves as genuine historical subjects who enact history by braiding into a whole the strands of events and circumstances handed them by the Age of Revolution. By situating the Haitian slaves as self-reflecting characters in the social text they co-wrote and produced with the principal movers of the French Revolution, James revises the definition of historical subjectivity.

In cliometric terms, Haiti's slave insurrection and subsequent War of Independence are unprecedented: "The revolt is the only successful slave revolt in history, and the odds it had to overcome is evidence of the magnitude of interests that were involved" (ix). How is the historian then going to explain such a revolution that has no model, without assimilating the force of its uniqueness into traditional conventions? James adopts two strategies: first, he explains the events with a Trotskyite variety of Marxian theory of class struggle, and second, he narrates the events in a self-consciously literary manner—using specifically the tragic form—to assign to the slaves critical roles without which the series of events would have been entirely unrecitable.[9] These are rather untraditional moves because (1) Haitian slaves, who for the most part have no property to their names, are made to bring about a "bourgeois" revolution; and (2) true tragic heroes do not normally come from the class of slaves. Haitian slaves, James argues, developed a common revolutionary purpose because their peculiar situation molded them into a form of working class: "The slaves worked on the land, and, like revolutionary peasants everywhere, they aimed at the extermination of their oppressors. But working and living together in gangs of hundreds on the huge sugar-factories . . . they were closer to a modern proletariat than any group of workers in existence at the time, and the rising was, therefore, a thoroughly prepared and organized mass movement" (85–86). With the explanation that Haitian slaves were not-quite-not-working class, but laborers nonetheless, James fashions out of slaves modern social agents (or "men") who could make history as their conditions of laboring permitted. The impact of this historiographic maneuver is that Haitians behave as living consciousnesses that can "accomplish intentional acts related by unity of meaning" (Mbembe 187). Furthermore, to make these "living" slaves credible historical actors, James's narrative presents the actions as "serious, complete, and of a certain magnitude," as Aristotle says of tragedy. I return to the question of tragedy below.

PROVERBS OF HISTORICAL INTERPRETATION

James outlines, as noted earlier, the enduring meaning of the Haitian events by connecting the eighteenth-century War of Independence to the future of colonialism. But he knows that influencing the course of African freedom was not the main consideration of the fighting Haitians. Hence James also lays out the "laws" he believes governed the complex dialectics of events the slaves were trying to control. These "laws" are registered in concise, neutral, timeless (with habitual verbs), and epigrammatic sentences I have called proverbs of history. They sum up the reasons that led Haitian slaves to create, under Toussaint's leadership, the specific world in which they found themselves. Without these proverbial "bookmarks," the story would have turned out a compilation of one fact after another, one skirmish after another, one battle after another, or one betrayal after another. I have termed these statements proverbs because they are literally true and mean what they say. But because they are also figurative, in that they apply to other moments besides the instance of their creation, they mean more than what they say and say less than what they mean.[10]

The most significant of James's great proverbs pronounces magisterially in the preface that "Great men make history, but only such history as is possible for them to make" (x).[11] It appears in abbreviated forms later as a conclusion to the description of slave conditions (25) and as a foreshadowing of the impact of Toussaint L'Ouverture's joining the war (91). Toussaint, the preface says, "did not make the revolution. It was the revolution that made Toussaint. And even that is not the whole truth" (xi). With these words, James memorializes the fact that both the revolution and its hero mutually make each other in their relationship to some third force that neither could totally control. The historian's "true business," he says, is to state those laws that govern the construction of a social text, "to portray the limits of those necessities and the realisation, complete or partial, of all possibilities" (x). Historical events, James seems to be saying here, are in their own right plot-making enterprises of which the most conscientious history writing can only be an approximation.

This view of plotting is, of course, as old as Aristotle's proposition in *Poetics* that poetry is more philosophical than history because literature handles better "how a person of a certain type on occasion speak or act, according to the law of probability or necessity." The revisionary element adopted by James regarding this age-old notion is that historical events are in themselves a form of real-life *writing*. In the original Aristotelian formulation, chroniclers only record and do not meditate long on the relation of events, whereas tragedians subject slices of social life to the rigors of genre/form. In James's revision, the good historian should see the subjects of chronicles as creators and not passive followers of circumstance. The Jamesian historian is, hence, duty bound to locate not just the sequence of events as they happened but the social "rhetorical" apparatus employed by historical subjects. Some parts of these instruments may have been handed down to the subjects by social circumstances, but a greater part, which may be nothing other than new usage of the handed down tools, has to be constructed anew within the particulars of the historical moment. African initiatives in modern history, James's study implies, have been neglected for so long by "regius professors" because they look for events that match preconceived notions of historically significant acts and not for the inventive "rhetorical" operations black subjects have been performing to create events.

Once he has established the general rule about history as active *plot making* by historical subjects, James goes on to explain why Haitians emphasize one event pattern (or plot element) over another. In what could be called James's first law of action choice, he says that slaves, being slaves, cannot create opportunities from scratch but can seize whatever chances come their way, many times through the miscalculations of their masters: "Men make their history, and the black Jacobins in San Domingo were to make history which would alter the fate of millions of men and shift the economic currents of three continents. *But if they could seize opportunity they could not create it*" (25; emphasis added). Haitian slaves, whose lives were defined by "docility and acceptance" (12) and could not start a revolution *ab initio,* recognized a schism in the hegemonic alignment of mulattoes, *petit* whites, and grand whites when mulattoes rioted against the governor's decision that only whites, even poor ones, deserve the benefits of universal liberty proclaimed in France.

For saying that slaves can only seize opportunities, James may be easily accused of capitulating to a fatalism that subsumes Haitian initiatives to European history. But that would amount to a grave error because the acting slaves remain the epicenter of interpretation for James. In the narrative elaboration, events in Paris only enlarged a "tradition" of what historians in the United States call "day to day resistance" (Bauer and Bauer). On African shores, during the Middle Passage, and on the plantations, slaves managed to poison their masters, vandalize property, slow down work pace, and, when all else failed, commit suicide. The most significant cause of slave rebellion, in James's blatant formulation, is slavery: "The slaves had revolted because they wanted to be free" (95).

The revolution in Paris added a huge qualitative difference to uncoordinated episodes of "day to day resistance." Among the many little revolts that sporadically broke out in the three centuries of Haitian slavery before the French Revolution, only the one led by Macandal approached being "an organised attempt at revolt" (21). Macandal was driven by a "boldness of spirit" (20) typically possessed by the unprivileged but desperate slaves who led maroon communities and carried out intermittent attacks on plantations.

Macandal, to whom we return in the next chapter, was different from the other maroon chiefs because he plotted a grand scheme that was to unite all the rebel communities and plantation slaves in a massive assault against the whites, all of whom he wanted to drive off the island. But Macandal, according to James, fell victim to his own "temerity" (21) and was burnt alive when caught. His campaign failed because both the leader and his followers seem to be "uninstructed" in the ways of the best of their enemies.

The events of 1789 began because a class of slaves that was fairly well educated in the ways of the planters had matured among the deceptively obsequious "house" slaves. These slaves, having "used their position to cultivate themselves, to gain a little education, to learn all they could" (19), were better positioned than any other group to understand and to exploit the opportunities provided by the internal political divisions among the master classes. The role of this class of slaves in the revolt leads James to propose another proverb of subaltern insurrection: "The leaders of a revolution are usually those who have been able to profit by the cultural advantages of the system they are attacking" (19). Without a Toussaint L'Ouverture, who had read Abbé Reynal's *Philosophical and Political History,* from which he had learned that "'natural liberty is the right which nature has given to *every one* to dispose of himself according to his will'" (25), the revolts that broke out in Haiti soon after the French Revolution might have become another unremarkable episode in the nation's series of vengeful violence.[12] Without the input of this group, the Haitian revolution would have been a short-lived massive bloodletting. Later in this chapter when I discuss Toussaint's fall, I return to the lesson of this proverb as it pertains to current theories of the colonized personality.

Boukman, who leads the revolt that precipitates the prolonged battle that will culminate in independence, is an intermediary character in James's scale of types of leaders who are capable of captaining a successful revolt. Boukman is a leader of field hands. His position allows him to follow the political turmoil of the ruling whites and their antagonists both in Haiti and in France. But Boukman is also a *vodun* high priest, a *papaloi,* which means that he has rejected the religion of assimilated field slaves and "big house" artisans. Boukman exploits his *vodun* connections to plot a massive revolt that is not detected until it actually breaks out. On the eve of the revolt, he uses his priestly office to mobilize the slaves, assuring them that "'the god who created the sun which gives us light, who rouses the waves and rules the storm, though hidden in the clouds, he watches us. He sees all that the white man does'" (87). Boukman tells his followers that black gods, in opposition to the white man's wicked god who "inspires" his people to "criminality," are now commanding them to avenge their wrongs with their own hands: "Our god who is good to us orders us to revenge our wrongs. He will direct our arms and aid us. Throw away the symbol of the god of the whites who has so often caused us to weep, and listen to the voice of liberty, which speaks in the hearts of us all" (87).

Boukman's speech suggests that he has some education in the ways of the whites. (He speaks of one God and of a feeling for natural liberty lodged in the hearts of all.) His campaigns are so widespread and the destruction so thorough that mulattoes, who "hated the slaves because they were slaves and because they were black" (89), join the battle. But James does not find the anger of Boukman's followers to be sufficiently political. The proverb he deduces from this says: "An uninstructed mass, feeling its way to revolution, usually begins by terrorism" (21). But terror is not quite a modern strategy of political struggle and can at best be seen only as a transitional act that must be complemented with more modern rational (ideological) calculations. That phase of the struggle will not be launched until the class best represented by Toussaint, the group that understands the issues at stake in less ethnocentric terms, joins the battle.

My casting Boukman's leadership as unmodern should not be construed as a negative comment, because James's proverbial generalizations about the propertied class show that whites too had very little comprehension of the events and how to respond to them. The masters' ferocious response to the unbridled terror unleashed when the slaves struck, as well as their incredulousness about rumors of slave uprising, reveals two other proverbial historical laws: (1) property "never listen[s] to reason except when cowed by violence" (70); and (2) "the cruelties [terrorism] of property and privilege are always more ferocious than the revenge of poverty and oppression" (88).

Toussaint L'Ouverture joins the war one full month after it has started. He knows from reading Reynal that the only thing needed is a "courageous chief" to direct the efforts of the enslaved toward reestablishing "'the rights of the human race'" (25). Toussaint does not report to camp to carry out a vengeance against the whites as Boukman's speech directs. That emotion is beyond him because he knows whites are not universally evil. He has even been a benefactor of their occasional and selective generosity. His father, who is allowed some relative measure of freedom, has "the use of five slaves to cultivate a plot of land" (19). At the time he reports to camp, Toussaint has acquired book knowledge of the politics, economics, and the history of France as well as of San Domingo. Because his plantation is close to Le Cap, he has been following keenly the intrigues among the Haitian whites since the fall of the Bastille. In addition to these factors, his sterling personal qualities—asceticism, orderly mind, and monogamous fidelity to his wife—prepare him to outshine those who preceded him into battle leadership.

With Toussaint's introduction, the narrative shifts from explaining the laws that govern the rise of historical actors to setting out those that determine successful actions. The successful Haitian leader, James shows, will have to know (1) the fundamentally antagonistic character of production in Haiti, and (2) the racial basis of the division of labor and expropriation of surplus. The governing system that perpetuates this order is designed and run by mulattoes and whites who consider themselves to be of a race (and not just of a class) separate from the laborers. This circumstance dictates that any liberation effort carried out by the laborers cannot but be racial, although the primary cause of the condition is economic. James summarizes this paradox in the book's central proverb: "The race question is subsidiary to the class question in politics, and to think of imperialism in terms of race is disastrous. But to neglect the racial factor as merely incidental as [is] an error only less grave than to make it fundamental" (283). No modern revolution—or counter-revolution, for that matter—will succeed without the formulation of an equation of actions that will balance the race and class variables. The masses of the slaves may comprehend their status from their race position, but the ultimate goal of their struggle cannot be racially limited. But as true as that is, the pervasive racialism that surrounds the struggle cannot be neglected since it too is a significant variable in the possible combination of actions. The leader who will sustain the slaves' rage for the duration of a successful revolt must maintain an unflagging focus on the racialist environment in which the sought-after freedom will be experienced. For that leader to think non-racially at the height of war, as L'Ouverture did, is to misunderstand his mission and to commit a tragic political error.

James's accounting for the collapse of L'Ouverture's regime is a lot less tidy than his historicist interpretation of the details of the revolt. In the latter case, the course of historical events seems fairly predictable and therefore susceptible to precise summations, and history appears to be the most meaningful "text" of events that fully conscious individuals construct out of the options available to them, in furtherance of their own class interests. Great men create the kind of history that is possible for them to have wrought, as one of the book's cardinal proverbs asserts. But Toussaint's fate also demonstrates that great men do fail in their efforts to make history even when they are very well placed strategically within the universe of events. How else can we explain the failure of a historical leader such as Toussaint L'Ouverture, who embodies the very essence of forces at work at the precise historical moment he occupies? When historical fortunes are reversed as in this case, James asks us to look for explanations in the kind of relationships that develop between the leaders and the masses of the people.

The same cultural and intellectual advantages that promote the group of slaves educated in the ways of the master class to the leadership of the rebelling blacks also paralyze it politically at the moment of victory when Toussaint begins to subordinate the slaves' desire for assuring comfort from their rulers to abstractions about the nation's progress. And these notions of progress come from what he has gleaned from his closeness to the master class he is trying to supplant. Toussaint's desire to rule from the standpoint of an unracialized republicanism confounds his suffering followers. James captures the logic of this development in the last of the proverbs of historical action: "To bewilder the masses is to strike the deadliest of all blows at the revolution" (287).

After Toussaint's forces have finally occupied all of Spanish San Domingo and ensured that no foreign attacker can use any part of the island as a staging platform to reintroduce slavery, the leader embarks on an ambitious nation-building exercise that relies heavily on the cooperation of whites, mulattoes, and "free" blacks, the most culturally and economically advanced sections of the society. Without asking them, L'Ouverture assumes the unwavering support of the masses of ex-slaves in "the colossal task of transforming a slave population, after years of licence, into a community of free labourers" (242). He permits the restoration of commercial farming done with "free," but involuntary, labor. Denied the chance to own abandoned plots of land, ex-slaves are herded into what remains of the large plantations. Although Toussaint passes a regulation that says a quarter of the farm produce be set aside for wages, he overlooks the very harsh conditions under which overwhelmingly black laborers suffer. Toussaint sets laborers to work twenty-four hours after he gains the control of any region, and he usually orders his military commanders "to take measures necessary for keeping them on the plantations" (156). The government also set up some other administrative and cultural machineries like a court system, a revamped Custom House, tax offices, new tax laws, schools, churches, and a dictatorial constitution. Under this law and order regime, "the poor sweated and were backward so that the ruling new class might thrive" (248).

For the first time in the revolution, Toussaint L'Ouverture, his generals, and advisers become defenders of state coercion against their erstwhile fellow fighters. The ex-slaves see a despotic, ruthless, and impenetrable leader who has an "unsleeping suspicion of everyone around him" (254). The ex-slaves, who believe that they fought a war of *racial* liberation, observe their leaders killing fellow champions of black interests and executing *black* dissenters "without mercy." When the black population in the district governed by Moïse, Toussaint's cousin, confidant, and trusted general, rioted against their harsh regimentation, Toussaint executed Moïse and "lined up the laborers and spoke to them in turn; and on the basis of a stumbling answer or uncertainty decided who should be shot" (279). Granted that all these events took place during Napoleon's final attempt to occupy the island and reintroduce slavery, the effect of the actions was that the revolution's leadership terrorized the revolutionary class and race while the reactionary class and race, by virtue of its immense cultural and material capital, enjoyed its confidence.

James's account of Toussaint's rise and fall deserves a little more attention, if for no reason other than its similarity to some governing axioms of contemporary understanding of the existential complexities of the postcolonial world. Toussaint succeeds in taking the lead because he put to inventive use some of the advantages he gained from his knowledge of French and European ways. He belongs to a group that is "able to profit by the cultural advantages of the system they are attacking" (19). To use Homi Bhabha's postcolonial concept-metaphors, Toussaint and his comrades succeed because they are "mimic" and "hybrid" men. It is fashionable in postcolonial discourse to agree with Bhabha that "the place of difference and otherness, or the space of the adversarial . . . is never entirely on the outside or implacably oppositional" (109).

James's interpretation of the Haitian revolt shows, however, that the in-between social position of the colonial hybrid should perhaps not be converted into a metaphysics of postcolonial identity, as is currently done. As James's report of the argument of the French bourgeoisie in the Constituent Assembly shows, behaviors generally made available for the colonized to mimic are usually those that can "reform, regulate, and discipline" (Bhabha 86). The slave can be encouraged to accept the Bible as literal words of God brought to light by the instrumentality of domination, but he cannot be encouraged at all to "know" liberty and "enjoy" its wisdom. The colonized that attains such knowledge does so illicitly. It is also very important to separate, as James does, Raynal's invitation to mimic *illegal* revolutionary actions from the one issued by the French maritime bourgeoisie to Haitian mulattoes to subvert the slaves; one is a call into selfhood and the other is not. James's narration of Toussaint's fall also shows that "mimicry," voluntary or forced, in the leadership of a revolutionary war of independence can exact a heavy sacrifice from the subaltern classes: Toussaint almost ruined the revolution because he would not make room for the difference between how counterrevolutionaries are treated in France and how loyal opposition should be handled in racially complex Haiti. Once the War of Independence is set in motion, James's narrative suggests, behaviors "copied" from the master require radical revision. When victory looms for the subaltern struggle, unrevised mimicry may become a source of stasis and outright betrayal of the slave's fight for life. One could say that the seemingly limitless crises of post-independence life in Africa, the Caribbean, and even Asia, those places whose future James tried to foretell from the details of the Haitian War of Independence, attest to the resilience of adulatory (unrevised) mimicry many decades after recent wars of independence.

POETICS AND HISTORIOGRAPHY

The explanation of the logic of Toussaint's fall still leaves some other textual questions unanswered. If historical actors choose their deeds rationally out of the competing options available to them, how does a great leader like Toussaint, who seems to be the man for the moment, commit such great errors? James summarizes the fall of the "great man" of Haitian revolution:

> The defeat of Toussaint in the War of Independence and his imprisonment and death in Europe are universally looked upon as a tragedy. They contain authentic elements of the tragic in that even at the height of the war Toussaint strove to maintain the French connection as necessary to Haiti in its long and difficult claim to civilisation. Convinced that slavery could never be restored in San Domingo, he was equally convinced that a population of slaves recently landed from Africa could not attain civilisation by "going it alone." (289)

L'Ouverture's political miscalculations are rendered here as dramatic acts. James uses more explicitly Aristotelian logic in the next paragraph: "[Toussaint's] allegiance to the French Revolution and all it opened out for mankind in general and the people of San Domingo in particular, this had made him what he was. But this in the end ruined him" (290). L'Ouverture rises because he cannot but do so; he also falls because he cannot but succumb to historical pressures around him.

Kara Rabbit has suggested that James's assimilation of Toussaint's political failure into Aristotelian tragedy "mythologize[s] and universalize[s]" the black hero, thus "allowing a *mimesis* of the historical events of the Haitian revolution to point toward the universals regarding the fall of colonialism and repressive hegemonic systems" (121). James's portrayal, she adds, indicates the historian's endorsement of Aristotle's dictum that poetry is superior to philosophy because "poetry speaks of universals, history of particulars." Rabbit believes that James recasts—especially in the 1963 appendix that directly traces the origin of the shifts in Caribbean history to Haiti—Toussaint's story as a tragedy to remind the reader, as a practical catharsis of some sort, that "hegemonic accountability and revolutionary pluralism" (126) cannot be abridged. Focusing on plot, Lopez-Springfield says: "James sees history as the unfolding of an action; in the Aristotlean sense, it has a beginning, a middle and an end" (89). In other words, James adopted Aristotelian poetics to universalize the Haitian War of Independence. Poetry is more philosophical than history, Aristotle wrote. We should not forget, however, that this statement is part of a philosophical argument.

But the connection between James's narrative and Aristotle is not that direct because the colonized writer first has to revise Aristotle in order to make heroes out of slaves. James's Toussaint, I would say, may be more correctly identified as a "high mimetic" hero rather than as a truly tragic figure. In Northrop Frye's famous reading of Aristotle, the hero of a "high mimesis" is superior to other humans but not to the environment. Such a hero has "authority, passions, and powers of expression far greater than ours, but what he does is subject to both social criticism and to the order of nature" (34). Because the high mimetic hero does not possess supernatural powers, his outstanding qualities derive from his superior intelligence and understanding of the laws of forces (the poetics, as it were) that govern societies. For the fall of this kind of leader to not degenerate into "romance," Frye says, the events that surround the decline are best read as *material* "social and moral fact[s]" and not human symbols in the broad sense. The fall of the tragic leader "is involved both with a sense of his relation to society and with a sense of the supremacy of natural law" (37). In high mimesis, the dramatic calamity is "causally related to something" done by the hero and "the tragedy is in the inevitability of the consequences of the act, not in its moral significance as an act" (38). Since the hero does not willfully cause the calamity, the "flaw" that brings about the trouble cannot be attributed to the will alone but to the operation of material social laws that are not subject to the particular combination of events being deployed by the hero. The calamity in high mimesis results from a miscarriage of desire and intention.

Virtually every term of Frye's adaptation and expansion of Aristotle has been formulated earlier in James's summary statements about Toussaint's misfortunes. "In a deeper sense," James says, the life and death of Toussaint L'Ouverture "are not truly tragic. Prometheus, Hamlet, Lear, Ahab, assert what may be the permanent impulses of the human condition against the claims of organized society" (291). L'Ouverture's misfortune arises not from fate but from historical miscalculations. He is not a victim of some universalizing force that is unrelated to the place of race in the class struggle of a people who for centuries have been victimized under race-based slavery. Like Frye's high mimetic hero, James writes about his L'Ouverture that "the harmatia, the tragic flaw, which we have constructed from Aristotle, was in Toussaint not a moral weakness. It was a specific error, a total miscalculation of the constituent events" (291).

Toussaint's "tragic" error—his inadequately discriminating allegiance to the French Revolution—is brought about by his actions and not the other way around. The tragedy flows from his inability to formulate the right equation for balancing the race and class factors in Haitian politics. To reiterate, James says that "the race question is subsidiary to the class question in politics. . . . To neglect the racial factor as merely incidental [is] an error only less grave than to make it fundamental." Toussaint discounts "race" and imperils his nation's historical fortune. For his country, he seeks an unracialized civilization, a plantation production system, and prosperity. Achieving any of these requires the coercion of the class of predominantly black free laborers for whom civilization, efficient plantation production, and palpable prosperity are intricately connected to racialized brutality. L'Ouverture cannot assume, as James shows abundantly, that the just-freed laborers will understand how a prosperous civilization that is decidedly European in outlook will justify the severe exactions expected of them. In other words, the masses of San Domingo, understandably, "speak" the language of *black* ex-slaves. Their leader, blind to his circumstances and loyal to the philosophy books he has read, speaks the language of a *French* revolutionary: "Knowing the race question for the political and social question that it was, he tried to deal with it in a purely political and social way. It was a great error" (286). But this is not a benign error. Moïse, his trusted general, cousin, and adopted son, advocates the allocation of "small grants of land for junior officers and even the rank-and-file" (277), but L'Ouverture believes that wage-based production will be more effective and efficient than free-holding land ownership. Moïse's racialism cost him his life. By the time L'Ouverture realizes the political wisdom of Moïse's thinking, Bonaparte is set to restore slavery, and L'Ouverture himself has lost the ability to galvanize the convergence of race and class-consciousness that fired up his followers in earlier struggles.

Evidence abounds in James's biography and his theoretical writing on Marxism[13] to support the idea that he subordinates race consciousness to an overriding class-consciousness in the mind of his L'Ouverture because he wants to prove the superiority of Marxist analysis. But L'Ouverture does not fall simply because he abandons his race, although that is what some of his followers think. He falls because he abandons the masses, which is a more fatal political mishap in James's reading of class struggle.[14] James's 1950 essay "Class Struggle" argues that the only sustainable true revolution is one in which dominant post-revolution production processes do not antagonize the interests of the laboring class. Whenever a bureaucracy, which for James "includes not only officials of government but the officials of industry" (*C.L.R. James Reader* 191),[15] takes over the decisions about the manner and goal of production, a social revolution is already becoming moribund, as was the case in Haiti during the waning period of Toussaint L'Ouverture's rule. The entire rebellion, in light of the "Class Struggle" essay, can be called "a revolution in production" in which ex-slaves intended to become independent workers who can "examine what they were told to do and then decide whether it was satisfactory to them or not" (193). Although these words condense James's thoughts on the failure of state capitalism in the Stalinist Soviet Union and the betrayal of the CIO's goals in the United States, they help us understand the later years of Toussaint L'Ouverture's rule in San Domingo. The curse on L'Ouverture's rule, in essence, comes from the government's seeking the "accumulated labour, science, and knowledge" of the planters and its organizing their use along the lines favored by the *ancien regime.* Toussaint's regime fails and the hero succumbs to a tragic fate because the leader abridges the course of the slaves' rebellion without the slaves' consent. That alone is the hero's moral and political flaw.

Writing the history of the Haitian slave rebellion allows James to meditate on how the War of Independence foreshadows the kind of battles that will have to be fought by twentieth-century colonized peoples, "those slaves of modern times" (Fanon, *Wretched* 73–74). Events in the colonized world about a quarter of a century after the book's initial publication have proved right James's historicism in virtually every respect. Independence came, as *The Black Jacobins* predicted, from the example set by Haitian slaves. Equally validated is James's fear that the "hybrid" men who led the decolonization struggle may succumb, like Toussaint, to their own historical hubris.[16] Overall, the thematic and narrative assumptions drawn from the historical laws believed to be at play in the Haitian struggles express a confidence in the ability of the subjugated to unite and exploit the contradictions that divide their rulers. In this narrative, the masses of the colonized will shape the course of their own history. The slave that fights has a chance to win the political battle. But in James's thinking, the battle for freedom is not fully won if, for whatever purpose, the leaders of the revolution adopt the production system of the defeated masters without restructuring it. Should this circumstance arise, the threat of another class of masters, as Moïse's supporters suspected, would develop.

6

SLAVE REBELLION AND MAGICAL REALISM
The Kingdom of This World

Tomi, ani oru beremane [It is men that make the Gods important].

—*Kalabari (Nigeria) proverb*

Seeds of the bloody slave revolts in Alejo Carpentier's *The Kingdom of This World* grow narratively out of Macandal's discovery of the enormous lethal power concealed in common plants. Prior to becoming the leader of Haiti's first nationwide slave insurrection, Macandal operates the sugar processing machine at the Lenormand de Mezy plantation until his left arm becomes mangled in an accident. The permanent disability leads him to be reassigned to the pastures. It is while working in the fields that "he develops a keen interest in the existence of certain plants to which nobody else paid attention" (23) and gets to learn of their hitherto unknown deadly chemical properties. As soon as Macandal notices hitherto unknown peculiar behaviors of the plants, he begins a systematic study that leads him to the discovery, among other things, that plants do shift shape and respond sympathetically to the needs of little ants. Macandal also discovers "sulphury capers," "solitary bushes with furry leaves that sweated at night," "pods that burst at midday with the pop of a flea cracked under the nail," and a vine that "made the head of anyone resting in its shade swell up" (24).

During experimentation and testing, he stumbles on the poisonous fungus that later becomes his weapon of choice in the anti-slavery insurrection he leads. Macandal refines the fungus's poisonous properties and increases its lethality with careful selection and crossbreeding. To use Carpentier's terms in the "Prologue to *The Kingdom of This World*," Macandal discovers the hidden marvels of his American environment by making himself at home there and taking advantage of his placement in the pastures. The "technical" marvels of making poisons out of plants and the life-changing political use to which they can be put during a slave insurrection are revealed to Macandal as a result of his "reflexive, self-conscious" studies.[1]

This chapter begins with a summary of Macandal's biography for several reasons, among them that Carpentier's representation of this "uninstructed" rebel contrasts with James's depiction in *The Black Jacobins*. There, Macandal is just a tad better than a charlatan and not an experimenter in poisons: "He claimed to predict the future; like Mahomet he had revelations; he persuaded his followers that he was immortal and exercised such a hold over them that they considered it an honour to serve him on their knees; the handsomest women fought for the privilege of being admitted to his bed" (21). Since he is no better than a deceiver, an Oriental despot precisely, James shows no sympathy for him when he is finally done in by his "temerity" (21). The difference between James's fearless rascal and Carpentier's rebellious scientist demonstrates the traditional nature of the kind of archives that James's historicism, in spite of its ground-breaking interpretation, trusts, what types of acts it considers heroic, and what types of narrative strategies it can allow to be deployed for depicting heroism. James's distrust of "folkloric" records of the "uninstructed" would only permit him to tell the history of the slaves' War of Independence from the standpoint of either great literate slaves or those that literate archivists found credible.

The discussion that follows demonstrates in part that James's representation of Macandal requires the supplementation provided in Carpentier's novel. Carpentier's depiction of Macandal speaks to the generally unacknowledged significance of the politics of the slaves' War of Independence to the formalization of "marvelous realism" (*lo real maravilloso*), a term that has come to represent the furthest-reaching Latin American—in truth, Third World—theory of high literary arts. Without his philosophy-inflected interpretation of the cultural circumstances of the Haitian slave revolt, Carpentier would not have been able to theorize marvelous (or magical) realism as the knowledge apprehension practice most appropriate for understanding the bases of late modern (or postcolonial) Latin American cultures. I argue that if the interpretation of magical realism in literary criticism is to reflect the spirit of Carpentier's initial conception, then the "unmodern" discovery processes which the enslaved put to liberating purpose in the Haitian War of Independence must be reckoned with. In the first part of the chapter, I propose that the "Prologue to *The Kingdom of This World,*" where Carpentier first outlined the tenets of magical realism, be read as simultaneously a theory of knowledge and of representation. The second part presents a close reading of the importance of "magical" perception and representation to the Haitian slaves' prosecution of the War of Independence.

MARVELOUS REALISM: KNOWING AND TELLING

In the 1949 "Prologue to *The Kingdom of This World,*" Carpentier recollects that a trip to Haiti "toward the end of 1943" made him feel as if he were walking on the same "earth where thousands of men eager for liberty believed in Macandal's lycanthropy, to the point that their collective faith produced a miracle the day of his execution" ("Prologue" 30). He reports finding in the ruins of Sans Souci an astonishing memento that stimulates a sensation of "the real marvelous": "With each step I found the *real marvelous*" ("Prologue" 30). Carpentier reads this feeling to be a symptom of something specific to the Americas: "The presence and authority of the real marvelous was not a privilege unique to Haiti but the patrimony of all the Americas, where, for example, a census of cosmogonies is still to be established" ("Prologue" 30).

At the time of the said visit, Carpentier, like other postwar Latin American intellectuals, was reexamining his view of European avant-garde arts, particularly surrealism's promise to reveal the "genuine enchantment" and "magic" underlying facile reality. Not quite trusting modernism's appropriation of European discoveries about the different worldviews of other peoples in ethnography and anthropology, Carpentier, like his other colleagues, was looking "for origins, the recovery of history and tradition, the foundation of an autonomous American consciousness serving as the basis for a literature faithful to the New World" (Echevarria 107). The search is enmeshed in two contradictory discourses. In order not to repeat the European cultural avant-garde's misappropriation of ethnography, Carpentier journeys, like the European ethnographers he criticizes, toward discovering Latin America's peculiarities. He wants to discover Latin American knowledge systems. Like Macandal, however, he wants to ground his discoveries on the gifts of the locality and privilege local measures of significance.

Being an ardent modernist, in spite of his differences with surrealism, Carpentier begins by comparing what he knows of surrealism to the empathy his Haitian travel provoked, and he concludes that the marvel embodied in the relics of slave insurrections is truer to reality. It is from this comparative standpoint that European avant-gardism, as a theory and practice of experiencing the genuine thrills of existence, appears plastic, overwrought, and excessively mechanical to the Latin American scholar.

Against surrealism's rote marvel, Carpentier describes Haiti's (America's) "unequivocally marvelous" reality: It "arises from an unexpected alteration of reality (a miracle), from a privileged revelation of reality, from an illumination that is either unusual or singularly favorable to the unnoticed riches of reality, from an amplification of the scale and categories of reality perceived with particular intensity by means of an exaltation of the spirit that lead it to a kind of 'limit-state' " ("Prologue" 29). This passage indicates that (1) realizing the world as a marvel (the "unexpected alteration of reality") comes at the end of a cognitive-sympathetic process; (2) the surprising perception about the environment is constituted by a new insight ("a privileged revelation of reality") into an aspect of nature's processes; (3) the new revelation about nature proceeds from the knower's especially peculiar ability, acquired either through training or intuition, to probe into nature ("an illumination that is either unusual or singularly favorable to the unnoticed reaches of reality"); (4) the newly discovered marvel about reality *materializes* not as something entirely novel but as an enlargement of known reality; and (5) for the enlargement to take shape and hold, the intensity ("exaltation") of the mind that articulates it must match the discovery. In short, the mind must be keenly predisposed and particularly trained to discover the marvels of reality and articulate its newfound knowledge as an amplification of the already known sensory environment.

The newly revealed marvelous dimensions of reality do not precede learning and expression but are produced by an appropriate predisposition. Also, the marvelous discovery is articulated through a linkage to some already known aspects of existence. The "unequivocally marvelous" that Carpentier speaks of is, in my reading, the knowledge of the operations of the American native environment expressed in a locally intelligible form. In Carpentier's scheme, the American locality is always imbued with fathomable and exalting "riches" native to it. The individual predisposed to cultivating the skills necessary for recognizing and apprehending them will revolutionize the "scales and categories," proportions, recurrence, regularity, flow, and extent of the state of the environment. In other words, with the spirit exalted such that it can attain a "limit-state," the trained sympathetic scholar can considerably amplify the scale and categories of discernible realities. The altered reality will be miraculous, of course, to tradition. Also operating in this conception of marvelous realism is a compelling trust in the ability of the keen observer to transform the physical world with or without the aid of a mechanical prosthesis. When Carpentier says that "the sensation of the marvelous presupposes a faith" ("Prologue" 29), he is prescribing not a dogma about the style of enlarged reality but the need for intellectuals of the Americas to believe that knowledge can transform life and vice-versa.

This reading of Carpentier's definition of the "marvelous real" implies two things: (1) The logical and representational distortions often associated with marvelous realism cannot and do not speak for themselves; and (2) whatever they express cannot be found "uncontaminated" outside the distortions in which they are constituted. Macandal's lycanthropy and Bouckman's *vodun* prowess appear magical in the novel because the manifestation of these powers confounds their comrades. Nevertheless, lycanthropy and *vodun* signify more than literal shape shifting and diabolical cursing because they are also a means of fomenting historically "incredible undertakings" ("Prologue" 30) during which a mass of slaves defeats its masters and creates a new nation. In other words, marvelous realism is not magic for its sake (or mere "sleight of hand") but an expression of the slaves' political praxis. Macandal and Bouckman, for instance, practice mesmerism because they want to lead their followers to overthrow the Master.

At one point in the "Prologue," Carpentier says all of the Americas are inheritors of a genuine "marvelous reality": "The real marvelous is found at each step in the lives of the men who inscribed dates on the history of the Continent and who left behind names still borne by the living: from the seekers after the Fountain of Youth or the golden city of Manoa to certain rebels of the early times or certain modern heroes of our wars of independence, those of such mythological stature as Colonel Juana Azurduy" (30). This passage risks falling into a troubling ahistoricism as it struggles for a language to name the revolutionary spirit native to the Americas. The passage does not distinguish between the historicizable faith that encourages a Macandal "to inspire one of the most dramatic and strange uprisings in History" (31) from the fantastic imaginings of European explorers. Carpentier writes ("Marco Polo allowed that certain birds flew carrying elephants in their talons; Martin Luther saw the Devil right before his eyes and threw an inkwell at his head" [29]), as if they are of the same order of marvel pondered by Macandal's followers.

Taken literally, some critical readers use these distortions and exaggerations inherent to the articulation of the marvelous to ascribe an autarkic nativism to the essay. William Spindler, for example, says "Carpentier's sense of amazement at the 'marvelous' reality of America . . . can be seen as a reflection of the European myth of the 'New World' as a place of wonders, based on a constant reference to European experience as a measure of comparison" (76). Marvelous realism thus becomes a nativist theory that unwittingly repeats the European projections of Latin America as the locus of what Europe has sought but could not find in the Americas. A more nuanced Echevarria argues that Carpentier's conception of the marvelous real derives from "an onto-theology" that assumes the ability of Latin America to "live immersed in culture and to feel history not as a causal process that can be analyzed rationally and intellectually, but as destiny" (125).

Equating representational habits of European records of the Americas and elements of the material form that Carpentier says the articulation of realized true marvel about the world can take amount, in my view, to dwelling in the maliciously "unreal" marvelous produced by a sleight of hand. The "history of all the Americas" adds up to "a chronicle of the real marvelous" (31) not because the concept is genetically native to the Americas. In my reading, Carpentier's point is that a genuine cultural history of the Americas will promote the appreciation of the continents' peculiar enhancements of the "scales and categories" of human understanding. Makers of the as yet unappreciated American marvelous reality are, according to Carpentier, those who "inscribed dates on the history of the Continent" and transformed the "scales and categories" of the Americas. The true patrimony that students of Carpentier's America must explore, if they were to make the continent yield its hidden wealth, are the uniqueness of its cultural landscape, the unprecedented diversity of its racial makeup, the historical insights revealed in its discovery, and the mythologies that derive from all these. That is the spirit in which I accept Echevarria's explanation that Carpentier's essay belongs to the post–World War II scholarly concert of efforts made to "formulate the basis of a uniquely American literature." I emphasize below the materialist/historicist import of Carpentier's conceptualization of magical realism because most critical commentaries too often neglect this aspect of the "Prologue." Usually, little is said about the history of slave revolts that surrounds the Haitian monuments which Carpentier himself posits as the instigator of his theoretical reflections in the first place. It is not totally fortuitous, I believe, that a slave rebellion, the greatest mass transformative experience in Haiti and arguably all the Americas in the late eighteenth and early nineteenth centuries, is the subject of the founding novel of marvelous realism as it was conceived by Carpentier.

MAGIC AND MAGICAL REALISM

Studies of Carpentier and magical realism often start with a comparison of the "Prologue" and the terms used by German philosopher of art Franz Roh to characterize European post-Expressionist art. According to Echevarria, Roh intended for his coinage to capture the magical phenomenology that encircles aesthetic perception. Echevarria says that for Roh, art's magic results from the transformation brought to the object by the viewer's perspective and the art object's ability to absorb and alter the perspective borne by the viewer: "the stance or the perspective assumed before phenomena, a perception which, by the unusual nature bestowed upon it by such a stance, casts both the gesture as well as its object into the realm of the miraculous and the devotional" (114–15). In Roh's marvelous realism, the object created in an artistic reflection "imposes itself on the observer, on the artist," whereas the Latin American observer or artist, whose magical realism is "onto-theological," seeks to discipline the character of his observation with subjective experience: "Roh's formulations do not have a greater impact in Latin America because the miracle that Latin American writers seek is not a neutral one but one through which they can fuse with a transcendental order—an order, however, that is no longer provided by Western tradition" (Echevarria 116). Latin American writers, in essence, are searching for a native ground for their explanation of the object-subject interaction specific to their environment. The problem with this search is that the nativist spirit that motivates it, the notion that there is a "peculiar Latin American consciousness devoid of self-reflexiveness and inclined to faith," cannot stand up well to a discursive analysis (Echevarria 125).

In a more sympathetic interpretation of the meaning of magical realism, Amaryll Chanady adduces a political reason for the differences between Carpentier and Roh. Territorializing the imaginary the way Carpentier does in the "Prologue," he says, defines post–World War II anti-colonial cultural practice. Carpentier, like other politically concerned thinkers in the postcolony, extols "national culture by demonstrating that it is equivalent and even in some aspects identical to that of the [European] metropolis . . . by emphasizing its difference" (130–31). According to early postcolonial theorists like Carpentier, knowledge of the world is multiple and so is the nature of the means of articulating this knowledge.

Constantly equating causality with nature, students of magical realism describe the manifest manipulation of causation, either by its defying logic or through some occultic wisdom, as its definitive feature. Echevarria, for example, says that in magical narratives "the relation between incidents, characters, and setting could not be based upon or justified by their status within the physical world or their normal acceptance by bourgeois mentality" (109). Some other critics argue that magical realism is defined not so much by its propensity for acts that defy physical laws but for representing the disruptions as if they were normal. Angel Flores says that the marvelous element in such narratives "happens as part of reality" (191); Luis Leal suggests that a magical realist writer need not "justify the mystery of events, as the fantastic writer has to" (123), because the writing presents itself as a search for "what is mysterious in things, in life, in human acts" (121).

William Spindler classifies magical realism into three: metaphysical, anthropological, and ontological. "Metaphysical" stories are largely realist portrayals that dwell on uncommon elements of familiar objects, acts, and events. Its masters are Kafka, Conrad, James, and Borges. Not too many postcolonial writers practice this mode. Their forte, and that of other writers in the Third World—places where "pre-industrial beliefs still play an important part in the socio-political and cultural lives of" the people (82)—is "anthropological magical realism," one in which a "a thematic and formal preoccupation with the strange, the uncanny and the grotesque, and with violence, deformity and exaggeration" (81) predominates. Spindler suggests that this form is more rampant in the Third World because the "collective myths" that obtain there are very useful for the forging of national and cultural identities that magical realists themselves help to construct. Magic in anthropological marvelous realism signifies "a process used to influence the course of events by bringing into operation secret or occult controlling principles of Nature" (80). To resolve the contradictions of magic and rationality cohabiting in a text, all that the artist needs to do is to bring ethnographic notions. In "ontological" narratives, which Europeans and Third World writers alike practice, magic is literal in that it names the "inexplicable, prodigious or fantastic occurrences that contradict the laws of the natural world, and have no convincing explanation" (82).

WHAT IS MAGIC?

Notwithstanding their different orientations these studies assume that magic is irrational, nonreferential, traditional, fantastic at best, and delusional at worst. They take magic to be an intellectual outlook not amenable to a rigorous philosophical inquiry and depict realism in the classical form Ian Watt argued for in *The Rise of the Novel:* a philosophical view that authorizes individuals to trust only the truths they discover with their senses "at a particular locus in space and time" (Watt 21). The universal supremacy of measured time and place in the production of a realist consciousness is not questioned by Carpentier's critics. Like classical sociology, the literary criticism of magical realism views magic as either a "fallacious science" or pure sorcery, or ethnographic fancy consistently trumped by unmagical "science," "philosophy," and realism.[2]

Some segments of African philosophical practice do not agree with this characterization of magic as a glaringly inferior reasoning. Unfortunately, literary critics have not allowed such writing to influence their assumptions. In 1978, for instance, a double issue of the philosophy journal *Second Order* was devoted to examining some of the questions that surround "magic" and other extrasensory phenomena like witchcraft. Some scholars, like Sophie Oluwole, call for further open-minded studies while others argue, not unlike Carpentier, that we must accept that "magic" (which includes witchcraft) may withstand a formal logical examination.[3] Albert Mosley, bringing developments in quantum physics to bear on his explanation of the elements of magical practice that trouble philosophy the most, defines magic as "an accumulated set of *beliefs and techniques* by means of which non-physical entities or forces (quantum mechanics shows that there need be no distinction between things and processes, matter and waves) can be used to achieve certain kinds of physically-manifested results" (12; emphasis added). He argues that twentieth-century scientific developments have made it possible to schematize the physical basis of some aspects of traditional magic and see psychokinesis, "spirits, souls, ancestors, demi-gods, and divinities," as not totally whimsical creations. They may, he says, be equivalents of "germs, genes, electrons, positrons, and neutrons." The most interesting issue in Mosley's essay is that he does not take "souls, ancestors, and divinities" literally. He calls them possible "theoretical posits" that function as mediators of cognition protocols whose internal workings are operated by "priests, medicinemen, sorcerers, rain-makers, and other specialists." The traditional scientific notions regarding the "natural" relationship between time and space, upon which literary criticism has based its skepticism about the plausibility of magic in magical realism, Mosley argues, have been revised.

Sodipo approaches the question from a different angle in his exploration of the differences in the use of "cause" and "chance" in formal logic and "Yoruba traditional thought," normally assumed to be "unscientific." According to Sodipo,

> The scientific man will push the application of general laws [of causality] as far as it can go; after that chance takes over. But not so in Yoruba traditional thought. Even if a general law says that only one person out of a hundred passengers in a lorry involved in an accident would be saved the Yoruba believe that the *gods*, not *chance*, decide who that lucky one shall be and it is certainly worth trying to make oneself the lucky one through a charm or through the necessary sacrifice to god or gods. (19)

In other words, the Yorùbá, who clearly understand the concept of causality, strive to eliminate chance by trying to cause general laws (or causality) not to apply indiscriminately. Gods, spirits, and ancestors, Sodipo says, do not respond to the question "how" but "why here now," which is the position of the person concerned in human experience (16). In this sense, Gods are meta-causative agents that can put chance to order. Invoking the Gods faithfully does not indicate that the believer is ignorant of chance but that he/she is just trying to make it less random or, we can say, uncontrollable. Sodipo adds that the magical means of subjecting chance to Gods' causative oversight are not in themselves magical because they are subject to knowable conventions: "Magic consists of socially standardized words, gestures, and procedures that man resorts to when, *having faithfully followed his technological processes,* he is left in doubt about the outcome of his efforts, when, that is, there is a gap between the point at which technology has taken him and the result that he desires" (20; emphasis added). The traditional *ifá* divination statement with which he concludes the essay confirms the meta-causal function of the Gods: "'If . . . you ask the Gods to make you invisible whenever danger threatens and you found a thicket to hide in effectively when danger did threaten, can you say that your prayers are not answered?'" (20).[4] Sodipo, Mosley, Oluwole, and other like-minded philosophers construe the rationality of magic in ways that neither oppose it to the known protocols of causation nor view it as unreal or irrational. To my mind, this is the idea of magic that is most amenable to the reading of Carpentier's marvelous realism.

In a paper he presented to the First Congress of Negro Arts and Culture held at the Sorbonne in 1956, Jacques Stephen Alexis, speaking on behalf of the Haitian cultural intelligentsia, described marvelous realism in terms similar to Carpentier's, but in a less philosophical language. Alexis characterizes the marvelous as "the *imagery* in which a people wraps its experience, reflects its conception of the world and life, its faith, its hope, its confidence in man, in a great justice, and the explanation which it finds for the forces antagonistic to progress" (270). Unlike readers, explicators, and critics of Carpentier's marvelous realism, Alexis takes the "magical" (or "non-realistic" content of Haitian cultural practices) to be figurative maneuvers and elements of an aesthetic movement. For him, literalizing magical realism seems to be out of the question because it is a literary-discursive prosthesis and not a naturally occurring machination.[5]

MAGICAL PERCEPTION AND STRIVING OUTSIDE THE MASTER'S ORBIT

At the end of the "Prologue," Carpentier says that American history, literature, culture, and philosophy—all discourses of expanding the "scales and categories" of existence—are yet to be fully studied for the marvels specific to them. To begin to remedy that scandalous situation, he offers *The Kingdom of This World,* a story whose retelling of selected aspects of the Haitian War of Independence (and early self-rule) subjects details of events to a peculiarly "non-chronological facade" or calendar ("Prologue" 31). In the remainder of this chapter, I examine Carpentier's representation of how Haitian slaves amplified—that is, made magical—the scale of categories available to them. I suggest that Carpentier's interpretation of Caribbean history in terms that defy ordinary chronology and modes of cognition reflects the marvelous historical beginning that the Haitians tried to inaugurate in the Age of Revolution. The narrative, I would say, demonstrates how the Haitian slave insurrection is sustained by those who believe, like Macandal and Boukman, that discursive norms must be altered such that the transformative hidden wealth of the American environment can be seized for advantage. The story's précis of Haitian history mirrors the efforts made by the slaves to alter the sociopolitical reality of the island through a studied manipulation of "unnoticed riches" of the environment and a huge "amplification of the scales and categories" of existence therein. Carpentier's "genuine" marvel makers begin their projects with a consistent (re)working of their native cultural forms and environment.

Known facts of the Haitian slave rebellion and War of Independence provide the narrative details—Macandal's poison campaign, Bouckman's rebellion, and so on—within which the significance of the marvelous orientation of the text should be sought. In the story, events deemed marvelous are executed to bring a new understanding to problems associated with the slaves' counter-violence. In every event that could be labeled magical, slaves and their leaders are engaged in either trying to acquire some subversive knowledge, to overcome the master's rule by some physical feat, or to mentally transcend the agonies of defeat after the failure of an attempt to topple the master. Each magical act or thought proceeds from a careful study of the natural, cultural, and *political* environments and a consideration of how each can be transformed. Marvels "emerge spontaneously," not to the rebellious slaves and their leaders but to those living contentedly in "bourgeois mentality" (Echevarria 109).

The first marvelous event occurs in the home of a free black woman who lives alone far away in the northern foothills. This Maman Loi (priestess) helps Macandal refine his concoction of poison and also teaches him some esoteric things about plants and animals. The narrator, Ti Noel, observes some of these teaching sessions where "at times the talk was of extraordinary animals that had human offspring. And of men whom certain spells turned into animals" (25). During one such session, the woman receives "some mysterious order" that commands her to dip "her arms in a pot full of boiling oil" (25). When she withdraws her hand, the woman's skin, "despite the horrible sputter of frying," is unscalded. As it is with other unusual occurrences in the novel, the Maman Loi's meddling with gross matter happens within the slaves' liberation struggle. Macandal visits the gifted woman in the course of his quest for new knowledge he can use to improve his discoveries about the toxicity of local plants. That Ti Noel calls her a witch (26) reiterates her high reputation as a person who has the ability to make matter obey her desires.[6] Indeed, the whole novel could be described as a story of the "sorcery" of rebellion, given the fact that it is about the efforts of slaves to occult freedom into reality.

Soon after the Maman Loi endorses Macandal's discovery, he tests the potion on his master's dog. He thereafter runs to the mountains to begin a detailed preparation for his "chemical warfare" campaign against slave owners: "That afternoon as they returned to the plantation, Macandal stood for a long time looking at the mills, the coffee- and cacao-drying shed, the indigo works, the forges, the cisterns, and the meat-smoking platforms"; he concludes that "the time has come" and then flees (26). The resolution sounds impulsive. But when the decision to run off to the mountains is juxtaposed to the meeting with the Maman Loi, the killing of de Mezy's dog, and the quick surveying of the condition of his servitude as nothing but soulless sugarcane processing, Macandal's rush to seek the end of slavery ought to be seen as the calculated judgment of a person compelled by the possession of a certified (by the Maman Loi) magical discovery.

In this and other exploits, Macandal does not proclaim himself capable of inexplicable powers. Rather, it is the stunning result of his painstakingly planned and executed deeds that leads other slaves to speak of him in terms of the marvelous beings in their *vodun* religion and other practices carried over from West Africa. When, for example, Ti Noel meets Macandal long after his fleeing de Mezy's plantation and learns that he has already recruited accomplices and selected targets, he is baffled by the "long, patient labor" (31) that Macandal has invested in his advanced plans for rebellion. Macandal's haggard look—a clear result of his Spartan living in the bush—furthers the appearance of awe: "Macandal was thin. His muscles now moved at bone level, molding his thorax in bold relief" (31). In the hills, Macandal's laboratory and residence is a dismal "narrow-mouthed cave covered with stalactites that pointed toward a deeper opening where bats hung by their feet" (30).

When the poison attack breaks out "invading pastures and stables" (33), it looks sudden, spontaneous, and miraculous to the plantation owners and slaves not privy to the planning. A slave forced to confess his knowledge of the workings of the poison campaign narrates his perception in the language of *vodun* religion and mystery:

> Macandal, the one-armed, now a *houngan* of the Rada rite, invested with superhuman powers as the result of his possession by the major gods on several occasions, was the Lord of Poison. Endowed with supreme authority

> by the Rulers of the Other Shore, he had proclaimed the crusade of extermination, chosen as he was to wipe out the whites and create a great empire of free Negroes in Santo Domingo. Thousands of slaves obeyed him blindly. Nobody could halt the march of poison. (36)

Going by his name, "the bowlegged Fulah," the person speaking here is probably a first generation slave.[7] He seems to have no knowledge of the mystery of poison beyond Macandal's direction. For him, the "Other Shore" and all the things associated with it signify freedom. The desire to keep replicating aspects of life on that "Shore" is manifest in his use of idioms of West African religions to depict Macandal and his efforts. After hearing the Fulah's account, the masters abandon their "prayers, doctors, vows to saints" (35) and mobilize "all available men" (37) to "track down Macandal" because they recognize the political essence of the Fulah's marvelous *vodun* speech. The masters' failed hunt reinforces the slaves' belief about Macandal's quasi-divinity.

It should not really be surprising that the slaves invest Macandal, the agent of social transformation, with the power of literal transfiguration. (For four years, Macandal visits his followers in whatever guise he chooses: a green lizard, a moth, a bird, or even a hoofed animal.) However, the slaves do not believe the metamorphoses are ends in themselves, or marvels for their sake, but means of upholding the vitality of the liberation spirit let loose in the poison campaign. For the slaves, the transformations express Macandal's strategic elusiveness in a culturally sensible form and foreshadow the great historical metamorphosis that will turn slaves to citizens, property to humans, and beasts of burden to human agents. The slaves believe that "one day he would give the sign for the great uprising" (42) that will end the tyranny of white rule. Macandal's ability to go and return at will, whether in animal disguise or human form, signifies the slave's deep desires to be free to behave likewise. When the slaves set eyes on Macandal in the flesh after four years of reported visits in disguises, their songs do not extol his wonderful transformations but lament their plight as slaves: "The chant became the recital of boundless suffering" (47). Macandal is not just a creator of poisons but also an embodiment of the will and transformations needed to breach the lines of servitude. So far as they extend the realm of possibilities or, to use Carpentier's phrasing, amplify the scale and categories of reality, both realistic poison making and mysterious lycanthropy are equally marvelous.

Macandal's execution scene provides a very useful comparison of the freedom-seeking *marvelous reality* of the slaves and the macabre *unmarvelous reality* of their owners. For the execution, white people, rejoicing at the chance to terrorize their slaves into believing in the futility of armed rebellions, deck themselves as if they are going to a carnival. The slaves, who do not share their owners' macabre enthusiasm, show up reluctantly. The joyful whites see ten soldiers hold and thrust Macandal "head first" into the execution pyre and notice that the noise made by the rebel's burning hair "drowned his last cry" (52). The slaves see Macandal transform himself on the pyre after "howling unknown spells" (51) that loosen the ropes used to tie him up. They see "the body of the Negro rose in the air, flying overhead, until it plunged into the black waves of the sea of slaves" (51–52), believing, as his most ardent follower, Ti Noel, says later, that "he would return to this land when he was least expected" (63).

If it is true that a "magical" experience cannot be followed at the primary sensory level, the slaves' perception is clearly delusional. The corollary of this "realist" reading should then be that the planter community's reaction, which derives completely from the senses, is unmagical. But our understanding of the differences between the communities of perception cannot stop here because literalizing Macandal's perennial metamorphosis as a delusion will amount to reducing both the act and its perception to the unmarvelous realism of the masters. The reader who does this will unwittingly devalue the slaves' politically inspired perceptual defiance and validate the masters' politics of counter-insurgence. As it is, Macandal's escape, figured in the transformation, realizes the slaves' hope in a form that is closed off to the planters. The slaves' structure of knowing, as Carpentier presents it, is not immediately accessible to the masters because whites exist in a universe that is far removed from the immanent culture and experience that affirm the slaves' subversiveness. Hence the slaves laugh heartily as they return to their plantations convinced that their hero has remained somewhere "in the Kingdom of This World" (52). For Lenormand de Mezy and other masters who came out to execute Macandal and reiterate, thereby, the futility of the slaves' counter-violence, the celebration of Macandal's "not-dying" demonstrates "the Negroes' lack of feelings" (52). Considered from the slaves' perspective, the celebration amounts to a peculiar orientation of the senses, an orientation that helps to shut out the terror let loose by the masters.

Bouckman's experience is a different matter. Like Macandal before him, he too seeks freedom for all slaves. Unlike Macandal, however, he is neither a chemist nor a discoverer of the hidden wealth of the local flora. Instead, he speaks rebellions into life, urging fellow slaves, with a verbal sophistication based on *vodun* religion, to emulate the Parisian masses that set the French revolution in motion.[8] At the great *vodun* gathering before the first Haitian massive slave revolt, Bouckman, in a speech that enrages and emboldens at the same time, joins the atrocities of slavery to Christianity and ties anti-slavery revolts to *vodun* obligations: "The white men's God orders the crime. Our gods demand vengeance from us. They will guide our arms and give us help. Destroy the image of the white man's God who thirsts for our tears; let us listen to the cry of freedom within ourselves" (67). "Magically," the gathered slaves, after submitting to an oath of allegiance sworn on the great Gods of West Africa, launch a massive mayhem. The magic of Bouckman's words emanates, I submit, from his cleverly analogizing the relationship of the two main religions in Haiti and the conditions of the two broad classes of people living there. The effective authority of his words does not derive magically from his diabolical "invocation" and spell casting. Speaking like a high priest in tune with the wishes of his deities, Bouckman reveals to his listeners "that a pact had been sealed between the initiated on this side of the water and the great Loas of Africa" to launch a revolution when the signal is given. The unification of determinant spirits from this shore and the other ends the division of being and aspiration for the initiates, and that coming together will, in the war bound to be won by the slaves, reconcile the masses too. It is easy thereafter for Bouckman to swear the assembled leaders to an oath of allegiance on Ogoun, the Yorùbá-derived god of war and creativity.

My main point is actually twofold: the slaves do believe that all the events that could be termed "marvelous" in the story are literally true, and they also know that nothing, even when literal, stands for itself. The slaves' actions show that they have always known what Lenormand de Mezy, for instance, will not recognize until after the Bouckman uprising breaks out, that "a drum might be more than just a goatskin stretched across a hollow log" (78). For the owners, the slaves' drumming means no more than frenzied slaps on a "goatskin stretched across a hollow log." The novel's clear stress on the immanence of culture and politics to scientific discovery, marvelous or otherwise, cannot be overemphasized, although that is the dimension conspicuously missing in the critical explanations of the novel's artistic realization of the theory of marvelous realism.

Echevarria's reading of Carpentier is perhaps the most rigorous attempt to sort out the objective principle of narrative and historical magic in *The Kingdom of This World.* His deconstructive interpretation, following Carpentier's claim that a hidden calendrical logic subtends the narrative, tries to set out the "principle, source, or reason" (135)—the writing system, as it were—that "rules history and the disposition of the story" in the novel (140). Matching events in the story with historical sources, Echevarria discovers that "Sunday will be the day of great propitiatory rituals; Monday the day of events and beginnings" (140). He further suggests that it is through this overwrought abstraction that Carpentier renders history as magic: "Magic, the marvelous, would be the relation between the numerical disposition of historical events and the text, a relation between those two orders whose transparent mediator would be Carpentier" (145). However, an additional, closer reading reveals to Echevarria that there are discrepancies between Carpentier's implied grid and historical facts and that the novelist is not a "transparent mediator" of a discovered occult calendar. Indeed, he has actually "force[d] history into the design of his own text" (146). Echevarria then concludes that the prologue "is the false formulation of an American ontology" (147). But Echevarria's demonstration of the disagreements between the "principle" and "practice" of Carpentier's historiography does not pay enough attention to the critic's own implied transparent mediation. He constructs what he calls Carpentier's mystical calendar out of patterns of events in the novel and other texts. When the critic's derived table does not fit the fact of Carpentier's novel, he blames the writer, forgetting that it is the critic that is actually looking for the story's "unmediated" principles of succession. Echevarria also assumes that Carpentier takes the slaves, who are the main historical actors, to be unknowing products of the hidden calendar that drives them.

In the reading proposed here, all marvelous acts attributable to the slaves appear so because they are inspired by the desire to scuttle the master's "unmagical" norms. Narratively, the story depicts the slaves' magical deeds with unmarked shifting of points of view. For example, the reporting of the unscalded hand episode discussed above goes thus: "Once Maman Loi fell strangely silent as she was reaching the climax of a tale. In response to some mysterious order she ran to the kitchen, sinking her arms in a pot full of boiling oil. Ti Noel observed that her face reflected an unruffled indifference" (25). Here the telling is distributed into two perspectives: one belonging to an independent reporter and the other to an eyewitness. The independent reporter's view is expressed by the third-person omniscient narrator's account of the Maman Loi's actions. This reporter distances himself, as it were, from the events by "quoting" Ti Noel as his eyewitness informant. A similar method is used to report Macandal's metamorphosis. First, there is a matter-of-fact account of the transformation: the one-armed Mandingue murmurs some spells and "the bonds fell off and the body of the Negro rose in the air" (51). But a second version crops up in the next paragraph: "And the noise and screaming and uproar were such that very few saw that Macandal . . . had been thrust head first into the fire" (52).

Both Steven Bell and Frederick de Armas ascribe the third-person "independent" perspective to Carpentier, the modern writer-interpreter, and the participant's view to the (oral) archives of the rebelling slaves. This division, they say, allows Carpentier to reflect the slave's worldview and also distance himself from the veracity, or otherwise, of the magical experience claimed in the oral archives.[9] Thus, the modern, skeptical, and reflexive Latin American writer separates his persona from that of his narrative subjects without discrediting the perspective from which the War of Independence was waged. This line of interpretation, like Echevarria's, reduces the slaves' worldview to a literally (in itself) true phenomenon—an unmarvelous realism.

Exposing Carpentier's "false ontology" and revealing the narrative prestidigitation of his novel as a peculiar virtuosity evade, I would say, the central concern of the truth status of the everyday forms of the perceptual processes of slaves. As the slaves show in the novel and the "Prologue," marvelous realism is a kind of "language" in social use. Carpentier conceives magical realism not as the philosophical opposite of realism, but as the "other" of dominant *unmagical* realism whose terror slaves must overcome in order to make the work of independence succeed. Unmagical realism operates as if genuine transcendence is inherently unachievable for the slave. When the masters realize rather late that there is a potential for deadly subversion (and transcendence) in the slaves' magical realism, the masters quickly consign Macandal and Boukman, simultaneously slave rebels and magical realists, to a doomed fate. Recognizing that Macandal's public execution is a death trap not only for their leaders but also for the independent spirit embodied in their audacity, the slaves continue to shun the master's worldview and adopt the outlook of the "Other Shore." Like James's *The Black Jacobins,* Carpentier's novel reinterprets the Haitian War of Independence mainly to abstract from events the enduring lesson they bear for historical posterity. In *The Kingdom of This World,* that lesson concerns the potential of the slave's perceptual strategies to upturn norms propagated by the master.

7

SLAVERY IN AFRICAN LITERARY DISCOURSE

Orality contra Realism in Yorùbá Oríkì and *Ọmọ Olókùn Ẹṣin*

The governing assumptions of orality scholarship have served theoretical constructions of the unity of precolonial and postcolonial African experience very well, probably because its paradigms are highly amenable to analyzing the raw materials of the history of peoples with a relatively short experience of writing. Adopting axioms of orality studies, particularly those that stress the functionality of oral texts and the dynamics of immediacy in oral communication, enables African critics to produce sophisticated explanations of what distinguishes African cultures from others, especially modern European traditions. Literary and cultural criticisms of this kind generally treat oral and folkloric forms as signifiers and carriers of Africa's *native* consciousness. Forms introduced under the aegis of European conquest, even when they are very old, are considered modern mainly because they are written. When such modern forms, such as the novel, enter wide usage and popular consciousness, critics account for their Africanness with the relationships they share with oral traditional practices. As a result, literary histories produced under the orality-literacy rubric assign textual "Africanity" by the closeness of each work to oral and precolonial forms.

In "The African Imagination," for example, Abiola Irele argues that "despite the impact of print culture on the African experience and its role in the determination of new cultural modes, the tradition of orality remains predominant, serving as a central paradigm for various kinds of expression on the continent" (56). He suggests further that the immanent dynamics of African textuality embodied in the performance practices of the nonliterate griot can yield valuable insights into the "phatic, ludic, aesthetic, didactic, ideological, and symbolic" dimensions of African cultural production in both precolonial and postcolonial epochs. Harold Scheub, in his own study of the general patterns of the development of African narrative arts, is even more emphatic than Irele on the dominance of orality in the evolution of African literature and culture. He advances the thesis that "there is an *unbroken* continuity in African verbal art forms, from interacting oral genres to such literary productions as the novel and poetry. The strength of oral tradition seems not to have abated; through three literary periods, a reciprocal linkage has worked these media into a unique art form against which potent influences from East and West have proved unequal" (1).

The tendency outlined by Irele and Scheub that oral traditions constitute the classics of African narrative aesthetics is also accepted by many influential historians looking for ways to demonstrate the truism that African history is deeper and vaster than the history of Europeans in Africa. Bọ́láńlé Awẹ́, a prominent member of the well-known Ìbàdàn school of African history, suggested some time ago that historians of nonliterate societies such as Africa should view oral literary traditions as valuable sources for chronicling the evolution of social and cultural consciousness. Her presumption is that oratures, like written creative artifacts, do sublimate the dominant mentalities of their production and consumption milieu, and that historians of oral epochs should be able to revive and make them useful for an enhanced comprehension of the moving spirit of such times. Oral traditions may not be very reliable for the literal facts they claim, but patterns of verbal stresses and aesthetic elaboration in them may disclose clues about measures of significance that determine historical deeds in times gone by.[1] Karin Barber's study of "the way language is used" in the praise poems of nineteenth-century Ìbàdàn war chiefs outlines, in the spirit of Awẹ́'s recommendations, the shifting contours of the concept of greatness at a precise historical moment among a Yorùbá people. Her well-received literary-anthropological study of oríkì, *I Could Speak Until Tomorrow,* demonstrates consistently how the content and form of oratures attest to the ideological machinations of the living societies that consume them.

The readings of Yorùbá lineage praise poetry, *oríkì orílẹ̀*, proposed in this chapter follow the Awẹ́ and Barber line of social inquiry and not the one that presents oral traditions as capsules of African "human essences." My main focus is on the marginal presence of subaltern social characters, particularly bondspersons, in these poems. The itinerary followed includes, first, a discussion of praise poetry—specifically lineage poetry and personal poetry of the eminent—as an instrument of hegemonic consensus building in old Yorùbá kingdoms. In the second part, I contrast the acquiescent depiction of slaves in orality to the rebellious postures slaves take in Adébáyọ̀ Fálétí's fictional recreation of social relations in a precolonial Yorùbá kingdom in *Ọmọ Olókùn Ẹṣin*.

The analysis set out in this chapter arises out of my contention that the relative absence of the topic of slavery in nineteenth- and twentieth-century mainstream African creative cultures is the result of a general anxiety of African intellectuals about the possible culpability of Africans in the Atlantic trade. Very few episodes in contemporary cultural and intellectual scenes illustrate this anxiety better than the flurry of critical exchanges launched by many outraged African(ist)s against Henry Louis Gates Jr.'s 1999 television series, "Wonders of the African World," which depicted relics of the means used to subject slaves on the African coast before exportation. Many Africanists criticized Gates for historical inaccuracies, especially his not showing clearly that traditional enslavement practices in Africa—or domestic slavery, to use the terms preferred by historians—were not as wickedly exploitative as the monstrous institution created in the New World.[2] To these scholars, it is close to a sacrilege to present on television Africans who claim that "without the participation of Africans there would be no slave trade."[3] Mass media summations like this, it is argued, may let descendants of European profiteers off the tenterhooks of culpability and unfairly hold Africans responsible for actions they were not in a position to control.

The tendency of most interest to me in the "Wonders" palaver is the repetition of the narrative that insists Africans of all social strata—kings, chiefs, and ordinary people alike—fought slavery gallantly but lost to an overwhelming force: "The majority of our ancestors fought against the evil and even European historians have paid homage to the heroic bravery of the African resistance in the fact of genocidal terrorist technology" (Agozino 45). The perspective I apply to the issue does not say that this interpretation is wrong but that something is amiss in the fact that popular African oratures do not preserve discursive[4] records of these struggles against slavery, especially domestic slavery, on the continent.[5]

WHAT IS *ORÍKÌ*?

Yorùbá praise poetry consists of three broad types: personal, lineage, and others. The subject of the first two are humans, and any being at all—animals, plants, prominent landmarks, and other objects that lineages and individuals relate to in the course of their daily lives—could be the topic of the third. Characteristic attributes of virtually all animals and birds are, for example, possible subjects of poetic contemplation in *ìjálá,* the hunters' chant (Babalola, *Content and Form*). Personal praise poems, functioning like elaborations of names, can contain epithets describing ancestry, circumstances of birth, remarkable attributes, network of influence, and peculiar weaknesses. The degree of elaboration and poetic quality of a person's oríkì vary according to the individual's social eminence and the kind of artistic capabilities the celebrated status can purchase. Lineage oríkì, comprising snatches of battles won and lost, condensed migration stories, enumeration of group characteristics, heroic accomplishments, and other features of a distinctive progeny, typically praise the achievements of social groups that can range from families to towns and entire kingdoms. Individual and lineage oríkì interrelate in that they both draw from one another. Performances of lineage oríkì can freely appropriate epithets of great men in the community in the same way that all members of a lineage, regardless of individual achievement or lack of it, can legitimately claim the general attributes commemorated in their kinship poems.

The oríkì poem, Awẹ́ says, "depicts the portrait of an object by giving its most salient characteristics in very figurative and hyperbolic language" (332); according to Karin Barber, "they are a highly charged form of utterance. Composed to single out whatever is remarkable in current experience, their utterance energises and enlivens the hearer" (*I Could Speak* 4). Adébóyè Babalọlá registers the ideal cultural function of personal and lineage oríkì in the following statement:

> A lè bèèrè pé kí ló wà nínú oríkì orílẹ̀ tó ń mú ìwúrí bá ẹni tí a ń fi oríkì náà kì. Ó jọ pé ohun náà ni ìtàn, ìtàn ayé àtijọ́, tí ó ń mú ẹni tí à ń kì kún fún ìgbéraga rere pé ẹ̀jẹ̀ akọni ló wà nínú ara òun; pé òun bá àwọn ènìyàn ńlá, àwọn tó ti ṣe gudugudu méje sẹ́hìn, òun bá wọn tan; nítorí náà ènìyàn pàtàkì lòun pàápàá jẹ́.
>
> We may ask what it is in lineage oríkì that inspires its addressee. It seems that thing is the knowledge of the history of ancient times that fills the addressee with pride that great blood flows in him; that he is related to accomplished heroes; a pride that makes the addressee himself feel very important. (*Àwọ̀n Oríkì Orílẹ̀* 13)

Regarding the nature of its cultural function, other scholars of oríkì agree with Babalọlá in almost every respect. Barber says they "are the principal means by which a living relationship with the past is daily apprehended and reconstituted in the present" (*I Could Speak* 15).[6] This view concurs with Awẹ́'s that the "head-swelling" effect of oríkì provides "a great deal of psychological satisfaction" to the listener ("Praise Poems" 332).

Personal oríkì induce these effects partly because they frame *everyone* affiliated to the praised person through lineage membership, or other social and kinship ties, as beneficiaries of the features of eminence extolled in the poems. Members of a lineage consume the oríkì specific to them partly by considering themselves literal inheritors of the past ruled by their ancestors. Poetic texts that recall the past constitute persons associated with the subjects of praise as units of continuity between the past and the present. The living addressee embodies the irrefutable evidence of the continuation of an enduring essence that the poem locates in the foregrounded kinship and personal attributes. In order to fully enjoy oríkì as stipulated one must, it seems, assume that time unfolds from the past to the present in one unbroken stretch.

Ordinarily, one would expect that the seamless concept of time required for the proper enjoyment of oríkì would carry over into the structure of the poems. But oríkì rarely narrate complete accounts of "historical" events and seldom linger on heroic deeds long enough for the purpose of imparting elaborate cognitive details about them. An inquisitive listener interested in the literal facts condensed in a performance would have to ask extensive questions from people knowledgeable about local histories, though they may not even be poets at all. An oríkì performance may consist of lines previously addressed to different moments and, not infrequently, other persons. The poem's internal order also does not cohere around one single subject besides assembling episodes that together affirm the addressee's eminence. According to Karin Barber,

> An oríkì text is not an "account." It is not narrative like a chronicle or consecutively ordered like a king-list. There is no necessary or permanent relationship between one item in an *oríkì* chant and the next: each may refer to a different topic. There is therefore no narrative continuity between them. The discontinuity arises from the fact that each unit has its own historical moment in which it was composed and to which it alludes. (*I Could Speak* 26)

Because the literal topics of oríkì lines do not cohere, they do not give substantive accounts of the subject's (the addressee's) coming into existence, but they summarize, with condensed references to unrelated events, essential qualities widely sanctioned as markers of social eminence. Lineage oríkì, for instance, will cite communal migration and dispersion but be brief about the causes. Also, the movement of detailed time, or any other form of chronological unity, is never the focus even when the texts speak of origin. Ecological shifts, extraordinary events, recurrent social events, and other traditional measures of *cognitive* duration[7] do not play significant roles in the textual structure. This is not to say, of course, that oríkì do not contain snatches of history as they concern the personality or lineage that is being praised. Personal oríkì, for instance, celebrate the social "largeness" of their subjects with the list of wives (sometimes chronologically), the children (not infrequently in the order of birth), and significant social deeds that demonstrate the subject's magnificence.

The main point pursued here is that oríkì joins the past to the present without unifying them rhetorically or historicizing their relationship literally. The addressee's "presence" which instantiates the performance seems to be all that the audience needs to connect the textual gaps. Whether the motivation for performance is a self-serving material gain, as is often the case with public professional oríkì performance, or altruistic, as is partly the case in the hailing of high-ranking officials, one's family members, and acquaintances, attention is always shepherded toward the addressee's eminence. The addressee's presence commands the constitution of a "useful past" and renders unnecessary the development of historical details. The robust verbal image of the wealthy man, brave warrior, or accomplished farmer is thus created at the moment of performance. A successful oríkì performance will conceal the manifest contradiction between the text's fragmented internal structure and the organic continuity implied in its cultural purpose. Barber attests to the hegemonic ends served by the environment described here when she writes that unlike genealogies that historicize individuals within a tradition, oríkì "create the impression that the big man [or woman nowadays] is at the center of everything, and, indeed, that the other members of the family tree exist only by virtue of their relationship to him" (*I Could Speak* 185).

THE RULER AND THE WARRIOR: TWO LINEAGE ORÍKÌ

The most enduring convention of nativist cultural and literary criticism will attribute the dynamics of the "swelling of the head" experienced by oríkì addressees to the inherently functional character of aesthetic practices in Africa. I think a proper question to ask at the present time is what specific function oríkì serves. It is also right to ask what cultural and political effects are produced by the reception disposition that demands the orientation of one's mind to an unbroken continuity between the past and the present. I return to these questions in the next section. Here I wish to illustrate how the general statements above are set out in the fairly standardized oríkì repertoire of the Olúfẹ̀ and Oníkòyí lineages. Although these two communities were in all likelihood deeply involved in domestic slavery, oral praise poems about them manage to gloss over internal divisions that slaveholding practices may have caused.

Olúfẹ̀ poems salute Ifẹ̀, the center of the universe in Yorùbá mythology. The Oníkòyí texts salute the warrior clan of the old Ọ̀yọ́ kingdom, Ifẹ̀'s rival in the leadership struggle for the control of Yorùbá cultural history and politics. The texts analyzed are taken from *Àwọ̀n Oríkì Orílẹ̀*, Adébóyè Babalọlá's anthology of lineage poems. This volume is a good source for comparative analysis: it covers sixteen major lineages found in the Yorùbá-speaking region of Nigeria and includes multiple versions of oríkì performed by different poets for several lineages. These recordings capture important variations that reveal the extent to which performers have control over their textual repertoire. Unlike personal oríkì that are constructed as the performance unfolds, the content of lineage oríkì is fairly standardized; in some formal situations a performance that deviates too sharply from the norm may be called to order by competing artists.[8]

In each of the four Olúfẹ̀ texts, the palace serves as the metonymy of the kingdom, and most of the aspects of social life highlighted as epitomizing the lineage radiate from the palace and its functionaries. The first Olúfẹ̀ text begins with an enumeration of the distinctive facial marks—an epithet repeated in the other three—whose remarkable symmetry beautifies only Ifẹ̀ people: "Olúfẹ̀ Akèjìọ̀mọ̀ / Àbú 'Ojú mi yẹ̀ṣọ́' / Ojú rábẹ / Ó lé gẹngẹ" (Olúfẹ̀ one who wears the bilateral ọ̀mọ̀ mark / Àbú "My face wears beauty well" / The face [that] anticipates the knife / With great eagerness) (15). The poetic persona then takes a walk through the palace as it summarizes the essence of the kingdom: "N ó rìn lọ́wá, n ó lọ Ìlákòko. / M'ọlọ́wọ́ẹdan" (I will walk around in the palace, I will saunter into the royal arboretum. / The offspring-of-one-with-a-wrist-of-masonic-bangles). The second section, in line with Barber's observation regarding oríkì's rhetorical heterogeneity, goes from the first person to the impersonal third person to list aspects of the royal environment that make Ifẹ̀ people proud.

Wọ́n lá ì í dúró á kí wọn ní'Fẹ̀ Ọ̀ọ̀ni.
A à gbọdọ̀ bẹ̀rẹ̀ kí wọn ní'Fẹ̀ Oòrè.
Bí o bá kí wọn ní'Fẹ̀ o ò tó̄ abẹ́rẹ́.
Ojúrábẹsá àwọn baba mi, ẹbọ ni ọ́n í fi ni í ṣe

You must not stand upright to greet them at Ifẹ̀ Ọ̀ọ̀ni
You cannot stoop to greet them at Ifẹ̀ Oòrè

> If you greet them at Ifẹ̀, you are less than a needle.
> My fathers will make a ritual sacrifice of you. (15)

These lines summarize the terrible fate faced by strangers and commoners who may become victims of ritual sacrifice should they wander into Ifẹ̀ at an inopportune time. Two sections down, the text returns to Ifẹ̀'s distinctive facial markings, depicted now as a possession envied by adjacent ethnic groups including the Hausa and the Nupe—people known, according to the poems, for the distinctly hideous marks they shamelessly parade on their cheeks—and people living within Ifẹ̀ under bondage, namely, vulgar slaves or *ẹrúkẹ́rú*. A person who wears facial marks other than Ifẹ̀'s is, in short, a little less than human.

The longest section of the poem, consisting of thirty-seven lines, describes definitive Ifẹ̀ rituals. The poet says, "Àbú làwọn apàpalàdọ̀ ènìyàn / Apàpalàdọ̀ ènìyàn ní í mú'lé Olúfẹ̀ í wù mí" (They are the ones who kill sacrificial helots with utter disdain / The sacrifice of helots draws me to the Olúfẹ̀) (16). This particular poet also praises the Olúfẹ̀ lineage for the way they dispose other sacrificial objects: "Bí 'ọn bá gbadìrẹ̀, wọn a jẹ ẹ́ torítorí / Bi 'ọn bá gbadìrẹ̀, wọn a jẹ ẹ́ toòrètoòrè" (When they accept roosters, they eat them whole, head inclusive / when they accept roosters, they consume them fully, the soul included) (16). In the lineup of sacrificial objects, the slave and the chicken, it seems, are of the same order in Ifẹ̀. In a kingdom in which a day will not pass without one ritual feast or another, priests show up in pristine white outfits (aṣọ funfun nigínnigín) and clean-shaven heads (orí kondoro) to kill slaves (and "cowards" [ojo] in one text) and offer their innards to the Gods. Ifẹ̀ witchcraft, the poem further says, is unparalleled: "Ẹ ẹ̀ rí ènìyàn tó mú yin lájẹ̀ẹ́ ò nírọ́ ńnú" (Whosoever accuses you of witchcraft cannot be lying) (16). The text, operating as if the entire kingdom is made up of priests and witches, depicts the Ifẹ̀ as a people not at all squeamish about their prolific practice of human sacrifice either in rituals or as part of witchcraft.

In the one major variation in the poems, the fourth poet makes a subtle reference to Ifẹ̀'s central role in a Yorùbá mythology of origin by linking the course of Ifẹ̀'s main river to several outlying communities. But for this instance, Ifẹ̀'s founding role in widely held Yorùbá myths of origin is left out of the oríkì.[9] Even without bragging about the primordial role myths assign to Ifẹ̀ in the pan-Yorùbá order of things, the celebration of the kingdom's royalty (the palace more than the personality of the kings), the priestly class (in relation to witchcraft and sacrifices), and the superiority of Ifẹ̀'s ways to those of other social and ethnic groups indicate that maintaining cosmic (which is to say political) balance is a paramount concern in the kingdom.

Where poems about Ifẹ̀ celebrate "peaceful" governance, Ìkòyí's lineage poetry commemorates war and brigandage, and extols hardness, sheer toughness, and the capture of slaves. The people love wars and live in a permanent readiness for them. They are greeted as "*adìílẹ̀kíkúótódé*" (those who are fully packed, ready for death's arrival), "*Ẹ̀ṣọ́ ò ríkú sá*" (the brave guards who do not flee when death approaches), and "*Ajàkẹ́rúwọ̀lú*" (warriors who arrive with swarms of slaves). Ìkòyí people, their epithets suggest, knowingly risk their lives and constantly court death in their pursuit of slaves. They adapt their lifestyle to fit the frequent movements imposed on them by their professional calling. According to one poem, they can with utmost ease make a home of grasslands, thick forests, high hills, large towns, and the sparsely populated countryside: "Ogun ló ká yin mọ́'gbó. / Lẹ dará igbó. / Ogun ká yin mọ́dàn. / Ẹ dèrò ọ̀dàn" (War duties take you to the forest. / You become forest dwellers. / War duties take you to the savannah. / You become grassland dwellers) (65). Ìkòyí praise poems are one stream of praises of warfare, arms and ammunition, transient living, looting, slave raiding, stealing, expertness in making protective charms in war, devotion to the God of war, ability to utterly inconvenience others. They are also defined by their ownership of vast possessions. Formulaic epithets that repeat these attributes mark shifts from the praise of one war-mongering ability to the other.

A section that depicts slave raiding as the Ìkòyí motivation for endless war making says:

Ènìyan ò ní jagun bí Olúkòyí kí ẹ má folè díẹ̀ kún un
Ọ̀ràn Ìkòyí ò lólè ńnú, Olúgbọ́n ní ńja olè ní kọ̀rọ̀ ti wọn
Tí nbá ńlọ ilé àwọn baba mi
Yánbíolú lọ ogun, ó lọ rè í mẹ́rú
K'Ólúkòyì tó dé, olè kó lé àwọn baba wa lọ
Ó pàdé baba olè lọ́nà
Ni wọ́n bá bẹ́ Yánbímlólú lórí
Orí Olúkòyì ró fiìrìpọ̀ ńlẹ̀
Mo mẹni Ìkòyí bẹ́ lórí, mo mẹni ó bẹ́rí ẹ̀
Mo mẹni tí Ìkòyí kó ńlé, mo mẹni ó kóle àwọn baba wa lọ

No one will fight wars like the Olúkòyí and not add a little pilfering
The Ìkòyí concern is not with stealing, Olúgbọ́n people are the real
thieves
When I salute my fathers.
Yánbíolú goes to war; he goes to capture slaves
Before the Olúkòyì returns, thieves invade our father's homestead
On the way back he crosses the path of a grand thief
Promptly, Yánbíolú is beheaded
Olúkòyì's head rolls freely on the ground
I know whose head Ìkòyí took, I know who took his
I know whose homestead Ìkòyí raided, I know who raided our
father's. (61)

In these lines, pilfering among the Ìkòyí is just a by-product of war mongering; the barefaced thieves come from the Olúgbọ̀n clan. (The poet euphemistically calls the Ìkòyí thieves ten lines later.) The principal reason Ìkòyí people go to war is to capture slaves, although livestock, women, and other items of war booty may fall into their hands as mere incidentals. Another Ìkòyí poem says, "Wọn ì í jíṣu, wọn ì í jágbàdo / Bí sànmọ́mí tẹ́ mọ ílẹ̀, tó jóbìnrin tó dáa / Wọn ó gbé e lọ" (They do not steal yams, they do not steal corn. / But if a seasoned highway robber has a beautiful woman / They will spirit her away). Ìkòyí are so fond of slave raiding that they would leave their homestead vulnerable to attack from burglars that seek less valued property. This reference is remarkable because it is about the only allusion to any opposition to Ìkòyí activities despite their being called "*ajàkẹ́rúwọlú*" (the warrior who arrives with swarms of slaves).

POETRY AND THE CONSTRUCTION OF CONSENT

According to Karin Barber, "Difference is what the oríkì celebrate" (*I Could Speak* 142). The poems reiterate, on one hand, the internal social stratifications that separate the freeborn (*ọmọ*) from the bonded (*ìwọ̀fà*) and the slave (*ẹrú*) and, on the other, the features that distinguish one lineage from the other. Within one locality, oríkì will differentiate (1) social classes and lineage groups, and (2) allow people of diverse classes who come from different places to relate to their different points of departure. Barber speculates that because some texts explicitly speak of outsiders in ways that indicate a desire for distinction, lineage oríkì probably developed "when towns began to define themselves in relation to their neighbours" (*I Could Speak* 146). With further expansion and dispersion, either through wars or voluntary migration, the differentiation first asserted in lineage oríkì remains the most permanent form of remembrance that allows people who may share origins to identify one another.

In the Olúfẹ̀ texts discussed above, for example, the commemorated attributes distinguish among the different classes of people within Ifẹ̀ and also identify the Ifẹ̀ as one people. Slaves who live within the kingdom, but not allowed to wear the lineage's distinct "*ọ̀mọ̀*" facial marks, are inferior to the freeborn Ifẹ̀. Further down the scale are the Nupe and the Hausa, who, according to the poem, wear unmentionable scars on their faces. The internal discrimination notwithstanding, all assimilated Ifẹ̀ descendents—whether of priests and kings or of slaves and witches—are supposed to be equally proud whenever they are hailed with the oríkì lines. Culture dictates that the ruling families, the priestly class that helps them to enforce the royal will, slaves, serfs, and witches, for as long as they claim a public relationship to Ifẹ̀, view themselves as inheritors of the greatness of the clearly stratified kingdom.

The oríkì form of circulating cultural and political consent is conducted poetically with the removal of references to *how things came to be* and a concentration on the way things *are*. To those who respond appropriately to the lineage oríkì, Ifẹ̀ was Ifẹ̀, and is still Ifẹ̀, because slaves were sacrificed by priests, and the king supervised everything for the good of all. Worthwhile dissent did not exist, slaves did not protest, and executed witches deserved their fate because they harmed the guiltless. Rivers moved, priests killed, and slaves served because that is the way things were. To cultivate the mood appropriate for enjoying Ifẹ̀'s oríkì, the listener must assume that priests and kings determined and kept cosmic and earthly orders to serve everyone's best interests. To effect this kind of reception, Ifẹ̀ poems construct the past as the location of a stable country in which citizens knew and played their roles with ease.

Social unanimity is also promoted in the Ìkòyí texts: warriors court death flagrantly and not because their enemies force it on them; they rarely face a serious opposition; and their captured slaves neither seek to escape nor to revolt. However, the other point I want to make with the discussion of Ìkòyí poems is that oríkì can also perform its cultural functions by softening discord. In one poem that closes with an unresolved tension between the warriors and a king who denies their request to go to war at a time of their own choosing, the text manages the conflict such that it does not escalate into a crisis. The king tells his warriors, for reasons not mentioned, to take a two-year leave, one for perfecting protective charms and another for creating plans that will mesmerize their enemies. In the third year, the king says, they can then go to war again:

> Wọn ì í jiyán.
> Wọn ì í jẹ̀kọ.
> Tójúmọ́ mọ́.
> Ogun n wọ́n í tọrọ.
> Lọ́wọ́ ọba.
> Ọbá kọ̀.
> Ọba ò ṣígun.
> Òòṣà ò ṣíkọ̀.
> Wọn ò pẹ̀ṣẹ̀dà.
> Ọba ní á fọ̀dúnnìí kàgbo.
> Fẹ̀míì ṣoògùn ọ̀wọ̀
> Bó ṣọdún mẹ́ta òní.
> Ogún yá.
> Ogun ḿbẹ lọ́wọ́ ọba. (64–65)

> They do not eat pounded yam.
> They do not eat corn meal.

Come sunrise.
War they do plead for.
From the king.
The king refused.
The king would not declare war.
The divine one does not say go.
They do not move a foot.
The king says make healing herbs this year.
Spend the next on perfecting mesmerisms.
When the third year rolls around
Let fighting begin.
Declaring war belongs only to the king.

In these lines, the warriors—who apparently do not live on the country's staples such as pounded yam and corn meal—and the king are at loggerheads. If the warriors do not fight, the poem implies, they would lose sustenance and the king's moratorium on fighting will amount to starvation. However, the poet represents this volatile confrontation ambiguously: "Ọbá kọ̀. / Ọba ò ṣígun. / Òòṣà ò ṣíkọ̀. / Wọn ò pẹṣẹ̀dà" (The king refused. / The king would not declare war. / The divine one does not say go. / They do not move a foot). Read one way, it seems as if the king has to invoke his quasi-divine authority as a living deity (òrìṣà or òòṣà) before he can stop his warriors: "Òòṣà ò ṣíkọ̀. / Wọn ò pẹṣẹ̀dà" (The divine one does not say go. / They do not move a foot). In another view, the warriors seem to remain adamant even after the king has invoked his quasi-divine authority. The line "Wọn ò pẹṣẹ̀dà" (They do not move a foot [without the king's approval]) may be reiterating the warrior's absolute loyalty to the king or toning down the warriors' recalcitrance. I prefer the latter reading because the poem indicates that the king, normally believed to be second only to the Gods, feels a need to justify his refusal to the adamant warriors. It is quite possible that the king is not satisfied with the warriors' recent performances. It seems, in short, the poem is repressing dissent rhetorically so that the king would appear as being in full charge.

The tendency to sanitize dissent and mute subaltern voices is also present in the Olúfẹ̀ lineage poems. In those texts, the pain and suffering of ritual human sacrifice and capital punishment are repressed. Executioners of political offenders are described euphemistically as "anítẹ́ojo" (those who have a burial ground for cowards). As noted below in the discussion of Fálétí's *Ọmọ Olókùn Ẹṣin*, this epithet that represents the trepidations of ritual sacrifice victims as something less than noble could only have emanated from among those to whom indiscriminate courage is very important. The so-called cowards are probably people who do not endorse the royal definition of bravery. Olúfẹ̀ poems also claim that human sacrifice victimizes only slaves and strangers who are either ignorant of Ifẹ̀ ways or have foolishly chosen to disrespect them. Overall, the poets rationalize Ifẹ̀'s routine killings. In effect, these oríkì represent mainly the ruler's sense of timeless good society: kingdoms form and disperse, diverse professional callings dominate social life in ancient lineages, power tussles are won by groups that are more adept in "medicinal" knowledge and diplomacy, and the ruthless attain civil eminence. The entire population is depicted as willingly participating in the construction of the defining ethos of the lineage.[10]

Oríkì's evidently hegemonic function poses considerable difficulties for a reconstruction of Yorùbá social and cultural history as experienced by "little" citizens who cannot access prominent representation in well-circulated verbal artifacts. Transatlantic slavery, for example, is not marked in oríkì. Slavery is mentioned numerous times, usually in passing, in both lineage and personal oríkì, either as part of the unique activities of a particular community or a wealthy person's retinue. Of course, by definition, an oríkì of the suffering of the poor will be a contradiction since the genre typically validates civil eminence, or *ọ̀lá,* as the ideal of citizenship.

Martin Klein notes in his study of the paucity of oral traditions of slaves and slavery in Senegal that oral traditions that are "formally preserved, not always as narratives, but in some fixed form" (209) tend to be very short on subaltern experience. Klein's research team observes that "slaves are present in oral traditions of the larger community, but only in passing. They are mentioned as followers, companions or victims. Traditions are concerned with the deeds of leaders, rulers, and founding heroes" (211). Oral traditions say little about slavery, Klein suggests, because slaves come to their places of servitude with little if any known progeny or other socially acceptable archival information on which personalized oral traditions depend:

> Slaves have little history. They often cannot give much of a genealogy. Many can tell you where their fathers came from but some cannot or will not tell even that. They will sometimes give a general picture of the hegemonic ideology. In a sense, servile informants can say a lot about "the world the master made." They tend to say very little about "the world the slaves made." (212)

Klein's team also discovers that Senegalese slaves, unlike other "low-status groups" like *griots* and blacksmiths, do not speak about their own activities and contribution to the society: "*Griots* will chat informally about great *griots* of the past. Blacksmiths can tell you where they came from and how they got where they are. Slaves cannot" (212). No matter how hard the research team tried, slaves would rather not talk about their communities.

Klein could have been working with Yorùbá traditions, for his findings are similar to Karin Barber's. In the personal oríkì of eminent persons in nineteenth-century Yorùbá country, oríkì subjects almost always emerge from among the freeborn; the bonded and slaves only show up in the texts as social appendages of their owner citizens. According to Barber, "Slavery was never mentioned except as a degraded and shameful status. Oral texts emphasised the disadvantages of slaves in comparison to ìwọ̀fà and free people. No mention was made . . . of slaves being able to redeem themselves by payments to their master" (*I Could Speak* 189).

Lack of civil eminence, in my view, may not be the only cause of the cultural elision of subaltern experiences in a society, like the Yorùbá's, where hunters eloquently salute the beasts of prey they encounter in the course of their daily activities. Trees, hills, palm wine, and virtually all inanimate objects also have dedicated praise lines. I am reluctant to agree with Klein that slaves do not have their own oral traditions because their lives are always in a flux. In communities where slavery was an integral part of the production and social systems such that slaves were assigned a place in civil hierarchy, as was the case in Yorùbá societies,[11] it is not inconceivable that slaves had traditions that reflect their own consciousness. They may not have a sociable genealogy at their place of servitude, but a past they must have had. According to a Yorùbá proverb about slaves, "ọ̀nà ló jìn, ẹrú náà ní baba" (The slave too has a father, although his location may be far). Another one speaks of slave genealogy directly: "bẹ́rú bá jọra wọn, ilé kan náà ni wọ́n ti wá" (Slaves that look alike [probably] came from the same household).

I return to these proverbs in the next chapter when I discuss subaltern presence in Akínwùmí Ìṣọ̀lá's usage of oral traditions in *Ẹ̀fúnṣetán Aníwúrà*. All that I need mention here is that subaltern oral traditions probably circulated internally among slaves and bondspersons who had neither the occasion nor the means to popularize them. "The poor man's proverb does not spread," says a Ghanaian meta-proverb. Unfortunately, the dominant traditions that have been collected and annotated for our understanding of African literary history contain very little of poor people's proverbs. The closest to subaltern "proverbs" are (trickster) tales of social metamorphosis often interpreted, in recent high literary theory, as embodiments of ontological indeterminacy. As Ropo Sekoni postulates, however, the Yorùbá trickster plays its "socially motivated" rebellious role partly because it is, like many slaves, of "unknown origin" and also "because of his marginalization in a world of hierarchy, size, and weight" (8).

The possibility also exists that traditions of the social underdog are not well preserved because the socially eminent squashed the development of texts that ventured beyond the trickster's ambiguous wiles. Bọ́láńlé Awẹ́

("Praise Poems") gives a revealing instance in Ìbàdàn. In 1946, many decades after the abolition of all forms of slavery in colonial Nigeria, I. B. Akínyẹ̀lé published an outline of Ìbàdàn history, *Ìwé Ìtàn Ìbàdàn,* using information gleaned from oríkì of prominent chiefs to augment evidence from other oral traditions, his own recollections, and written records. He included texts of the oríkì of founding Ìbàdàn generals in the published book. Some descendants of Olúyọ̀lé, one of the warrior chiefs, did not like the unflattering parts of the oríkì and successfully made the author, himself a prominent Ìbàdàn chief and future king, to "withdraw the yet unsold copies from the market and remove two pages of the oríkì" (Olatunji 85). The offending lines, expunged from subsequent editions, seem to have been lost completely. According to Awẹ́, "It has been impossible to get any of his [Olúyọ̀lé's] descendants to recite [those] four pages" ("Praise Poems" 335).[12] It is not unreasonable, therefore, to speculate that the type of censorship exercised by the powerful in this instance, close to a century after the death of the subject of the oríkì text, may not have been uncommon in earlier times. This episode of censorship may not be that unusual, if we consider the implications of the Yorùbá adage that advises tact when one speaks about the powerful: "ẹ̀ni tí yóò sọ pé ìyá baálẹ̀ lájẹ̀ẹ́ kò níí sọ ọ́ láàrin ọjà" (Whoever would proclaim that the chief's mother is a witch would not do so in the marketplace).

THE SLAVE'S NARRATIVE IN ADÉBÁYỌ̀ FÁLẸ́TÍ'S *ỌMỌ OLÓKÙN ẸṢIN*

Contemporary African realist historical fiction accepts the possibility that expressions of subaltern discontent did exist, although oral traditions maintain textual silence about them. For two quick examples in Anglophone African writing, we can consider Ayi Kwei Armah's marking historical shifts in his *Two Thousand Seasons* with subaltern rebellions, or how Buchi Emecheta, in *Joys of Motherhood,* imposes severe sanctions on the warlike chief Agbadi, whose troubled daughter is the reincarnation of a slave woman killed as part of a funeral ritual. *Two Thousand Seasons* progresses narratively on the premise that Africa would suffer degradation for one millennium and reconstruct itself in another. The novel ends with the beginning of reconstruction started by ex-slaves who liberated themselves from a slave ship bound for the Americas. In order to maintain consistent cultural reference points, however, I use a Yorùbá historical novel of slave rebellion to illustrate how contemporary writers negotiate the persistence of the oríkì view of African traditional society.

Ọmọ Olókùn Ẹṣin traverses the royal domain of the Olúmokò, where the most important activities are about the smooth running of the Òkò empire, and Òkè Ògùn slave colonies, where people groan under the severe rule of Òkò administrators. According to Bísí Ògúnṣínà, Òkò is none other than the nineteenth-century Ọ̀yọ́ kingdom, and Òkè Ògùn refers to northwestern Yorùbá towns subjugated by the Ọ̀yọ́ kingdom in precolonial times (130–31). Òkò's representatives, stationed permanently in Òkè Ògùn towns, collect for the royal city myriad taxes, dues, and tributes. Periodically, princes and other palace functionaries organize arbitrary tribute-gathering stomps all over Òkè Ògùn. During such visits, palace officials behave outrageously, raping women, seizing properties, and assaulting people any time the urge catches them. A major grievance of Àjàyí, the leader of the Òkè Ògùn rebellion, against Òkò is

> bí a ti tóbi tó nnì, ẹrú ni wá. Ìgbèkùn ni a jẹ́. Oúnjẹ Òkò ni wá. Bí ẹgbẹẹgbẹ̀rún àwọn ọmọ-ọba Òkò ni wọ́n máa ńwá sí Òkè Ògùn ní ọdọọdún, tí wọ́n yóò gba oríṣiríṣi nǹkan àlejò, tí wọ́n yóò máa ta ènìyàn ní ìtàkutà, tí wọ́n yóò máa jẹ̀ ayé ìjẹkújẹ.
>
> as many as we are, we are mere slaves. We are a people under bondage, and we are fair game for Òkò. Countless Òkò princes raid our towns every year to collect gifts, sell people without the slightest regard, and arrogate to themselves unbelievable privileges. (3)

The daughter of an Òkè Ògùn chief summarizes the relationship thus: "Ewúrẹ́ Olúmokò ni Ọlọ́run dá gbogbo wa, àrà tí ó bá sì wù ú ni ó le fi wá dá" (God has made us all Olúmokò's goats; he can do to us whatever catches his fancy) (22). The ill usage of Òkè Ògùn people by Òkò princes shows that Ìbíwùmí's animal imagery is not far from the truth. One heinous instance that shows Òkò people's utter contempt for their Òkè Ògùn slaves occurs when prince Lágboókùn orders his entourage to torch farms and villages to light his way after dark!

Compared to oríkì's adulatory orality, Fálétí's realist portrayal of the Òkò-Òkè Ògùn relationship gives us a different perspective of operations in a traditional principal city. As noted earlier, oríkì simply excludes slaves from consideration. Fálétí's realism, in contrast, brings into full view the sufferings of Òkè Ògùn vassal slaves in whose voice the story is told. Further, the novel shows that the well-being of Òkò, whose political status is analogous to Ifẹ̀'s, derives from the suffering of its outlying slave communities. Òkò thrives because compulsory work orders are being carried out in Òkè Ògùn.

Being a "colonial" overlord, the Olúmokò, as the British rulers of Fálétí's Nigeria did historically, governs his slave territory indirectly with local chiefs. This political arrangement means that while Òkè Ògùn people are undoubtedly slaves, they are also colonials, and especially that they own a vast territory to which they claim natal rights (3), albeit under terms imposed by an alien force. They own farmlands, keep families, and worship their own deities, and their chiefs are appointed from among their ranks. Even so, Òkò slaves are freer than native Òkè Ògùn chiefs from whom, as Mbembe would say, practically "no rational acts with any degree of lawfulness proceed" (183). The people cannot make any long-range decisions about their own affairs without Òkò's approval. They cannot use the resources of the land in the way they see fit unless the ruling alien force permits them. The people cannot, for example, thatch their roofs with the most durable leaves in their country (3), whereas they gather and ship the same roofing material to Òkò for royal usage. In Orlando Patterson's characterization of slavery, Òkè Ògùn people may not be "natally alienated," but they are socially dead on their own soil. The Olúmokò has seized their territory and curtailed their sovereignty to enrich his own kingdom.

The Òkè Ògùn struggle for freedom begins with Àjàyí's spontaneous refusal to work on his hometown's annual contribution of roofing materials to Òkò. Àjàyí is convinced that the injustice of Òkè Ògùn's service to Òkò would be clear to everyone, once he leads by his own example. Unfortunately, no one comes to his side because most of his people have come to believe that the prevailing social order is natural. Before her conversion to the rebellion, Ìbíwùmí, the daughter of the head chief in Àjàyí's hometown, chides him while he is held in jail: "Baálé ilé ju ọmọ ilé lọ, Baálẹ̀ ju Baálé lọ, Olúmokò sì ju Baálẹ̀ lọ, Ṣísẹ̀-n-tẹ̀lé ni Ọlọ́run dá gbogbo nńkan láyé" (The head of the household ranks higher than other residents of the family compound, the village chief ranks higher than heads of household, and the Olúmokò ranks even higher than village chiefs; God has ordered everything in the world into a hierarchy) (22). Using different words, but angling for the same effect, a village chief rebukes Àjàyí: "Òkò ni àtìrandíran àwa á sìn, Ọlọ́run kò sì ní jẹ́ kí a yé wọn ọ́n sìn tí a ó fi kú ní tiwa" (We've been serving Òkò since the beginning of time, and may God never make us incapable of serving them) (11). With the opposition to rebellion so deeply entrenched, Àjàyí's spontaneity fails. The local authorities arrest him and decide to send him to Òkò to face the music. He would have been promptly executed had Ìbíwùmí, now converted to the cause, not given him the file he used to saw off his chains, for which she gets in trouble.

Meanwhile, Àjàyí realizes the very limited usefulness of spontaneity during his detention: "kí ènìyàn tó dáwọ́lé ìjà gbígba òmìnira lọ́wọ́ ará òde, òmìnira ti inú ìlú ni ó kọ́ ṣe pàtàkì ná" (prior to embarking on the struggle for freedom from external forces, one must first secure internal emancipation) (15). Hence, after his escape from jail, he starts a "mind opening" project, traveling all over Òkè Ògùn territory to educate fellow slaves and to instigate them to rise up against the Olúmokò. Àjàyí, like Martin Delany's Blake, puts the rebellion on the road and constructs the insurrection as he moves around, launching sporadic skirmishes along the way. Eventually, the widespread Òkò security apparatus ensnares him and his leading accomplices, who are all arrested and sent to Òkò for execution. It is while on death row that the four principal leaders of the insurrection—Àjàyí, Ìbíwùmí, Kọ́lájọ̀, and Àyọ̀wí—meet for the first time as a group and recount the different first-hand experiences that make up the greater part of the novel.

A widespread slave rebellion actually breaks out while Àjàyí and his Òkè Ògùn "free born" insurrectionists are in detention. This revolt is launched by the personal slaves Ìbíwùmí had freed earlier in defiance of her father. The combination of the pressure mounted by the little army of Ìbíwùmí's emancipated slaves and the protesting band of some brave Òkè Ògùn people finally convince Òkò authorities to grant freedom to their slave colony. However, they first negotiate a lucrative deal that would continue their parasitic exploitation of the "free" Òkè Ògùn. Before granting emancipation, the Olúmokò makes Òkè Ògùn people pledge that they will supply annually, for ten years, fifty bags of money to the king, another fifty to his chiefs, twenty to the crown prince, and two bullocks. In the most shocking part of the "freedom" charter, the slave communities grant the Olúmokò the right to keep up to twenty slaves at one time. Àjàyí goes home with Ìbíwùmí and they are married at a festive ceremony!

The melodramatic ending orients the story toward an allegorical depiction of Africa's recent colonial history in which the recreation of Yorùbá slave-holding practices of the nineteenth century—a historical period dubbed the "Age of Confusion" in Yorùbá history because of the nearly unremitting upheaval created by internecine wars that invariably fed the slave trade—are mere narrative incidentals. This is not to say that some of the details are not historically accurate: To rebuke Àjàyí, a chief asked him: "'A kò sin ará Òkò mọ̀ tàbí kín lo wí? Ará Ìbàdàn kí a ó wá máa sìn?'" (We should not serve Òkò? Is it Ìbàdàn that we should serve?) (11). This statement reflects the principal role Ìbàdàn played in the reconstitution of power politics in nineteenth-century Yorùbá land when Ìbàdàn became an imperial entity sustained by constant war making. The destabilizing impact of Ìbàdàn's warring activities all over the Yorùbá country is the principal reason J.D.Y. Peel names 1820–1890 as the "age of confusion" in Yorùbá history (47–88). The "confusion" of that age is further revealed in the reluctance of Ìbíwùmí's freed slaves to return "home." They say: "'Bí a bá kúrò níhìn-ín, ìyà ni à ńlọ jẹ un. Níbo ni a lè gbé mọ́ tí yóò rí bí ilé Baálẹ̀. . . . A kìí wulẹ̀ fi ìyà jẹra ẹni'" (If we leave, we are going to suffer. At any rate, where else can we live that can give us the comfort of the Chief's household. . . . There is no point in going away only to suffer needlessly) (82–83). Although Ìbíwùmí interprets these words to be a sign of the slaves' reluctance to give up their corrupt privileges of being the head chief's operatives, it is quite possible that the slaves are genuinely afraid of returning to the uncertainty of "home" in the "age of confusion."

Historical veracity notwithstanding, the most important point to note is that Fálétí corrals the slave rebellion plot into a *decolonization* narrative; Òkè Ògùn starts out as a slave colony and ends up a neo-colonial territory. The slave rebellion settles exploitative "transnational" relations but leaves the equally repressive intra-national relations unexamined. The story, for instance, gives no explicit indication as to what will happen to domestic slaves in the newly independent country. In short, Fálétí's novel successfully assimilates the question of slavery into an indictment of colonization and a critique of the shortsightedness of those who negotiated instruments of Òkè Ògùn's (Africa's) independence. I need not say that this tale has been told many times over in African literature and criticism.

REALISM CONTRA ORALITY

But we cannot leave alone the story of slave rebellion in this novel. Its realist interpretation of Yorùbá domestic slaveholding practices affords us, in the way oral literary traditions like oríkì cannot, a glimpse into how slavery is internalized culturally. Let us consider how slaves are acquired in those wars about which Oníkòyí lineage poetry speaks very highly. In both Òkè Ògùn and Òkò, war captives, kept for either personal use or for sale in the open market, are the main source of slaves. Òkè Ògùn region was apparently run over by Òkò forces that subjugated it. Going by the terms of the proverb used to admonish Àjàyí for instigating a rebellion, slave raiding is one important reason for waging wars at that time and place: "'Ọba kò bí ni ká rè 'mẹ́rú'" (Offsprings of the king have no business going to the place of plucking slaves) (11). "The place of plucking slaves" is, according to the novelist's gloss, a synonym for war. We can, in light of this term, describe Ìkòyí's fondness for war as a love of "slave plucking."

An incident that occurs when the Òkè Ògùn rebellion finally spreads to the royal city of Òkò gives an indication as to how slaves are made in war. Òkò forces, realizing that the rebels are going to overwhelm them, surrender, screaming, "'A ti dẹrú yín o! A dẹrú yín o!'" (We have become your slaves! We are now your slaves!) (139). On one hand, the surrender convention, "We are now your slaves," shows the defeated as accepting their fate and deflects the responsibility for whatever might happen later onto the victim.

We may assume that before the novel started Òkè Ògùn people lost their right to self-government when they declared "We are now your slaves" to their Òkò captors. I submit that this is the "oríkì" view of the slaves' motivation. If we read the convention from the perspective of the enslaved, we could say that the statement is not a sign of cowardice but an effort of the defeated to create a retreat. The warriors are not making their captor's job easy but negotiating a passage for themselves. The defeated know that their time is up; they also know, however, that the bloody deeds of war are not really aimed at killing them but to capture them. The captors themselves, I would add, know that the defeated proclaim "We are now your slaves" not because they have suddenly discovered the grace of servitude. In the types of oral traditions discussed earlier, unfortunately, the captive's perspective is not entered into cultural records.

The surrender convention is a plot—*ọ̀tẹ̀* in Yorùbá—being devised by the defeated to organize a retreat and not the ceding of a right—*ẹ̀tọ́*—to the victor.[13] In words that closely resemble terms used by Gabriel's interrogators in *Black Thunder*, the Olúmokò, the principal slaveholder, once tells Àjàyí, the leading slave rebel, "'Béniyàn ń fún ẹrú lóyin jẹ̀ níjoojúmọ́, nígbà tí ó bá di ọjọ́ kan ni yóò máa sunkún ilé rẹ̀" (If one serves honey to the slave every day, he/she would still one day demand to return to his/her natal home) (129). If pampering a slave, as the Olúmokò suggests, would not quench the desire for freedom, it should mean that a declaration of sincere self-enslavement by the defeated is most likely a slaveholder's fantasy. These words also imply that the anxiety-free bravado of Ìkòyí warriors and the agon-less peace sought in Ifẹ̀ rituals, as celebrated in oríkì, are hegemonic constructs that repress seething antagonisms running beneath the governing structures praised in oral traditions.

The realist narrative of *Ọmọ Olókùn Ẹṣin* also allows us to fill other textual gaps in oríkì's orality. As it is in the Ifẹ̀ of the oríkì, warriors are absent in Òkò's daily affairs. We only see the king enjoying the fruits of the warriors' slave taking. A different picture emerges when the narrative shifts to the provinces. Àjàyí tells readers, for example, that roofs in the capital city are thatched with the durable materials gathered in the provinces under harrowing conditions, and that Òkò's abundant food supplies are provided by starving slaves: "A ó pa bẹẹrẹ tí ọba yóò fi kọ́ ilé, a ó ru ẹran ìgbẹ́ tí ọba yóò fi ṣe ọdún lọ. Ẹran tí a bá rù, a kò gbọdọ̀ jẹ níbẹ̀, ebi ì bá fẹ́rẹ̀ pa olúwa rẹ̀ kú" (Annually, we gather and send to the king sheaves of leaves for his roofing needs and meat for him to entertain his guests during festivals. We cannot eat the game we kill, even if we are dying of hunger) (3). In oríkì, nobody is ever undeservedly hungry.

Àjàyí arrives in the capital city in chains at the time of a festival analogous to the ones praised in Olúfẹ̀ poems. This particular festival, at which slave colonies present their levied tributes, is represented as a celebration of renewal. A high point of the festivities includes an elaborate cleansing ritual during which miscreants gathered from the provinces, along with other "wrongheaded" strangers, are sacrificed to Òkò's great deities. Fifteen Òkè Ògùn rebels, including Àjàyí's father and brother, are scheduled to be killed at the king's principal Ògún (the God of war, among other things) shrine. Other classes of victims include strong people, captured top warriors of other lands, and disloyal citizens (146).

The realist depiction of the regal pageantry that fills the air at Òkò during the days that lead to the cleansing festival provides a fuller alternative to the dense allusions, disjointed historicity, and many ellipses of oríkì's high poetry. At Òkò, as in the poetic Ifẹ̀, human sacrifice is a daily affair during festivals: "ojoojúmọ́ ni wọ́n ń bẹ́ ènìyàn lórí" (beheadings go on everyday), Àjàyí observes from jail. The Ògún priest, like the main persona in the Olúfẹ̀ lineage poem, refers to the victims of ritual sacrifice as "páńdukú" (136), or worthless ruffians. Slave rebels and others to be killed are referred to as "ẹran òrìṣà" (meat for the Gods) (147). They are fed yam peelings (131), treated like domestic animals, and tethered to posts like beasts. In contrast, Àjàyí, who has an intimate knowledge of the noble cause for which his fellow dissenters are fighting, describes the victims as "*akọ̀ni*" or braves (138). Because oríkì presents only the priestly view of human sacrifice, the kind of alternative terms used by Àjàyí did not get to the public domain controlled by promoters of high praise poetry. Hence oríkì speaks only of the ostensibly universal communal good to be served by the killing of vulgar slaves (*ẹrúkẹ́rú*).

The Olúmokò's justification for sentencing Àjàyí to death reveals the connection between bondage or servitude and good governance in a kingdom like Òkò. The king says Àjàyí's treasonable rejection of slavery constitutes a direct challenge to the Gods: "'irú àwọn tí ń fa ìbínú irúnmọlẹ̀ ni irú àwọn abẹnu ṣùàṣua yìí'" (This foul-mouthed bumpkin is of the kind that provokes the wrath of the Gods) (129). In other words, dissent against the king constitutes an offense to the Gods. The Olúmokò's interpretation of Àjàyí's rebellion literalizes the popular oríkì of kings as "aláṣẹ èkejì òrìṣà" (the authoritative one second only to the Gods). Since the king is the supreme earthly master and defying him amounts to challenging the Gods, executing insurrectionists like Àjàyí would be divine justice. The narrative further connects ritual sacrifice and slave rebellion in two statements used by Àjàyí and Ìbíwùmí at different times to justify their actions. While in jail in his hometown pending transportation to Òkò, Àjàyí resolves to die, if need be, in the course of fighting for freedom: "A kìí kú lẹ́ẹ̀mejì" (Dying is not done twice) (29). Shortly before she is to be sent to Òkò for trial, Ìbíwùmí thinks about the death sentence she may receive and reconciles herself to that fate by telling herself, "Ẹbọ kan kìí le kí ó kọjá ikú" (No blood sacrifice is graver than death). In these instances, the rebels are rendering very explicit the meaning of the literal death that royal authorities, acting under the guise of appeasing Gods and affirming peaceful order, visit on their slaves.

It would be extremely difficult to grasp the messy nature of human sacrifice just by reading or listening to the Olúfẹ̀ lineage praise poetry. The poems repeatedly affirm the pristine beauty and serene appearance of Ifẹ̀ priests to conceal the brutality of some of the things they do in the course of their duties. Olúfẹ̀ epithets say, "Ṣẹ́ṣẹ́ẹ̀fun bu iyì kóòṣà" (White beads add to the gracefulness of the Gods) and "Aṣọ funfun nigínnigín bu 'yì kóòṣà" (Spotless white attires add to the gracefulness of the Gods) (16). In Fálétí's Òkò too, priests make strenuous efforts to put forward a clean face. On the day Àjàyí and his co-conspirators are first scheduled for execution, the priest in charge shows up thus: "Ó da aṣọ àlà onírọ̀rọ̀ kan báyìí bora. Ó wa ìlẹ̀kẹ̀ funfun gòdògbà gòdògbà sí ọrùn, ó mú ọ̀pá ṣẹ́ṣẹ́ẹ̀fun lọ́wọ́, gbogbo ara rẹ̀ ni ó ń dán rokoso fún osùn tí ó kùn" (He wraps himself in a spotless white toga. He bedecks himself with large white beads, he carries a whitewashed staff in his hand, and his painted body shines in camwood red) (145). The white apparel, usually associated with Ọbàtálá, the deity that created the world in one Yorùbá creation myth, signifies stable serenity and spotless continuity. The white cloth contrasts with the red camwood lotion with which the priest's body is painted. The red color here is not an iconic acknowledgment of the blood sacrifice that the priest is about to make but a reinforcement of the communal rebirth that the sacrifice is intended to cement. Camwood lotion is traditionally associated with new mothers who, after the birth of a newborn, color their hands and feet with it. The Òkò high priest is, in essence, decked as a male "mother" devoted to social rebirth.

Ọmọ Olókùn Ẹṣin complicates the celebration of priestly functions with descriptions of the conflicts inherent to ritual human sacrifice. While the priests are very calm, their subordinates who lead the victims to the stakes are much rougher. Representing the traditional boisterousness of Ògún, the God of War,[14] these petty functionaries wear very skimpy shorts like warriors and gird their waists with a tight band: "Ojú wọn pọ́n koko bí ojú ẹ̀gà, ìrìn wọ̀n kò sì jọ ìrìn ọmọlúàbí" (Their eyes are ember red, and their swagger is far from a gentleman's) (145). These rough operatives, whose attire and comportment vulgarly signify the war-making spirit that led to the subordination of the socially discontent about to be sacrificed, did not make it into Olúfẹ̀ praise poetry. Furthermore, resistance is out of the question for victims of human sacrifice in oríkì. In Fálétí's Òkò, however, victims do not accept their fate. Àjàyí attacks a priest at the Nààrì shrine (147). Granted that this may not be a typical act, Ìbíwùmí's fainting when she is dragged to the execution stake certainly contradicts the clockwork smoothness depicted in oríkì. The postponement of the rituals because Ìbíwùmí faints shows that the Òkò royal establishment is invested in presenting an image of the victim's calm acceptance of her fate exactly as oríkì depicts it. The priests haul Ìbíwùmí and others back to their cells to better prepare them for a stoic acceptance of their tragic end.

After having said all of the above, it would be misleading to suggest that Fálétí's realism is meant to subvert the oríkì perspective of Yorùbá traditional society. Like oríkì, the melodramatic ending of *Ọmọ Olókùn Ẹṣin* blunts the sharp edge of its allegorical exposure of traditional slave relations. When representatives of Òkè Ògùn rebellious slaves intrude on the rescheduled execution of Àjàyí and his compatriots, the symbolic "confusions" that have bedeviled Òkò's aborted human sacrifice of its slave rebels assume "literal" dimensions. The Olúmokò's own slaves turn in their "ààsó" (160) insignia, the token of their authority to act with impunity on the king's behalf. When these privileged slaves repudiate the king, it becomes obvious that the Òkè Ògùn rebel movement has reached decisive historical proportions and that an epochal turn is about to occur.

But the novel reverts to the conciliatory and non-adversarial model of conflict resolution said to be African in nature.[15] The Olúmokò rules that the slaves that were nearly executed for offending the Gods of social peace and good governance be released immediately and changes the basis of good governance from forceful enslavement to exploitative persuasion. The hitherto blatantly imperial Olúmokò eases himself into the rhetoric of family relations when he addresses restless Òkè Ògùn crowds:

> Mo kí yín o, gbogbo ẹ̀yin òṣèlú. Ẹ kú osi. Ẹ kú iṣẹ́. Mo sì kí ọ, ìwọ Àjàyí, ọmọ Olókùn-Ẹṣin. Ọmọ ọkọ ni ọ́. O kú iṣẹ́, o kú àfaradà. A ti ro ọ̀rọ̀ yìí lọ síwá sẹ́yìn, kò sí ibi tí a lè yẹ̀ ẹ́ sí mọ́—àfi kí a fún yín ní òmìnira tí ẹ̀ ń fẹ́. Nítorí náà, ẹ̀ máa lọ. Gbogbo orílẹ̀-èdè yín di òmìnira láti ààrọ̀ yìí lọ. A kò sì ní í fi ìjà túká. Ti-bàbá-tọmọ tí a jẹ́ láti òwúrọ̀ wá náà ni a ó máa jẹ́ títí di alẹ́. Ṣùgbọ́n kí ẹ tó lọ, ẹ ṣe ètò: Kín ni n ó máa jẹ, kín ni n ó máa mu, ta ni n ó máa ránni sí? Gbogbo ètò wọ̀nyí ni kẹ́ ẹ ṣe fún mi kí ayé leè gbà fún yín pé ẹ ja ìjà òmìnira náà dópin.
>
> Greetings to you all. I particularly salute you, Àjàyí, a true son of the king's horseman, for your forbearance. We have deliberated long on this matter, and there is no other thing for us to do but to grant you the freedom you seek. From this morning on, your province is free. We should part ways amicably. We shall forever remain fathers and offspring to one another. But before you go your own way, you must make plans for my well-being. It is

> only after you have done this that we can say you have fought the freedom fight to the good end. (161)

At his defeat, the ex-master transforms himself into the father and makes the ex-slave into the child. Surprisingly, Àjàyí and his people, being "good Yorùbá citizens," accept the rhetoric of paternalist privilege and agree to keep sustaining the royal "father." In nineteenth-century Yorùbá sociology, the position of the father, according to Peel, implies "priority, dominance, leadership, or superior efficacy in any sphere, human or otherwise" (72).[16] Fálétí's view of the historical change brought about by the Òkè Ògùn slave rebellion, I conclude, ultimately endorses the oríkì version of society, one that transmutes the subaltern's yearning for freedom and renewal into the father's gift of cultural peace and orderliness.[17]

8

PRYING REBELLIOUS SUBALTERN CONSCIOUSNESS OUT OF THE CLENCHED JAWS OF ORAL TRADITIONS

Ẹfúnṣetán Aníwúrà

The "negative" readings of the previous chapter highlight covert and overt strategies of excluding unruly subaltern presence in contemporary constructions of African traditions. That the reading exercise is even possible indicates that slaves and other bonded classes are not completely removed from cultural view after all. This chapter proposes a more positive interpretation in that it ascribes rebellious intent to what is there in Akínwùmí Ìṣọ̀lá's depiction of the tragic fate of a nineteenth-century Yorùbá leader in *Ẹfúnṣetán Aníwúrà.*

THE PLAY: THEATER CONTRA HISTORY

Disagreements over the proper control of slaves in nineteenth-century Ìbàdàn constitute the primary means of reflecting on the nature of absolute power in *Ẹfúnṣetán Aníwúrà.* The play, which won the top prize of the Ẹgbẹ́ Ìjìnlẹ̀ Yorùbá (Yorùbá Studies Association) in 1966, dramatizes the political in-fighting that led to the assassination of the very wealthy and powerful Ẹfúnṣetán Aníwúrà, the city's *Ìyálóde,* or leader of women, or "mother of public affairs."[1] The play is a standard in the curriculum of the public school system in Yorùbá-speaking areas of Nigeria. It has been performed many times for television by a variety of troupes. Bankole Bello made a feature-length movie based on the play in 1981. The same year, an Ìṣọ̀lá Ògúnṣọlá Theater production of the play was performed to "an audience of more than fourteen thousand spectators" who watched "in a festive, holiday mood" at the Liberty Stadium in Ìbàdàn. That was a record attendance in the history of the Yorùbá traveling theater movement (Jeyifo 115). Although the source of the play's popularity is not the subject of discussion here, I would like to say that the depiction of Ìyálóde Ẹfúnṣetán as a wealthy but childless and cantankerous woman accounts for a good part of the play's attraction. The play may also have been very popular because it revives a version of glorious local history in its effective use of oral traditions like oríkì, spell-binding incantations, and the spectacular presentation of Ẹfúnṣetán's tradition-defying aggressive mien.

In his preface to the first edition of the published play, Ìṣọ̀lá states that his motivation for writing about Ẹfúnṣetán is to comment on the unspeakable wickedness history accuses her of perpetrating on her slaves.[2] A part of oríkì traditions about her is quoted as:

> Ẹfúnṣetán Aníwúrà, obìnrin mẹ́ta
> Adé-káyà-ó-já!
> Ẹ̀rùjẹ̀jẹ̀ tíí fẹrú paléyá!
> Ẹfúnṣetán ọ̀kan, Ìbàdàn ọ̀kan.
> Abàyà-gbàǹgbà tí í p'Olódùmarè lẹ́jọ́:
> Ọba òkè kò tètè dáhùn,
> Ẹfúnṣetán gbéra láyé, ó lọ̀ bá A lọ́run
>
> Ẹfúnṣetán Aníwúrà, the one woman worthier than three
> Whose arrival sprouts fear
> The fearsome one who kills slaves for Eid
> The brazen one who challenges the Almighty to a palaver:
> The king above is slow to respond,
> Ẹfúnṣetán goes up there to hurry him up.

Ìṣọ̀lá uses three interlocking themes to dramatize Ẹfúnṣetán's high-handedness: the inhuman regulations under which her slaves serve and their expressions of discontent about these rules, Ẹfúnṣetán's complete disregard for kinship and family ties, and lastly her frontal rejection of her male colleagues in the political hierarchy. Ẹfúnṣetán owns many slaves, all of whom she uses like pieces of farm tools and keeps in check with draconian regulations. One of her peculiar rules stipulates capital punishment for any slave, male or female, caught trying to have a child. With this law, she shares with her slaves the sanction of childlessness she believes God has inflicted on her.

With this rule, she mocks God by trying to play one: "Èmi kò mọ ohun tí mo fi ṣe Elédùwà / Tí ó fi fọmọ lá mi lójú báyìí. / Ṣùgbọ́n kò burú, ohun tí à á ṣe kù, / Kí òun mú òkè Rè̩ lọ́wọ́ lọ̀hùnún / Kí èmi náà mú ilè̩ lọ́wọ́ níhìnín" (I don't know what I've done to offend God / That he would deny me children / But all is not lost / Let him hold his heavens / I will hold the earth here) (9).

In the process of enforcing this merciless rule, Ẹfúnṣetán pays no regard to family and the concerns of fellow chiefs. When a slave puts another in the family way and solicits the help of Ẹfúnṣetán's brother, whom he begs to claim responsibility for the pregnancy, she refuses all entreaties. When her slaves kill an old man they believe is trespassing on her farm, Ẹfúnṣetán scorns the council of chiefs' request for explanation. In the end, the male chiefs conclude that she has become a political menace that must be removed by force. They attack her person, raze her compound, free all her slaves, and then arrest her. Unable to bear the humiliation, Ẹfúnṣetán commits suicide. From her tragic death the play draws a very clear moral lesson about gross misuse of power: "Má fagbára dẹ́rù bà mí, / Ejò tí ńlọ́pọ̀lọ́ lè ṣe déédéé ọdẹ" (Frighten me not with your might, / The snake chasing the hapless frog may yet fall victim to the hunter's snare) (79). The play insists in many ways that Ẹfúnṣetán deserves her fate, most effectively in the contrast established between her egregious excesses and the usually good-natured deliberations of her opponents. The gleeful victory parade of her opponents after her deposition is not protested by anyone.

Probably because the play, usually read as a historical reenactment, projects a negative perception of powerful womanhood in traditional Yorùbá society, a different interpretation of oral traditions regarding Ẹfúnṣetán has been proposed by Bọ́láńlé Awẹ́ in an essay that could be easily read as an extended correction of Ìṣọ̀lá's play. Awẹ́ rebuts Ìṣọ̀lá's statements on Ẹfúnṣetán almost point for point, from her allegedly excessive cruelty, the motivation of male chiefs who killed her, through her relationship to her family, down to the details of how she died. In an apparent reference to Ìṣọ̀lá, Awẹ́ derides "one tradition which has now been reinforced in a Yorùbá play that claims Ẹfúnṣetán was unpopular because she was cruel to her slaves. She was alleged to have refused to allow them to get married and to have brutally killed one of them who became pregnant" (69). Using evidence that "gives a contrary impression," Awẹ́ demonstrates that the historical Ẹfúnṣetán, unlike the one in tales preserved by her political enemies and perpetuated unwittingly by Ìṣọ̀lá's play, was not cruel and did not misuse her powers. On the contrary, "she was so powerful that no one dared to take liberties with her female slaves" (69). Ẹfúnṣetán's slaves, whose descendants still live in Ìbàdàn, actually married "other slaves or contracted marriages with free men outside Ẹfúnṣetán's compound on the payment of the usual redemption price" (69). These indisputably loyal slaves always returned home to her after long trading trips outside Ìbàdàn.

According to Awẹ́, the male chiefs moved against Ẹ̀fúnṣetán for reasons other than the unbridled high-handedness for which the play charges her. She was attacked because her independence, marked by her blunt speaking, threatened the men's financial and political interests:

> For instance, after the Ado war of 1872 when Ogidan, her [Ẹfúnṣetán's] slave, has led 100 of her slaves to battle under Are Latosa, she gradually got disenchanted with the idea of continuous warfare, particularly as the warriors, especially Are Latosa and Balogun Ajayi Ogboriefon, stretched increasingly her credit facilities and failed to pay their debts. When Are Latosa launched another expedition in 1874, she therefore refused to field any solders, to give ammunition on credit and to declare her solidarity with him along with the other chiefs at the gate to the town as was her wont. Thereafter it was an open declaration of hostility between her and Are Latosa. (69)

In this version, Ẹfúnṣetán got in trouble with her male compatriots because she tried to protect her financial well-being. She could not physically prevent the men from going to war, but she can withhold her personal investments in crucial war supplies.[3]

In history, Awẹ́ further says, Ẹfúnṣetán did not commit suicide, although the male chiefs did all they could to drive her into either depressive despair or exile. Her defiance baffled the male warriors who construed her continuous presence in town "as an indication of their own weak position" (70). They refused her gestures of reconciliation and succeeded in getting one of her relatives to betray her. They then unleashed on her "the masquerade charged with the responsibility of killing women offenders" (70) who, with the help of three slaves, crushed her to death with an "imported Portuguese cask" (70).

The oríkì fragment Awẹ́ uses for her epigraph shows most poignantly her divergence from Ìṣọ̀lá:

> Efunsetan Iyalode
> One who has horses and rides them not
> The child who walks in a graceful fashion
> Adekemi Ogunrin
> The great hefty woman who adorns her legs with beads
> Whose possessions surpass those of the Ààre [Commander-in-Chief]
> Owner of several puny slaves in the farm,
> Owner of many giant slaves in the market
> One who has bullets and gunpowder.

> Who has gunpowder as well as guns,
> And spends money like a conjurer,
> The Iyalode who instills fear into her equals.
> The rich never give their money to the poor;
> The Iyalode never gives her wrappers to the lazy. (57)

These lines stress Ẹfúnṣetán's wealth and say nothing about her treatment of the slaves she holds in such large numbers.

Both Ìṣọlá's play and the contradiction of its main plank in Awẹ́'s biographical sketch offer object lessons in the preservation of slave experience, especially their expressions of dissent, in hegemonic oral traditions. To Awẹ́, Ìṣọlá's meditation on power, in which everything is right until Ẹfúnṣetán recklessly arrogates the right of life and death to herself, repeats the traditions encouraged by Ẹfúnṣetán's political enemies who called her an implacable witch. For example, she is described in the play as "ìkà" (wicked one), "ìyá àjẹ́" (mother-witch), and "arẹ́nijẹ" (blatant cheat). But Awẹ́'s biographical sketch, written to redeem women's cultural representation from the male biases of certain traditions, succeeds partly by promoting a view that erases the specific concerns of Ẹfúnṣetán's slaves—among whom many were women. She suggests that the burden of a country's political imbalance is unfairly dumped on a great woman when, in reality, the problems are caused by a few greedy male chiefs. Ẹfúnṣetán, from this perspective, was simply a great merchant; her slaveholding practices being no more inhumane than what prevailed in all of Yorùbá land where, generally, "slaves could be more appropriately regarded as the domestic servants of today" (63). In the preface to his English translation of the play, Niyi Oladeji repeats Awẹ́'s explanation of slavery in Yorùbá country: "In reality the characters called 'slaves' in the play are not 'slaves' in the Western sense of the word. The characters are indentured persons, providing interest in kind with their labor for sums of money borrowed from Iyalode Efunsetan Aniwura by their fathers, mothers or other relatives" (vii). While Awẹ́'s referring to "slaves" as "servants" can be overlooked because she is working from her own cultural translations, there is no basis for Ọládèjì to rewrite Ìṣọlá, who does not describe his characters with the Yorùbá term for debt peons, ìwọ̀fà.

SLAVERY AND SOCIAL DEATH

Ìṣọlá clearly privileges the traditions preserved by Ẹfúnṣetán's enemies. Nevertheless, his representation of the treatment of slaves as the primary subject of the power play between Ẹfúnṣetán and her male rivals shows the palimpsestic way subaltern consciousness survives in what we now call African traditions. In the remainder of this chapter, I focus on the slaves' role in the play by examining the import of their words for what they think of their servile status, their role in the plotting of Ẹfúnṣetán's fate, and how the chiefs' removal of Ẹfúnṣetán actually preempts a slave uprising against her. I want to read the play as if it is as much about the slaves as it is about high-stakes political contests between two main centers of power, one controlled by Ẹfúnṣetán (as Awẹ́ reads the tradition) and the other by the male chiefs (as the scenes foregrounded by Ìṣọ̀lá indicate). The play, I am suggesting, is about an aborted slave rebellion.

Orlando Patterson's definition of slavery can help us settle the social status of Ẹfúnṣetán's men and women, whom Awẹ́ represents as domestic servants and Oladeji pleads are debt peons. As noted earlier, slavery involves the continuous exercise of the power of life and death over a class of people whose certain death has been commuted in exchange for exploitation in whatever ways the overlord, in agreement with the larger society, chooses. To recall Patterson again, slaves are different from other types of servants and bondsmen and women because they are "genealogically isolated" and excluded from all rights pertaining to claims of birth: they cannot "integrate the experience of their ancestors into their lives, to inform their understanding of social reality with the inherited meanings of their natural forebears, or to anchor the living present in any conscious community of memory" (5). Finally, Patterson suggests, "Slaves were always persons who had been dishonored in a generalized way" (10).

Ìṣọ̀lá's depiction of Ẹfúnṣetán's slaves leaves no doubt as to their chattel status. Adétutù, whose slave partner's efforts to save her from being executed gives the male chiefs the last excuse they need to attack Ẹfúnṣetán, constantly speaks of the "generally dishonored" lives she and others live. One of her introspective speeches at the beginning of the play lists the indignities that define a slave:

> Ayé ìyà mà ni ayé *ẹrú* o!
> Bí inú ḿbí *ẹrú* kò gbọdọ̀ fi hàn.
> Bí inú *ẹrú* dùn àdùndẹ́hìn, èèwọ̀,
> *Ẹrú* kò gbọdọ̀ rẹ́rìnín àṣàṣàmọ̀ṣì
> Ṣebí ara *ẹrú* ni a ti í dán ọrẹ́ tuntun wò!
> Ẹrú ni ó le *ru ẹrù* tí ó wúwo,
> Ẹnu rẹ̀ ni eegun ti ńdùn;
> *Ẹrú* kì í jẹ *irú* lọ́bẹ̀,
> Ìdí *ẹrú* ni àkísà ti í dára.
> *Ẹrú* kò lọ́rùn ìlẹ̀kẹ̀, àfi tokùn. (1–2)
>
> The slave's life is full of suffering!
> Profound happiness is out of bounds for her,
> A hearty laughter, she cannot enjoy.

> Isn't the slave's body the testing instrument of new whips!
> The slave is the one for whom the heaviest burden is reserved,
> Meatless bones taste marvelous in her mouth;
> The slave's soup is never spiced,
> Her body wears rags.
> The slave's neck is never fit for precious beads;
> But for tethering ropes.

This speech correlates rhetorically the vocal similarities between *ẹrú* (the slave), *ẹrù* (burden), *rù* (to carry on the head), and *irú* (a spice) to contrast what the slave has to what she lacks: she carries (*rù*) the heaviest burden (*ẹrù*), but the simplest pleasure (*irú*) is out of her reach. The slave cannot voice her sadness, nor can she sing her joy. To her belongs heavy lifting; denied to her is the laughter that seasons life. Materials that disfigure the body and offal that people ordinarily shun are forced on her. Another slave supports Adétutù's observations by describing the slave as a person on whom another can spit (ẹni à ńsíntọ́ lé lórí) with absolute impunity.

That the slaves are living through a deferred death sentence is obvious in Ọ̀ṣúntúndé's questions to another slave on the frustration of being a human chattel: "Bí ayé ọ̀hún kò ṣe é gbé mọ̀, / A kì í wá kú?" (If life is this unlivable / Why not die?) (6). Adétutù has asked herself earlier, "ǹjẹ́ kò tilẹ̀ yẹ kí n kúkú kú?" (Shouldn't I have died after all?) (1). But as Ọ̀ṣúntúndé observes after Adétutù's execution, slaves, under normal circumstances, live or die by the grace of their owner: "Ọmọ ènìyàn wá di adìẹ tí à ḿbọ́, / Ó di àmúpa níg-bàkugbà" (Humans become like hand-fed chickens, / Only to be killed at arbitrary will) (59).

Obviously, the slaves' words signify depressive despair, but they also attest to the heavy toll slaves pay for the obligation to which they are subscribed after being captured. The most extreme expression of social death is the draconian decree that bans Ẹfúnṣetán's slaves from having children. Adétutù, the last victim of the law, says, "Àwọn èkúté ilé ńbímọ lálàáfíà / Ṣùgbọ́n ọjọ́ tí ẹrú bá lóyún pẹ́rẹ́ / Ẹlẹ́kọ ọ̀run á bẹ̀rẹ̀sí polówó" (Rats give birth without hindrance / But the day the slave conceives / She will respond to heaven's herald) (28). One proverb used repeatedly by Ọ̀ṣúntúndé, and variously echoed by all the other slaves, reflects the profound natal alienation imposed on the slaves, their Yorùbá names notwithstanding: "ọ̀nà ni ó jìn, àwa náà ní baba" (It is the distance that is great, we too have fathers) (6). This proverb shows that the slaves have some natal memory, although it carries no social advantage in the land of servitude. The fact that Àwẹ̀ró is a chief's daughter in her homeland, and that Ọ̀ṣúntúndé is the son of a "compound" [clan] head is irrelevant to their current status.

Ẹfúnṣetán's own words indicate that the slaves are not simply embittered individuals overwhelmed by their wicked fate. She calls them "ọmọ àlè" (bastards) repeatedly to reiterate their social illegitimacy. She constantly uses the Yorùbá idiom of distinguishing the bonded from the freeborn to remind her slaves that they came to her household on their feet (as full-grown humans) and not on their head from a mother's womb (as native-born babies).[4] Besides conveying Ẹfúnṣetán's all-around wickedness, these blunt expressions also reveal the true character of slavery in Ẹfúnṣetán's Ìbàdàn. For her, slaves are "nǹkan" (things) and not humans. When approached to spare Adétutù's life for the sake of her brother, who has been begged by Adétutù's slave lover to claim their child, Ẹfúnṣetán says, "Gbogbo nǹkan le padà ní ayé, / Bí-n-ó-ti-ṣe-nǹkan-mi-nìyí, kò mà padà" (Everything in the universe may change, / This-is-how-I am-going-to-dispose-my-thing will not) (46).

The central conflict thrashed out between Ẹfúnṣetán and the male warrior chiefs revolves around the manner of making slaves accept their condition. Normally, slaveholding succeeds only to the extent that the society helps slave masters combine physical coercion with subtler methods in their exercising authority over their bondspersons who, in Patterson's words, are "enemies within." Slaveholders should be able to transform force into right "and obedience into duty." In other words, slave societies have to make slavery cultural and then initiate the bondspersons into their roles. Within the play, Ẹfúnṣetán's recalcitrance on this front is the cause of her slaves' open discontent and also of the chiefs' disagreements with her. Ẹfúnṣetán treats "culture," as it concerns slavery, with great disdain: against the desire of other chiefs, Ẹfúnṣetán executes her slaves for breaching her idiosyncratic decree against slave reproduction; her male slaves beat a freeborn to death; she rebuffs every "cultural" gesture made by family members to work around her decree against slaves' having children.

As it is betrayed in the oríkì of the male chiefs, all these "cultural" infractions take place in an already unstable political atmosphere. The male chiefs earn their living from frequent war making. Because this way of subsistence often takes them away from the seat of government, the chiefs have to ascertain that "cultural" stability prevails at all times, particularly when they are out of town. In this circumstance, it makes political sense that the warlike chiefs should move to curtail the influence of a civic leader who dares to contradict them. Whether the person concerned is a demon, as some elements of Ìṣọ̀lá's play emphasize, or an astute trader reluctant to subordinate her interests to the ego of the warrior chiefs, as Awẹ argues, the material excuse for the political conflict that destroys Ẹfúnṣetán is the culturally acceptable treatment of slaves.

The general tyranny that hovers around the Ìyálóde's household reverberates in the male chief's consciousness, too. At one of the male chiefs' meetings, Lálùwọyè rings an alarm about Ẹfúnṣetán's privately enacted laws: "Ìyálóde mà ti wá di ẹ̀rùjẹ̀jẹ̀ sí ààrin ìlú . . . / Ẹfúnṣetán fẹ́ tú ìlú yìí o, àfi kí a ṣọ́ra" (The Ìyálóde is becoming an unapproachable object of fear in this town . . . / Efúnṣetán will destroy this city, if we are not careful) (17). Ayọ̀rìndé reminds the other chiefs that her execution of forty-one slaves (thirteen women and twenty-eight men) two years earlier went unchallenged (18), although her office lacks the authority to administer capital punishment. Àjàyí Ògbóríẹ̀fọ̀n's rhetorical question at this meeting also points to the fact that the male chiefs are afraid that Ẹfúnṣetán's "cultural" violations will make her into a law unto herself. At another meeting, Àjàyí says: "Ẹfúnṣetán ti di ejò, / Kò ṣe é fi sórí òrùlé sùn. / Ó ti di iná, kò ṣe é gbé sábẹ́; / Ó ti di ìkookò, / Kò ṣe é fi sáàrin agbo ẹran" (Ẹfúnṣetán has become a snake, / We cannot go to bed knowing she is lurking in the rafters. / She has become the blazing fire that cannot be used to warm the body's nether region; / She has become a wolf, she cannot be allowed among the flock) (56). Láwọyin, accusing her of being intoxicated by power (57), urges his brother chiefs that "A kò le tijú ẹni tí kò pọ́n wa lé" (There is no deferring to someone who scorns us) (57). Since she refuses to honor the codes of dealing with slaves, or to relate to the other chiefs over the matter, the resolution to remove her from office passes easily.

For the "culturally" informed reader or spectator of Ìṣọ̀lá's play, the chiefs' oríkì suggest that they have a reasonable ground to be concerned by the excesses of the leader of women. Látóòsà, the commander-in-chief whose name translates literally as "Wealth-is-enough-a-divinity," is "praised" with these words: "B'áàrẹ ńṣe ọ́, o má bọ̀ṣun, / Ọ̀ràn kò kan tòòṣà; / Ò báà bọrìṣà, ò báà bọbàtálá, / Aṣúbíaró níí ṣe ni kánrin" (If the generalissimo is set against you, do not seek divine help, / That is not a case for the Gods; / Worship you Ọbàtálá, be it the òrìṣà, / He-who-is-unfathomable-like-a-pot-of-black-dye will annihilate you) (12). At a later meeting, another senior chief, Àjàyí Ògbóríẹ̀fọ̀n, is saluted as follows: "Ẹni tí ńjẹun nílé Gbóríẹ̀fọ̀n / Nísàlẹ̀ Ọ̀ṣun / Oríta ọ̀run ni ó gbé ńjẹun / Béniyàn ńmu ọtí Òìbó / Nílé Gbóríẹ̀fọ̀n / Nísàlẹ̀ Ọ̀ṣun / Ẹ̀jẹ̀ èniyàn ní ńmu sùn" (Whosoever eats a meal at Gbóríẹ̀fọ̀n's house / In valleyside Ọ̀ṣun / Dines at the crossroads to heaven / Anyone who drinks bottled spirit / In Gbóríẹ̀fọ̀n's household / In valleyside Ọ̀ṣun / Guzzles human blood for dinner) (53). In these "praise" lines, Àjàyí's homestead is not different from Ẹfúnṣetán's in that both can be rightly described as a "crossroads to heaven" (oríta ọ̀run). The case is even worse for the freeborn in Àjàyí's home because the pathway to death that his house has become claims its victims without regard for distinction of birth. The gruesome tone of Àjàyí's oríkì, recited extensively at the chiefs' second meeting, belies the chiefs' expressed concern for the peace and orderliness that they believe Ẹfúnṣetán's execution of another pregnant slave would threaten. The city governed by these men is not a peaceful domain.[5]

Ẹfúnṣetán's control of her slaves, because it reveals the unseemly side of the institution, is interpreted by the male chiefs, perhaps rightly, as a behavior that might cause political unrest. At the meeting where the male chiefs decide to attack her, General Látóòsà says in exasperation, "A kò tilẹ̀ wá mọ ẹni tí ó ni ìlú yìí mọ́!" (We don't even know who are the true owners of this city!) (55). This is an exaggeration, of course. Nonetheless, it appears that Ẹfúnṣetán's treatment of her slaves questions the fundamental grounds of Ìbàdàn slaveholding rules. Látóòsà's statement and the decision to remove Ẹfúnṣetán reveal that the men are anxious to reestablish unmistakably the identity of the true "owners" of the town, those whose cultural dicta must be obeyed by all. To restore the proper slaveholding order, Láwọyin accuses Ẹfúnṣetán of godlessness: "Ó ti ṣẹ Ọlọ́run, Ọlọ́run ti kọ̀hìn sí I" (She has offended God, and God has turned his back on her) (57). In my view, God here is a synonym for the rule of the warrior chiefs who want to safeguard "normal" slaveholding practices.

Why are the male chiefs acting at this moment when they, and everyone in the city, know that Ẹfúnṣetán has always controlled her slaves in very unorthodox ways? The male warrior chiefs were not, for instance, unaware of the Ìyálóde's rules when she killed thirteen young women and twenty-eight men. Since then, nothing obviously different has happened to warrant the urgency of the chiefs' deadly resolve. If one were to accept as the truth the words Ẹfúnṣetán speaks after she has been removed from office, the chiefs are not acting in the interest of the slaves, nor in the interest of the city, but for their own selfish ends. According to Ẹfúnṣetán, "Látóòsà kò fẹ́ ẹnìkejì. / Nígbà tí mo ṣẹ̀ṣẹ̀ joyè nílẹ̀ yìí. / Tajá tẹran ló ḿbá mi jẹ. / Nígbà tí wọ́n rí i pé owó mi ya mìrá. / Inú ṣẹ̀ṣẹ̀ wá ḿbí wọn" (Látóòsà hates competition. / When I was an unknown chief. / All sorts of people befriended me. / Once I became wealthy. / They turned bilious) (76). From these words we know that Látóòsà, who cannot tolerate a rival authority, is displeased, as Awẹ́ argues, at Ẹfúnṣetán's wealth and dominance of the city's internal affairs. Her last words after poisoning herself are: "Látóòsà mo lọ fún ọ o! mo lọ o" (Látóòsà, you can now have the place to yourself) (78).

More important than personal jealousies and high-stakes political rivalry, either as the case is made by Awẹ́ or dramatized by Ìṣọ̀lá, is that the chiefs' resolution to depose Ẹfúnṣetán preempts the revolt being planned by her slaves. That is to say that Ẹfúnṣetán's deposition only concludes what the slaves themselves began. Before the chiefs act, Adétutù's friends, including her lover, have started to plot a little mutiny. After Adétutù's execution they put the plans in high gear. Ìtáwuyì, the lover, asks fellow slaves, "Kínni àwa gan an tilẹ̀ ń̄ṣe?" (What are we really doing about the matter?) (59). In the course of the slaves' discussion of how to respond, Ẹfúnṣetán, hitherto just a wicked person (ìkà), is called a witch (àjẹ́) for the first time. By so naming her, they make her destruction imperative. To poison the witch, the male slaves set aside their arrant sexism to enlist the cooperation of Àwẹ̀ró, Adétutù's close friend, who also happens to be the slave in charge of Ẹfúnṣetán's meals.

The slaves employ strategies they have learned either before their enslavement or from their interaction with the freeborn after capture. Àwẹ̀ró reminds others that poisoning a highly accomplished "witch" like Ẹfúnṣetán requires that they should first plead, with oríkì, for the help of more powerful witches euphemistically called great mothers: "ìyá mi òṣòròǹgà, / Àwọn a japá jorí, a jọ̀rá, jòróǹro" (My unfathomable mothers, / who consume the whole body; head, arms, and bile) (63). This confidence-boosting "praise" of life-taking "mothers" does not appear to be enough for Àwẹ̀ró to act. She moves against Ẹfúnṣetán only after ruminating on the fate that awaits the slaves for as long as the woman lives. Then, she resolves to dare death, like Ìbíwùmí in *Ọmọ Olókùn Ẹṣin:* "N ó mọ́kàn le, bí a ó kùú, ẹ̀ẹ̀kan ni à á kú" (My mind is made up, death comes only once anyway) (63). Unfortunately, Ẹfúnṣetán detects the poison and kills Àwẹ̀ró with it. In utter desperation, Ìtáwuyì attempts to behead her. But as his machete goes up to strike, Ẹfúnṣetán binds him with a fast spell and commands him to stay still, drop his weapon, and lick up the poisoned dish prepared by Àwẹ̀ró. When the male chiefs show up soon after this confrontation, the putsch against a heartless slaveholder and wicked witch is a justified act to the audience.

On the surface, the similarity in the concert of actions taken by the slaves and the male chiefs confirms Ìṣọ̀lá's emphasis on the moral universal repugnance of Ẹfúnṣetán's misdeeds: she is so bad that she outrages slaves and masters equally. But a comparative analysis of the motivations of these different strata of the social spectrum will show that the two groups attack her for different reasons. When Látóòsà's forces appear, their excuse is Ìbàdàn interest: "Ìlú Ìbàdàn ni ó ṣí mi nídìí" (I have been sent by the city of Ìbàdàn). The general's spells are actually ineffective until he invokes the name of the entire city, indeed the entire universe: "Bí ayé bá ḿbẹ lẹ́hìn aláǹtètè, / Yóò pa adìẹ. / Ọwọ́ ìlú ni ó tẹ̀ ọ́" (If the world stands behind the grasshopper, / It will kill the rooster. / The long hands of the city now grasp you) (74). These are rulers who can divine Ìbàdàn's will. Unlike the chiefs, Ìtáwuyì and Àwẹ̀ró are not fighting Ẹfúnṣetán to save the "world." Nor do they want to save Ìbàdàn. Their immediate goal is to reclaim the dignity crushed by slavery. The main goal of the chiefs' war against Ẹfúnṣetán is to teach other slaveholders that they will suffer greatly if they govern their slaves in ways that contradict the chiefs' will. During the assault on her, Ẹfúnṣetán is told, "Ìjòyè tí ó bá bú baálẹ̀, / Yóò jẹ pàṣán ọmọ olóko ẹṣin" (The petty chief that defies the head chief / Will receive the scourge of the king's horseman) (73). There is no indication in the play that slavery was abolished in Ìbàdàn after Ẹfúnṣetán's ouster, detention, and then suicide. Only a potential slave uprising was squashed.

The point of the foregoing reading is to show that in a slave society, hegemonic "cultural" discourses can easily sublate subaltern discontent. Ìṣọ̀lá claims, for example, that the play is inspired by an episode from Ìbàdàn "history" (v). But the notion of history he dramatizes is one driven by conflicts of "good" and "evil," stability and instability, excess and moderation, with chiefs and slaves unevenly divided between the forces. Lost in this moral drama are the material denominators of the primordial struggles. It has been the argument of this chapter that we can recover, if only for juxtaposition, aspects of traditional African subaltern consciousness if we read between the lines of the canonical texts as they are being retranscribed in modern discourses.

Ẹfúnṣetán dies partly because her slaves revolt against her rule. Although Awẹ́'s historicist correction of the play's overdramatization of women's power as diabolical witchcraft provides a welcome alternative to the acutely masculinist viewpoints promoted by the play, her efforts to repress the role of slavery and slave revolt in the power play that caused Ẹfúnṣetán's historical demise cannot be overlooked. Awẹ́ considers demonstrating that Ẹ̀fúnṣetán was not a cruel slaveholder to be very significant. However, she finds no reason to believe that the slaves might have a good reason to want to kill her. According to Awẹ́, after Ẹfúnṣetán's death, her powerful friends accused Látóòsà and Àjàyí Ògbóríẹ̀fọ̀n of murder. Indeed, a "civil war was only averted when [the chiefs accused of killing Ẹ̀fúnṣetán] protested their innocence and those who actually perpetrated the deed were brought to book" (71). As it happens, the culprits are one avaricious relative and "*three slaves* who actually committed *the crime*" (71). I am unable to find much solace in the criminalization of the slaves' deeds. As it were, both Ìṣọ̀lá's theater and Awẹ́'s history cannot depict the oppositional inspiration of Ẹ̀fúnṣetán's slaves. Rebelling slaves are either pawns in the governing tactics of the powerful or criminals who deserve their fate. In one recollection, rebelling slaves are victims of an evil female chief; in the other, they are simply criminals. Either way, the oríkì sentiment about tradition holds strong.

9

REITERATING THE BLACK EXPERIENCE
Rebellious Material Bodies and Their Textual Fates in *Dessa Rose*

Sherley Anne Williams's novel about a female slave rebel appeared in 1986 amidst two auspicious developments: the domestication of poststructuralist theories of textuality for African American literary criticism was at its height, and the admission of black women writers into the American national canon was under way. The publication history of *Dessa Rose*, its dominant themes, and its narrative structure all indicate that the novel was aimed at nothing less than a redirecting of African American literature in the wake of the civil rights era's reign of black aesthetics. "Meditations on History," the story on which the novel is loosely based, first appeared in Mary Helen Washington's 1980 anthology, *Midnight Birds*, consisting of the works of black women writers who would define many of the main concerns of both late-twentieth-century American feminist writing and post–civil rights African American literature.[1]

Signs indicating the coalescence of black women's writing into a major force began to emerge a few years earlier in 1977, when Alice Walker received the Pulitzer Prize for *The Color Purple*. (In 1975, Sherley Anne Williams's first collection of poems, *The Peacock Poems*, was nominated for a National Book Award.) The steadily increasing recognition of black women writers reached unmistakable significance when Toni Morrison's *Beloved* (also a fictive recreation of a slave woman's ordeal) received the Pulitzer, just a year after *Dessa Rose* came out to critical acclaim.[2] As black women's writing gained national prominence and critical acceptance, critics looking for ways to make sense of African American writing within poststructuralism and deconstruction translated the traditional materialist language of interpreting canonical black American literatures into textualist idioms and reformulated the dialectics of text and society that has dominated black critical discourse into accounts of textual, authorial, and tropological relations.[3]

The textual (ex)changes that mark the march of Williams's book from a short story to a novel appear to be an accreditation of the dominant creative and critical concerns of black American post–civil rights literature, particularly issues of reckoning with feminism in the reconstruction of black subjectivity.[4] The short story is structured with the diary entries of an ambitious white writer gathering materials for a book about the causes of slave rebellions and how to prevent them. The full-fledged novel edits down the diary entries of the story to privilege the viewpoint of the white writer's principal informant, a pregnant slave rebel awaiting execution. The meaning of these textual changes has been the main issue critics find most engaging about the novel: locating the tropes of "white" writing, recovering the history of women's participation in black resistance projects, the denigration of oral slave culture in written records,[5] the literary character of history writing,[6] and the subjective construction of gender and other identities.[7] In short, critics tend to see *Dessa Rose* as a "theory" novel, specifically black feminist metafictional historiography.[8] That critical consensus is supported by Williams's admitting in an interview with Shirley Jordan that she used the novel to address some of her interests in literary theory: "I have been influenced to some extent by the kind of debates that are going on in literary circles about the uses of history, deconstruction, and other aspects of contemporary critical theory" (290).

The main proposition of this chapter is that the novel's relationship to (black) poststructuralism is not fully affirmative. I am going to argue that although the narration is done in a perspective that is amenable to deconstructive analysis, the story of the slave woman's heroic rebellion revamps the spirit of militant politics of the civil rights era and questions the political responsibilities of (black) poststructuralism. The novel's revision of the traditional black resistance narrative from a female slave rebel's point of view represents the survival and preservation of the material body as the ultimate aim of black textual ventures.

WRITING PROCESS: FROM STRUGGLE TO TEXT, FROM INTERVIEW NOTES TO BOOK

Adam Nehemiah (Nemi),[9] a white professional writer out to ride the forward momentum of his modestly successful slave management book, *The Master's Complete Guide to Dealing with Slaves and Other Dependents,* researches a new "black book" he expects to earn him fortune, fame, and access into respectable social circles. The (cultural) capital accumulation project, to be titled "The Roots of Rebellion in the Slave Population and Some Means of Eradicating Them," intends to clue white "non-slave holder and slave holder alike" (19) to counter-measures they can use to reverse the escalation of slave uprisings in the Deep South. To ground his work empirically, Nemi, son of a slave-abhorring Calvinist, studies the trial records of accused slave rebels and interviews imprisoned slave insurgents for crucial leads into the machinations of their psyche. Unfortunately, he is repeatedly frustrated by "outdated reports, principals who were dead or moved from the neighborhood" (21), and the studied silence of his interlocutors. One uncooperative informant he characterizes as a giant imbecile presents him with an impenetrable "smiling vacuity" (20). His growing despair is relieved when he meets Dessa Rose in an Alabama county jail, freshly convicted for her role in a slave uprising.

Williams's first version of this research project, "Meditations on History" (a parody of the subtitle of William Styron's *The Confessions of Nat Turner*), is structured as selections from Nemi's journal summaries of Dessa Rose's recollection of slave life on the Vaughm plantation. Most memorable among Nemi's writing are snippets of how the deep affection Dessa shared with Kaine, a fellow slave, threatened to disrupt plantation order. The notes also contain observations about Dessa Rose's frustration at Nemi's repeated probing into how the slave revolt broke out and how the ringleaders escaped. Besides recounting the events that led to her being sold to Mr. Wilson, the trader who prides himself on his acumen about discount slaves, Dessa does not reveal any critical information not yet in the trial records. She speaks about Kaine's failed efforts to get her assigned light duties, his confrontation with Master Vaughm, who broke his beloved banjo and then killed him when he protested, her own physical assault on Mrs. Vaughm, who accused her of adultery, and the cruel punishment she received for that effrontery. In both the short story and the novel, Nemi tips off the local militia that Dessa had mentioned a "place without whites" as a possible refuge for her comrades after their fight with Wilson's slave traders. With the authorities of law and hegemonic social research now on what turns out to be a "wild goose chase" (68), Dessa's comrades descend on the sheriff's home and spirit her away to their maroon camp at Sutton Glen.[10]

Only eight of Nemi's dated thirteen notes in "Meditations" make it into the novel. The revised and updated narrative explains her evasions of Nemi, brings to plain view her activities after the rescue, and integrates Nemi's proslavery research into Dessa's allegory of the slave's resistance to domination. The revision and expansion of Nemi's journal by the new narrator allegorizes many facets of the sociology of knowledge about slavery. The narrator ties the doomed fate of Nemi's research to his inability to elicit useful responses from Dessa because his preconceptions stand in the way of honest questioning and listening. For example, Nemi repeatedly presses Dessa to reveal the source of the file the slaves used to break their chains when none existed; and for a long time he could not believe that Kaine's fight with his master over a broken banjo has anything to do with Dessa's rebelliousness.

The novel's revelation of the short reach of Nemi's inquiries also highlights in part the necessity of Dessa's corrective "Black Studies" counter-narrative, intended to expose the muddy underbelly of "mainstream" social science about black people.[11] The intent to dramatize the impact of entrenched interests in the production of knowledge about slavery goes further. As we see in Nemi's stated intentions and methods of gathering facts, "white" social science, motivated by the need to devise methods of disciplining and punishing freedom-seeking individuals like Dessa, services slaveholding interests. Hence the daring removal of Dessa from jail marks both the end of the hegemonic writer's quest for the secret of black resistance and the dividing line between the story his diary tells in "Meditations" and the fuller account rendered in the novel. Rescuing Dessa complements the strategic defenses she put up earlier in the form of her "silence, nonacquiescence, evasion, and dissemblance" (Henderson, "(W)riting *The Work*" 647) while answering Nemi's questions. The language used to describe Dessa's disappearance indicates that modern law and social science lack rational terms to describe the slave's striving for freedom: Nemi, for instance, characterizes the rescuers as "not human blood, human flesh, but sorcerers" and Dessa herself as "the devil" (69).

The novel also explicitly questions the excision of women's contributions from the Black Power critique of American history. In "Author's Note," Williams indicts the entire history-writing enterprise: "I loved history as a child, until some clear-eyed young Negro pointed out, quite rightly, that there was no place in the American past I could go and be free" (ix–x). However, when in the next sentence she praises Angela Davis's analysis of the injustice done to black women in standard American (national) and African American (ethnic) accounts of black heroism, the missing subject in heroic history, one would have to say, is specifically the black woman. The Davis essay that Williams invokes as the novel's main ante-text argues, against dominant Black

Power axioms, that the female slave could never have been a collaborator (silent or otherwise) with plantation owners in the oppression of fellow slaves. Two facts of slave life, Davis indicates, suggest that sustained resistance could not have developed outside of women's view: (1) the traditional male provider, who is also the dominant moral figure, was not a typical feature of the black slave household, and (2) the main pillar of the slave household was a woman whose role did not conform "to the historically evolved female" (8). Slave women labored in the field like slave men and, in addition, held the key to social and cultural continuity. In the slave society, "by virtue of the brutal force of circumstances, the black woman was assigned the mission of promoting the consciousness and practice of resistance" (5). Davis further argues that the male-dominated black nationalist tendency which promotes the view that plantation social structure nudged slave women to cultivate damning "relationships with the oppressor" and "enchain" black men ought to be repudiated or they would continue to impair black "capacity for resistance today" (14):

> The myth must be consciously repudiated as myth and the black woman in her true historical contours must be resurrected. . . . Our fight, while identical in spirit, reflects different conditions and thus implies different paths of struggle. But as heirs to a tradition of supreme perseverance and heroic resistance, we must hasten to take our place wherever our people are forging on towards freedom. (15)

Writing about a decade later within the poststructuralist milieu in which *Dessa Rose* was published, Hortense Spillers's rebuttal of the pathologization of the black family reiterates Davis's analysis but without the activist's imperative language:

> The African American woman, the mother, the daughter, becomes historically the powerful and shadowy evocation of a cultural synthesis long evaporated in law—the law of the Mother—only and precisely because legal enslavement removed the African-American male not so much from sight as from mimetic view as a partner in the prevailing social fiction of the Father's name, the Father's law. (80)

Williams's most obvious homage to Davis's critique of Black Power gender bias is the conception of Dessa's story around one of the actual instances of the slave woman's heroic resistance cited in the essay (11). A less apparent, although equally strong, complement of the Davis thesis is the novel's critique of the discursive choices (and exclusions) that produce the "misrepresentation and misreading" (Henderson, "(W)riting *The Work*" 640) of black women perpetuated in androcentric history.[12] Nemi's record, the novel demonstrates, subjects Dessa's words to a hermeneutic framework suited to allaying "the secret fears of non-slave and slave holder alike" and convincing slaves "to be happy in the life that has been sent them to live" (41). Initializing and then aborting Nemi's quest for Dessa's story and the subsequent privileging of Dessa's *telling* her story to a writer of her choice allegorize the *reinterpretation* of written archives that is needed in order to compose the correct history of black women's heroic tradition.[13] To construct this story, Dessa's preferred narrator preserves parts of Nemi's written research notes for purposes of cross-reference and as a supplement to Dessa's more complete oral retelling of her struggle, especially the difficulties and triumphs experienced after freedom, practically beyond Nemi's intellectual reach. By juxtaposing fragments of Nemi's written notes and Dessa's oral contestation of what is recorded, the narrator enacts the "rewriting" and "rereading" of Nemi's intellectual legacy. The traditional axioms of telling and writing are reconstituted to lend prestige to oral testimonies and to question the reliability of written constructs. In Henderson's words, the novel "shifts emphasis from the authority of the written, and closed, solipsistic text (i.e., the official record) to the oral, and open collaborative text" (Henderson, "(W)riting *the Work*" 655).[14]

"'CAUSE I CAN'"

A crucial element of the novel's textual politics that does not receive the critical attention it deserves is the rebellion story, at which no professional historian or sociologist is present originally. That struggle involves a band of about 100 slaves being transported from Alabama to Louisiana mutinying against their handlers, killing five men, and maiming their owner, who goes incurably mad after the fight. A guard mistakenly left for dead wakes up and runs to a surrounding settlement to rally the local militia for help. The escaped slaves are chased down and most of them recaptured: thirty-one are executed and nineteen branded or flogged. In all, "some thirty-eight thousand dollars in property [was] destroyed or damaged" (38).[15]

By itself, the *accomplished* revolt is unique in African American fiction of slave rebellion because successful land-based slave insurrections on U.S. soil have been somewhat unimaginable. Of greater significance, however, are the narrative innovations Williams uses to speak about the causes of slave rebellion and the places that can nurture it within the geographical boundaries of the United States. Unlike Nat Turner, Dessa Rose does not invoke the biblical apocalypse; unlike Bontemps's Gabriel, she is not instigated to act by a mysterious spirit of Jacobinism. Dessa Rose rebels simply because she finds slavery unbearable. She fights her masters because they, by virtue of their being masters, deny her the ordinary desire to choose a lover freely. Asked why she attacked her owners, Dessa says, "'I kill white mens cause the same reason Masa kill Kaine. Cause I can'" (13).[16]

The shocking starkness of this simple motivation is captured in Nemi's persistent disbelief that craving for reciprocal affection can move a black person, generally thought capable of only carnal pleasures, to risk being killed: "The master smashed the young buck's banjo. The young buck attacked the master. The master killed the young buck. The darky attacked the master—and was sold to the Wilson slave coffle" (34–35). Reduced to a single unthinking "attack" is the desperation of unrealizable inner yearnings that led Dessa and Kaine to fight their master. What transpired before the master broke the banjo, as well as the tyranny that provoked that act, is left out. As Dessa says, however, Mr. Vaughm breaks Kaine's banjo and kills him because he "can." We should recall in this regard Colonel Franks's words in Delany's *Blake*: "If slavery be right, the master is justifiable in enforcing obedience to his will; deny him this, and you at once deprive him of the right to hold a slave" (13). For slaves to attack the person of the master "cause [they] can" is to question the slave owner's fundamental right to exist as master. But because Nemi fails to grasp the logic of the slave's counter-violence, he attributes Kaine's anger to the restless miscegenated blood in him;[17] unnamable evil forces that possess uncontrollable black women, he says, influence the "unmixed" Dessa.[18]

Revealing the discrepancy between Nemi's misconceptions and Dessa's comprehension of plantation normativity—if the master "can" wreak violence willfully, the slave too "can"—reflects the awareness of Williams's speakerly writer (and writerly speaker) of the exploitative character of knowledge produced about subaltern classes. This narrator, a subaltern scholar of sorts, asks the right questions, is predisposed to accepting the slave's explanation that she does not need any special reason to rebel, and has been acculturated into accepting that fighting back is a defining condition of slavery. This "native" writer is unlike the narrators of stories of slave rebellions analyzed in previous chapters in the crucial respect that he enjoys the double privilege of gleaning excerpts of Nemi's notes and speaking to a slave rebel. Although Nemi too speaks to Dessa, in that project "the rebel has no place . . . as the *subject* of rebellion," as Ranajit Guha says for colonialist historiography in India (71).

PLACING REBELLION

Dessa's freedom goal is fulfilled on her native soil, and storytelling and intellectual traditions upturned in the process, because the novel secures for the rebels a strategic retreat at the Sutton Glen farm when they need it. The freedwomen and men of Sutton Glen build a maroon community out of the poorly managed farm abandoned by its white male leader to his wife and black maid, Dorcas (a.k.a. Mammy). The ex-slaves take over crop management under Dorcas's leadership: they expand the potato fields and replace cotton, Bert Sutton's "vanity" crop, with corn, oats, hay, peas, and other produce more suitable for the soil in that region. The free laborers make all production schedules: "They seemed to work with a better will than darkies on the place had ever done," Rufel says (116). At the revamped plantation, the white master and provider is absent; the white mistress wet nurses a black infant; the black workers are free to go and come as they wish; and, according to the white "mistress," these blacks do not know how to treat a white person right. This unique place, based on the historical case of a white woman who gave "sanctuary to runaway slaves," brings about very unusual meetings: Mrs. Sutton (Rufel to the blacks) and Dessa, two women representatives of different races and classes, walk a very stressful path that culminates in the complacent white woman realizing the character of the racial deprivations that ensure the privileges people like her enjoy, and the militant black woman recognizing that cooperation and understanding across racial lines is not impossible.[19]

Except for the mother-daughter team of Ada and Annabelle, bound by blood ties, the ex-slaves form loyalties on the basis of their escape experiences. "A special feeling" (160) that is "as tight as bloodkin" (188) is forged among the slaves in the ordeal of escape, capture, and rescue. Nathan, Cully, and Dessa, all survivors of the Wilson coffle, cling to each other. Harker, who later becomes Dessa's lover, is admitted into this group partly because he participated in Dessa's rescue. When he is teased by Rufel for his obvious admiration for Dessa, Nathan replies, "'You been through with someone what we been through together and you be 'sweet' on them too'" (160). In African American fiction, utopias of this kind are typically found (or thought to be possible) only in Canada or other offshore locations "without whites," like Haiti and Africa. (Dessa's group actually considered finding its way to Haiti after the first fight with the guards on the Wilson entourage [61].)

Going by Herbert Aptheker's studies, however, enclaves of subversion like Sutton Glen are not quite rare in U.S. history. Runaway slaves formed, not infrequently, independent all-black communities that "offered havens for fugitives, served as bases for marauding expeditions against nearby plantations and, at times, supplied the nucleus of leadership for planned uprisings" ("Maroon" 151). Exceptional communities built permanent camps where families thrived. The most famous, those in the Dismal Swamp straddling Virginia and North Carolina, had about 2,000 fugitives at some time and "carried on a regular, if illegal, trade with white people living on the borders of the swamp" (152). These "pugnacious and migratory" communities usually existed undisturbed until either accidentally discovered by the outside world or when the maroon raids become so brazen or too frequent that threatened plantations felt compelled to counter-attack. Aptheker reports that no fewer than fifty such communities were known in the slave states between 1672 and 1864, mostly in the "mountainous, forested or swampy regions of South Carolina, North Carolina, Virginia, Louisiana, Florida, Georgia, Mississippi, and Alabama (in order of importance)" (152).[20]

The swampy environment of Sutton Glen, located six miles from the nearest road, resembles the typical historical maroon camp as outlined by Aptheker. Other features of the fictional locale recall historical camps: the area is sparsely populated, a great part of the land is undeveloped, and "hills rose behind it, heavily timbered, stretching without break to the far horizon" (109) to provide natural barriers against intrusion. (The soil does not support cotton and, to worsen matters, rust and boll weevil thrive in the region.) Even before Dorcas and Mrs. Sutton convert Sutton Glen into a maroon camp, Bert Sutton's maltreated slaves have always found it easy to escape; as Ada, the earliest of the fugitives to arrive, recollects, "White folks there didn't keep too close watch over black people; they thought it was so few up that way that they knew them all" (190).

Aptheker's study further shows that a maroon community within a slaveholding society can only be a temporary refuge unless it becomes so strong that slaveholding interests figure that the cost of destroying it exceeds that of tolerating it. The threat of this peril is not lost on the refugees at Sutton Glen. Harker asks his comrades to move camp before Bert Sutton returns or the suspicion of their neighbors dooms them. To finance the move to a more secured place, Harker proposes a scheme he used to run with his old master: "'They would go into a strange town and his master'd sell Harker, auction him off. After a couple of days Harker would run off and join him at a place they'd already picked out'" (162). As Dessa recollects, Harker believed that the ex-slaves "'could go down in the black belt and run that scheme three or four times using me and him, maybe two or three others, we could make maybe nine or ten thousand dollars'" (162). The plan succeeds beyond Harker's imagination, and the fugitives use the proceeds to pay for their move from the almost exclusively black Sutton Glen to the western United States where, although whites are present, there are no slave catchers and patrollers. The fugitives are initially concerned that there are whites in the West. But living with Mrs. Sutton has taught them that the master's color is not the main cause of their enslavement. They are indeed emboldened by the Sutton Glen experience to reject offshore black utopias on "'some islands way out to sea . . . where black peoples had made theyselfs free'" (201). As far as the freedwomen and men of Sutton Glen know, "no black man come back free from these so-called islands" (201).

TELLING, WRITING, AND READING *DESSA ROSE* IN THEORY

The golden age of black deconstruction, which reached its crest with the publication of Henry Louis Gates Jr.'s *The Signifying Monkey,* witnessed the production of grand statements that endure until today about African American writing. Besides Gates's book, two other watershed texts of that age are Robert Stepto's *From Behind the Veil* and Houston Baker's *Blues, Ideology, and Afro-American Literature.* Each work attempts to capture in one explanation the internal textual features—and ideological ones in Baker's book—that define black American writing. With the exception of Baker's, the "grammatological" themes of deconstruction shape the reading methods these texts deploy to overturn the traditional materialist concerns of African American criticisms. Stepto and Gates, both working in the shadow of Yale deconstruction, convert the traditional black American writer's concerns with pressing political questions into discussions of the writer's self-reflexive engagements with the materiality of writing, textual influences and their historiographic import, and the mythographic basis of plot patterns. They propose in their deconstructive use of the themes of writing, structuration, and rhetoric that black orature and literature are repositories of second-order linguistic and philosophical operations and not simply cultural appliances that black writers bring to bear on political problems.

I want to pause over Gates's book because its terms of reference have dominated, implicitly and explicitly, the critical discussions of *Dessa Rose.* Gates derives his terms of theorizing black writing from his interpretation of the relationship between African American orature, self-referential commentaries on the orature, a deconstructive interpretation of the commentaries, and an intertextual reading of selected black texts. The literary history and practical criticism his book outlines link—straightforwardly in some sense—folk culture, vernacular metacommentary, poststructuralist theory, and modern black writing. For Gates, vernacular rhetoric, because it stores both private and communal rituals that cannot but influence writers and critics familiar with the tradition, is "the black person's ultimate sign of difference." Gates presupposes that if one studies the evolution of black verbal arts and artists from oral epochs to literate times, from folk expressions to literature, from animist chants to Christian syncretisms, one can enrich literary theory with some vernacular notions on both the nature of rhetoric and the principles of textual relations. The insights yielded by a vernacular reading of theory and literature will enable the critic to locate, as the writers themselves have done, the points of difference and convergence of black literature and criticism with other American literatures. In short, elevating vernacular terms to the level of high literary discourse will nativize the philosophical approach necessary for fully appreciating the complexities of African American literature.

African American vernacular speech, more than its white counterpart, allows greater play with concepts even in non-artistic contexts. In nonliterary "white" language "signification depends for order and coherence on the exclusion of unconscious associations which any given word yields at any given time." The black equivalent, Signification, "luxuriates in the inclusion of free play of these associative rhetorical and semantic relations" (49). African American speech, in the general sense, like the historically antecedent practice in Yorùbá divination procedures, is "style-focused" (78), allows unauthorized, many times critical, revisions of a received utterance, and indulges dialogues that exploit the substitutive dimensions of language.

Black American writers share, repeat, critique, and revise (124) each other's use of literary language in ways that follow the generally unmalicious manner of everyday linguistic interactions observed in Signification. Because the most important African American writers consciously mark their awareness of developments in the oral and literary traditions—that is, "become fluent in the language of the tradition"—by reworking different prominent tropes already well known in existing texts, Gates argues that the true measure of textual ethnicity ought to be located in literary language and how such is "shared, repeated, critiqued, and revised" (121). With incessant self-conscious "revision of tropes" black writers acknowledge, criticize, and extend how "the received textual tradition" represents "its ostensible subject matter, the so-called Black Experience" (124).

Analytical paradigms honed by black poststructuralisms such as Gates's have helped readers to identify the (ante)-textual genealogies of Williams's novel and to explain its cultural purpose. The information exchange relationship between Nemi and Dessa shows, for instance, that the hegemonic social scientist would like to extract from the condemned rebel any information that could be used to preempt insurrections. The interaction also demonstrates that the rebellious "native informant" would refuse to fully cooperate in order to keep her resistance project alive. The story of the rebel's eventual triumph would not be written until the emergence of the native scholar who is free to "Signify" on previous authors. The allegory of significations that results from the interaction of these principal "writers"—Dessa, Nemi, and Dessa's preferred narrator—reiterates the author function in truth-telling projects, be they subversive or hegemonic (Sánchez 25).

In my view, however, a novel of slave rebellion, its primary subject being the survival of the slave's material body, cannot but be critical of deconstruction. To be properly construed, I would say, the struggle to live, carried on relentlessly by Dessa and her compatriots, is a criticism of the terms of bloodless discursivity and textuality used by black poststructuralism to rewrite the traditional critical terms of African American cultures. The move away from the evaluation of literature for its position on what Gates calls "the so-called Black Experience" to a near-exclusive focus on styles of black literary speech is questioned in Dessa's escaping precisely at the point Nemi is about to fix her textually. The writers with the final say in this novel, Dessa and her grandchild, relate "insider" versions of militant black history not simply because their narrative styles "signify" on Nemi's but because their goal is to not reveal the secrets of slave rebellions prematurely.

Nemi fails, it is worth repeating, because Dessa and her comrades find "a place without whites" where they could live free. Dessa's punditing on records of slave life only after she has secured the survival of her corporeal existence suggests the inseparability of material survival from textualization. Dessa Rose's story becomes a textual reality only after she has won the primary battle against literal and "social death." To her, preserving a record, in whatever signifying strategy, is secondary to ensuring a successful waging of the slave's counter-violence against the master. The ex-slave's desire to take charge of the dissemination mechanisms of the records of the slave's counter-violence develops only after her victory against bondage is no longer in doubt. The protagonist in this story of slave rebellion, Dessa Rose, does not set out to re*write* history—that is a game for the "living" to play—in the literal sense because she knows, like every slave rebel, that her struggle for social rebirth may easily lead to her literal death. Hence, as Williams presents it, the "interruptive" writing and telling that readers encounter in the novel about her develop in the course of her struggle to elevate her material body out of the tomb of social death. The ultimate theme of this textual structure is that the nature of the irreducible material signifier of black experience cannot be separated from the fate of the gendered black laboring body.

It is necessary to insist on the meaning of this aspect of the novel because most of the critical writing about the story speaks only to the implications of its textual intrigues for historiographic meta-discourse and neglects the meaning of the material struggles that contextualize those metafictional concerns. Readers of *Dessa Rose* rewrite the slave's striving to become a citizen and subject in her own right into rhetorical struggles, or "textual healing," as Griffin says. Some representative quotes should suffice: Williams "represents the process by which Dessa uses her voice to gain her actual and representational liberation from the prescriptive pen of Nehemiah's written record" (Rushdy 140); "The novel signifies on the history it records—both on history as event and on history as text" (Fox-Good 12); "The violence done to the image of the black slave woman by historians corresponds to the violence done to her literary voice by (black and white) male authors" (Henderson, "(W)riting *the Work*" 640).

Paying close attention to Dessa's chosen writer may be helpful in our understanding of the critical relationship of Williams's story to these textualist formulations about the book. Dessa dictates her story to this writer in order to "live" for her people—specifically the community of ex-slaves (and their descendants) living out in the West—the way they have done for her and to apprise generations that did not experience slavery of what their ancestors endured: "'This is why I have it wrote down, why I has the child say it back. I never will forget Nemi trying to read me, knowing I had put myself in his hands. Well, *this* the childrens have heard from our own lips. I hope they never have to pay what it cost us to own self'" (260).

Although the chosen narrator proceeds from Dessa's point of view, the story of insurgency he relates entails more than rhetorical resistance despite the many references to verbal tests of will between Dessa and Nemi. This narrator shows repeatedly how Dessa dodges Nemi's probing and irritates him with the story of the deep love she shared with Kaine (34–35). Even Nemi's journal says that she "answers questions in a random manner, a loquacious, roundabout fashion" (16). However, the native historian does not position, in the way critical commentaries about the novel do, the verbal giving and taking between the subject of study (Dessa) and the hegemonic scholar (Nemi) as struggles for sheer *political* power. In some instances, as noted above, Dessa simply does not have the information Nemi needs. According to Dessa's chosen writer, she escapes and beats Nemi largely because her comrades reciprocate the sacrifice she has made earlier to save them during the second fight with slaveholding forces. Dessa knows that being pregnant is slowing down the escape of her comrades and so she volunteers to return to the main group still fighting with patrollers, despite the knowledge that she may be killed. She goes back into battle, fights fiercely, and gives the breakaway group the chance to escape without hindrance. These are the "prefigural" and "literal" heroic passages that culminate in Dessa's escape from the reach of law and hegemonic social science. Without these heroic deeds, Nathan and Cully would have been killed, and Dessa herself would have been executed. These facts precede the discursive struggles allegorized in the contrasting of hegemonic and resistance historiography.

The struggle for the control of the history of slave rebellions becomes an explicit topic again at the end of the novel when Nemi, still carrying his interview notes around, surprises Dessa on the streets of Arcopolis, Alabama, as the Sutton Glen refugees prepare to move west. Nemi convinces the sheriff to detain Dessa, claiming that some scars burned into Dessa's thigh before her master sold her off will corroborate his accusation that Dessa is a dangerous jail breaker. Earlier in the story, we have learned that the scars now developing into a "text" of contention look like "a mutilated cat face," that the mutilation has grown into a "tissue [that] plowed through her pubic region so no hair would ever grow there again" (166), and that the letter "R" is also burned into the inside of her thigh.[21] Nemi bases his claim on his knowledge of these scars that demonstrate, as Henderson suggests, white patriarchy's inscription of its supremacy and contempt for the black woman's femininity. The mutilation and inscription, Henderson says, "deprive the slave woman of her femininity and render the surface of her skin a parchment upon which meaning is etched by the whip (pen) of white patriarchal authority and sealed by the firebrand" ("Speaking in Tongues" 26). Nemi's asking the sheriff to look under Dessa's dress for a confirmation of his claims supports Henderson's interpretation. Nemi believes that when an appropriate reading authority views the scars, their meaning will be obvious and, in effect, Mr. Vaughm's original intention to communicate his evaluation of Dessa as a dangerous woman will be safely delivered to any pro-slavery reading authority.

But what transpires henceforth shows that meaning, in spite of Vaughm's intentions and Nemi's proper education in the protocols of interpretation, cannot be *written* beforehand. Slavery's violent ritual of inscription may register the master's feelings, but the master's conscious meaning cannot be transported unhindered. After Mrs. Sutton protests that men should not be allowed to search a woman even if she is under suspicion of a capital crime, the sheriff, against Nemi's protest, asks a trusted old black slave, Aunt Chole, to decide the competing claims. The old woman, bribed with a knowing look and a quarter, examines only Dessa's back and declares there are no scars there: "'I ain't seed nothing on this gal's butt. She ain't got a scar on her back'" (254). Writing, her conspiratorial acts show, does not predetermine reading and meaning.

This episode, the last before the epilogue, carries great implications for the reading of *Dessa Rose* and its commentary on histories of slave rebellion. Had Aunt Chole not deliberately misread Dessa's scars and the slave master's writing, the story of rebellion would have been irreparably aborted and Nemi would have gone on to complete his counter-insurgency narrative. Dessa too would not have lived long enough to dictate her story to her writer. Aunt Chole's misreading saves Dessa's body, and thereafter her words and deeds become parts of the record available to the "native" historian.

But records on their own, even when they are in the custody of participants, cannot narrate histories the way writers do. The difference between Nemi and Dessa's chosen narrator, therefore, is not about the choice of "one form of representation . . . and another" (Rushdy, "Reading Mammy" 366), nor is it a struggle between "literacy and orality." It is more a matter of relating the imperatives of material survival (righting slavery's injustice) to discursive signification (writing about the righting project).[22] Dessa and her rebellious colleagues are not engaged in a struggle over *representation,* per se, but the willful appropriation of, first, their persons and, then, their labor. Dessa speaks and dictates a fuller and counter-hegemonic version of her story only after she has attained physical freedom. Nemi fails "to capture Dessa in print" primarily because striving for physical freedom triumphs over the desire to enslave. The escape experience textualized by Dessa's preferred writer owes its existence to the prior literal correlate executed by the rebellious slaves: Dessa rejoins her fighting colleagues in order to give Nathan and Cully the chance to escape; these two later join Harker to get her out of the sheriff's basement cell; the runaways bail out of Sutton Glen at the appropriate time; Aunt Chole deliberately misreads the tracking device left on Dessa's body. Nemi's failure does not result fully from his wrongheaded poetics and politics of inscription. He fails because the slave rebel's will to freedom is always one step ahead of the scholarly aid to policing, disciplining, and punishing he sets out to write.

Williams, in "Lion's History," describes her novel as a story "that focused not on slavery as an institution but on slaves as people, the major actors in their own stories" (250), driven by "the intimate history that had escaped the formal historians" (253). According to Deborah McDowell, "Contemporary Afro-American writers who tell a story of slavery are increasingly aiming . . . to reposition the stress points of that story with a heavy accent on particular acts of agency within an oppressive and degrading system" (161). In *Dessa Rose,* the most important "particular act of agency" is the premium that slaves placed on material struggles to be free. To the free descendants who should not have to pay the steep price that liberty cost their ancestors is left the task of putting the archives bequeathed them—including Nemi's writing notes—to hegemonic contests. Dessa's writer, Williams's allegorical coordinate in a sense, is not competing against Nemi (who has failed, anyway) but with other readers of Nemi's notes.

CONCLUSION

What Is the Meaning of Slave Rebellion

In the late spring of 1841, about the time the U.S. Supreme Court freed the Amistad slave rebels, a wealthy, free black man from Philadelphia, Robert Purvis, commissioned Nathaniel Jocelyn to paint a portrait of the leader of the revolt, Singbe Pieh, also known as Cinque.

> On the day Purvis received the painting, he had a visit from Madison Washington, a slave whom Purvis had helped escape to Canada two years earlier. He was headed south to smuggle his wife out of Virginia, and sought the abolitionist's aid. During the visit, Purvis displayed Cinque's portrait, telling the story of the Amistad Incident. Washington became "intensely interested. He drank in every word and admired the hero's courage and intelligence." (Alexander 48)

The listener-response to this story of rebellion was almost immediate. Later aboard the Creole, after his plans to free his wife had gone awry in Virginia, Madison Washington found himself aboard a slaving vessel, where he, like the Amistad Africans, mutinied. Like Singbe Pieh, he demanded that the slave ship be steered to a free port rather than to New Orleans. Washington and fellow rebels reached free land in the Bahamas without the tortuous detour suffered by Singbe and his comrades.

In this instance, the purpose of retelling stories of slave rebellion is so apparent as to need no glossing. With a few provisos, the most significant being that slaves were predominantly illiterate, it could be said that Robert Purvis's instruction in self-liberation reflected the intention of antebellum stories of rebellion analyzed in the opening chapter of this book. Purvis's narration of the Amistad rebellion and his portrait of Singbe Pieh facilitated, like the novels discussed above, a cultural exchange that presented to Madison Washington a model of action.

After Emancipation, stories of rebellion have to serve purposes other than directly urging slaves (who do not exist, in theory, any more) to imitate narrative heroes. The new function can be illustrated with an episode from Steven Spielberg's movie *Amistad.* As the story moves toward closure in the U.S. Supreme Court, John Quincy Adams briefs Singbe Pieh on what the court may do:

> Adams: The test ahead of us is an exceptionally difficult one.
>
> Cinque: We won't be going in there alone.
>
> Adams: Alone? Indeed not. No. We have right on our side. We have righteousness on our side. We have Mr. Baldwin over there.
>
> Cinque: I mean my ancestors. I will call into the past, far back to the beginning of time, and beg them to come and help me at the judgment. I will reach back and draw them into me. And they must come, for at this moment, I am the whole reason they have existed at all.

The screenwriters probably intended this dialogue to nativize Singbe Pieh's understanding of the trials and to present him as a full participant in the defense of his own cause. In court, Adams represents the rebel's words as a sign of anthropological specificity: "When a member of the Mende . . . encounters a situation where there appears to be no hope at all, he invokes his ancestors. Tradition. See, the Mende believe that if one can summon the spirit of one's ancestors, then they have never left, and the wisdom and strength they fathered and inspired will come to his aid."

A lot more than mere cultural belief is at play in this conversation, although the contrast between Adams's conception of a person and Singbe Pieh's would cause a viewer to pause and recognize, following Adams himself, the depth of Singbe Pieh's mind. In relation to the goal of post-Emancipation narratives of slave rebellion, Singbe Pieh's language of invocation indicates a self-willed effort to claim an ancestral legacy of freedom. Ancestors are symbols of inspirational antecedence that can be summoned when needed. They also signify the integrity of the line of communication between the past and the present. The present is meaningful because ancestors existed; without them the future is unimaginable. That present actions promise a free future means that ancestors (or the past) are not (and cannot be) completely gone. Hence, Singbe Pieh could say with confidence, "I am the whole reason they have existed at all." Walter Benjamin, speaking a different language, might say, "Every image of the past that is not recognized by the present as one of its own concerns threatens to disappear irretrievably" (255).

Variants of Singbe Pieh's metaleptic "historical imagination"—"a retrospective assignation of a relationship between present and past" (Bahti 9)—are present in the stories of slave rebellion analyzed above. Writers invoke Gabriel Prosser, Nat Turner, Toussaint L'Ouverture, and other unnamed rebels to conjure, like Singbe Pieh, images capable of lighting the path to a free present (and possibly future). In some of the texts, the slave rebel's story abets the formation of realist fiction in nineteenth-century African American stories. For later epochs, the slave rebellion theme enables the articulation of historical realism (*The Black Jacobins*), magical realism (*The Kingdom of This World*), anticapitalist critical realism (*Black Thunder*), and historiographic metafiction (*Dessa Rose*). The elision of the slave's subaltern presence in Yorùbá oral tradition has also been explained as playing a key role in the dissemination of hegemonic poetry. In all these texts, the slave's rebellion is recalled for refashioning the present as much as for preserving the past and for sketching the trajectory which each writer prefers that the future developments should follow.

Some peculiar features make slave rebellions amenable to figurations of change. As narratives, stories of rebellion portray the careers of individuals who strive to alter the social order of things in ways that make them either godlike to their sympathizers or devilish to their detractors. This is to say that slave rebellions epitomize either noble deeds or despicable ambitions. In the stories analyzed in this book, even when the results are tragic, the ennobling elements of slave rebellions give each writer the chance to express his/her dissatisfaction with the social reality he/she confronts and also to indicate ways of changing it. In these texts, slave rebels march on the public sphere ready to disrupt the "continuum of history" performed there and to launch a "new calendar" (Benjamin 261). Nineteenth-century American writers positioned rebellions as a means of ending chattel slavery, mid-twentieth-century writers found in slave rebellions germs of working-class revolutions, and a late-twentieth-century writer like Sherley Ann Williams used the slave's rebellion to symbolize the material ends that textualized struggles should serve.

Slave rebellions are attempts by the underclass to effect fundamental changes in relations of social and material reproduction. Nat Turner wants to introduce a "new heaven and a new earth," Douglass's Madison Washington wants to claim the fruits of freedom promised by American founding fathers, C.L.R. James and Arna Bontemps try to herald the "cataclysm to come" with the stories of Gabriel Prosser and Toussaint L'Ouverture, and Ìṣọ̀lá's slaves want to kill their owner and stop her blood-sapping "witchcraft."

That the slave's rebellion exemplifies an attempt to redefine social relations both in theory and in concrete terms is demonstrated in Susan Buck-Morss's historicization of Hegel's philosophy of recognition: "The actual and successful revolution of Caribbean slaves against their masters is the moment when the dialectical logic of recognition becomes visible as the thematics of world history, the story of the universal recognition of freedom" (852). The Haitian War of Independence, Buck-Morss argues, is the real event that led Hegel to the modern theory of recognition summarized in the allegory of Lordship and Bondage:

> Prior to writing *The Phenomenology of Mind,* Hegel had dealt with the theme of mutual recognition in terms of Sittlichkeit: criminals against society or the mutual relations of religious community or personal affection. But now, this young lecturer, still only in his early thirties, made the audacious move to reject these earlier versions (more acceptable to the established philosophical discourse) and to inaugurate, as the central metaphor of his work, not slavery versus some mythical state of nature (as those from Hobbes to Rousseau had done earlier), but slaves versus masters, thus bringing into his text the present, historical realities that surrounded it like visible ink. (846)

These ideas did not sprout spontaneously from the philosopher's fertile brain but developed out of an interpretation of the practical struggles he encountered in reports of the Haitian War of Independence. Unfortunately, Buck-Morss also noted, the philosopher "becomes obscure and falls silent" when it comes to exploring the implication of the slaves' demonstrating through revolt, and not just work, "that they are not things, not objects, but subjects who transform material culture" (848). I hope I have shown in this book that the philosopher's silence has not barred more sympathetic students of the slave's revolt from squeezing meaning out of the struggles.

Revisiting stories of the slave's counter-violence is apposite at this moment because a critical complement is needed, I believe, to counterbalance the hue of "bloodlessness" which surrounds late modern (black) Atlantic intellectual histories that call on all communities to either find their ways within postmodern norms or risk total irrelevance. The analysis in this book has been carried out in full agreement with Gayatri Spivak that "if we only concentrate on the dominant, we forget that the difference between varieties of the emergent and residual may be the difference between radical and conservative resistance to the dominant, although this is by no means certain" (314). The critique *Dessa Rose* mounts against black poststructuralism well illustrates the way stories of slave rebellion aid the formation of an alternative view of the dominant. Stories of the slave's counter-violence remind us that we can exclude antagonisms from the relations of (textual) communities that shaped (and are still shaping) late modern history only if we want to tell the Master's version of how things came to be.

Tzvetan Todorov has suggested that we should not put too much stock in worldviews that represent social interaction as landscapes of deadly mutual antagonisms because they do not "tell the truth of the human condition" but portray "a relatively particular relationship" (13). It has not been my intention, I should say, to isolate the single seed of all modern black existence in the slave's counter-violence. My plan has been to recount one fundamental theme in the efforts of an enslaved people to establish an identity different from the one given them by their masters.

NOTES

INTRODUCTION

1. Darwin Turner and Sherley Ann Williams ("The Lion's History") say as much.

2. Earlier in 1934, Guy Endore's *Babouk* had examined the Haitian revolt from a class-conflict perspective.

3. An excellent study of the anthropology of oríkì is to be found in Karen Barber's *I Could Speak Until Tomorrow.*

4. For the Styron controversy, see Albert Stone, John Henrik Clarke, and also the report of a symposium organized around the novel at the 1968 annual meeting of the Southern Historical Association, in Ellison et al.

5. Albert Stone's opening chapter provides a good study of how civil rights cultural politics affected the reception of the novel.

6. There is a very obvious British tendency—actually a specific class therein—in the provenance of that apt phrasing of Gilroy's. The two words operate homonymically only in the upper-class British way of speaking English. In American speech, for instance, "route" is not always homonymous with "root." In England and the United States, "rout" may also mean total defeat, which would amount to an uprooting of some sort.

7. I have not read any proposition strong enough to contradict Eric Sundquist, *To Wake the Nations,* on this subject.

8. Armah's "histories" include *Two Thousand Seasons* and *The Healers.* For Ouologuem, see *Bound to Violence.*

9. For Aidoo, see *Anowa;* for Sutherland, see *Edufa* and *The Marriage of Anansewa;* for Emecheta, see *The Slave Girl* and even *The Joys of Motherhood.*

10. See *A Theory of Literary Production,* pp. 82–84.

1. HEGEL'S BURDEN

1. Habermas says a modern society is defined by Hegel as that which "has to create its normativity out of itself" (7).

2. I owe this formulation to my colleague Anna Brickhouse.

3. Two good examples of Black Atlantic works are Charles Piot and Lorand Ma-

tory. The phrase is also sometimes used to name the work of "nation-less" eighteenth-century black writers like Equiano and Cugoano. As it happens, "Black Atlantic" is replacing what used to be called diaspora studies. See Brent Edwards and James Clifford in this regard.

4. The handling of "origin" is, in my view, the most convincing criticism of the transnationalist tenets of "Black Atlanticism." See Laura Chrisman; Joan Dayan; Simon Gikandi, "Introduction"; and Ntongela Masilela.

5. The words are Hegel's, as quoted by Habermas (16).

6. Simon Gikandi made this point in his review of Gilroy ("In the Shadow of Hegel" 146). See Gilroy, chapter 2.

7. I consider very tenuous Gilroy's evidence for the notion that Douglass may have been literally influenced by a reading of Hegel. For the 1845 edition, at least, it is not very likely that Douglass would have read Hegel.

8. Gilroy also cites in this regard the case of Margaret Garner, the Cincinnati, Ohio, fugitive slave woman who in 1856 chose to kill her children rather than let them be returned to slavery. For Garner and Douglass, "the repeated choice of death rather than bondage articulates a principle of negativity that is opposed to the formal logic and rational calculation characteristic of modern western thinking and expressed in the Hegelian slave's preference for bondage rather than death" (68).

9. Mbembe stresses, in my view, that this kind of answer will be a miscomprehension because Africanists have not even begun to consider deeply the ramifications of what it means to be a slave.

10. The concept of "social death," the most intriguing part of Orlando Patterson's formulation, emanates from the slave's double alienation from the land of capture and the place of servitude. The slave must first be "violently uprooted" (38) from his natal community and then introduced to his new status as a nonbeing in the new society. Many times, especially in the case of criminals, the changed social status takes place in the same locale.

11. Patterson could thus be said to conceive slavery as the result of "an act of force, hence a *political* act" (Engels 202).

12. Hence slaves embrace Christianity and create another universe that demonstrates their worldly inability to realize freedom literally.

13. See Gibson.

14. See Behrendt et al.; Richardson; and Bailyn.

2. NAT TURNER AND PLOT MAKING IN EARLY AFRICAN AMERICAN FICTION

1. The discussion carried out in this section relies on the methodological suggestions in Ranajit Guha, "The Prose of Counter-Insurgency," and Pierre Macherey, *A Theory of Literary Production*, pp. 82–101.

2. See Aptheker, *American Negro Slave Revolts*, chapters 1, 7, and 13; Harvey Wish's two essays; and Higginson, pp. 208–13, 265–75, and 306–26.

3. Lydia Maria Child, "To Harriet Jacobs," 13 August 1860, in Linda Brent [Harriet Jacobs], *Incidents*, p. 244.

4. Mrs. Child included the ex-slave's memories of the aftermath of the Turner

revolt in her 1839 biographical piece on Charity Bowery, also originally of Edenton, North Carolina. Charity Bowery's son was killed by his master because he resisted punishment. As recorded, Bowery's recollection is considerably shorter than Jacobs's but agrees with it in all respects. Mrs. Child's editorial representation of Turner in that piece is consistent with the advice she was going to give Harriet Jacobs twenty years later. Juxtaposed to the one-paragraph recollection of the mayhem unleashed on black people is the full text of a hymn sung by the terrorized folks. The song that practically closes the article is prefaced thus: "In a voice cracked with age, but still retaining considerable sweetness, she sang. . . ."

5. See Scot French (65–73) for a summary discussion of changes in abolitionists' position on anti-slavery violence.

6. See Goldstein for how Frederick Douglass dealt with the same question. Scot French details how radical blacks, including Douglass, negotiated Turner's name in speeches (73–120).

7. See Howard Jones, "The Peculiar Institution."

8. See Richard Yarborough, "Race, Violence, and Manhood."

9. See Killens, *The Trial Record of Denmark Vesey,* and Eggerton.

10. Eric Sundquist argues that the sea-based rebellion allows Douglass to pursue a natural law proposition (*To Wake the Nations* 115–17).

11. Thomas Higgins says that the story was most probably invented in the aftermath of the Turner revolt. See also Davis, "Arna Bontemps' *Black Thunder.*"

12. The main sources of the summary in these paragraphs are Mary Kemp Davis, "Arna Bontemps' *Black Thunder,*" Tragle, and Higginson's chapter on Gabriel Prosser.

13. See French (107–112) for a discussion of how other black writers and commentators used the occasion of the Brown incident to bring back Nat Turner.

14. Two novels written by white writers addressed the Turner episode in the 1850s: Harriet Beecher Stowe's *Dred* and G.P.R. James's *Old Dominion.* Mary Kemp Davis (*Nat Turner Before the Bar of Judgment*) discusses these two stories in great detail along with other nineteenth-century novels about Nat Turner by white writers.

15. See Olney, "'I Was Born.'"

16. See Eric Sundquist, *To Wake the Nations,* p. 81.

17. See Sundquist, *To Wake the Nations,* pp. 27–82; Clarke; and chapter 1 of Albert Stone's book. These questions are revisited with new evidence and fresh analyses in Greenberg's *Nat Turner,* especially Greenberg's own "Name, Face, Body" and David Almendinger's "The Construction of *The Confessions of Nat Turner.*"

18. Sundquist says that "Turner was far more than Gray's *equal,* as a man and also as an 'author'" (*To Wake the Nations* 39). Andrews says the "literary antagonism" between the two turns them "into inadvertent collaborationists, whose defense against each other ironically leads each into a reasonable cooperation with the other" (*To Tell a Free Story* 76–77).

19. See William Andrews's "Novelization of Voice" for a discussion of the importance of truthfulness in early African American fiction.

20. Walter Rucker argues that the situation may not be that simple because scattered episodes of rebellion in the United States always involved the use of African religious beliefs.

21. Genovese, pp. 587–98.

22. John Zeugner thinks the undisclosed secrecy "summons up narrative tension"

(101). Ernest says it makes the novel mysterious (112). Sundquist suggests that the "strategy underlines the fluid nature of the conspiracy that Blake envisions" (*To Wake the Nations* 198) and is a move calculated to escalate the panic of white readers.

23. The one major theme accentuated about the journey is the extreme danger "free" states have become to runaway slaves after the Fugitive Slave Act. The gang's escape also shows that whites will ease a fleeing slave's passage if the slaves are able to pay the right price. According to John Ernest, episodes in which the slaves pay their way through demonstrate that in slavery money supersedes morality and/or legality.

24. Interpretations that are less distrustful of the influences of pressing mid-nineteenth-century U.S. nationalist controversies about slavery and abolition on the novel will be found in Sundquist, *To Wake the Nations*, pp. 221–22, and Levine, p. 216.

3. REVERSE ABOLITIONISM AND BLACK POPULAR RESISTANCE

1. See Edmonds, pp. 136–77; Hayden; Prather; and Yarborough, "Violence, Manhood, and Black Heroism," pp. 231–37.

2. Major Carteret responds positively to an invitation to invest in an out-of-state project "which promised large returns" (29). The changing South is also a theme in Chesnutt's tales of "conjure."

3. See Glenda Gilmore for a discussion of the sexual anxiety repressed in this vampire image.

4. See Prather, p. 18, and LeeAnn Whites for the role of the *Wilmington Daily Record* in the events that led to the 1898 riots.

5. See LeeAnn Whites and also Gilmore for discussions on the role of the virtual war created by the historical *Wilmington Daily Record* editorial that condemns the moral inconsistencies of lynch and miscegenation laws.

6. Knadler reads Green's boast of having beaten up a South American dockworker as an example of his exclusivist view of the races. He fails to point out that Green fights black workers, too.

7. A similar sentiment organizes the plot structure of Frances Harper's *Iola Leroy*, published roughly a decade earlier.

4. SLAVE REBELLION, THE GREAT DEPRESSION, AND THE "TURBULENCE TO COME" FOR CAPITALISM

1. For the relation of *Black Thunder* to the Scottsboro trials see Sundquist, *Hammers of Creation*, pp. 118–19; for a summary of the trials see Douglas Linder; for the aggravation of black people in the Great Depression, see Sundstrom and also Charles Martin.

2. Barbara Foley classifies the story as a "proletarian social novel" (chapter 10).

3. See also W.E.B. Du Bois, "Criteria of Negro Art."

4. See Countee Cullen's "Heritage" and Bontemps's "Return."

5. The best example would be the mini–slave autobiography Nanny recounted to her granddaughter, Janie, in Hurston's *Their Eyes Were Watching God* to explain her concerns about the latter's sexual awakening and her reasons for desiring a conventional marriage for her (16–18).

6. See chapter 5 of Bernard Bell's book.

7. See pp. 181–89 of Harold Cruse's *Crisis* for a critical interpretation of the de-

bilitating effect of doctrinaire communist activism on Wright's inability to properly implement the materialist nationalism he recommends to other writers.

8. For a nationalist study of the dilemma of blacks in the Communist Party in the 1930s, see Harold Cruse's *Crisis,* particularly all four chapters of section II.

9. This event is comparable to Frederick Douglass's famous eavesdropping on Captain Auld about literacy and freedom.

10. Foley, "The Uses of the Documentary Mode," p. 397.

11. See Davis, "From Death Unto Life"; Campbell; and Weil for other discussions of the importance of the elaboration of folk life to the plot.

12. In "Reading, Revelation, and Rebellion," James Sidbury analyzes how nineteenth-century American slave rebellions were fostered by "'textual communities' integrated through a shared interpretation of sacred script" (120).

13. I have quoted the New International Version because the diction is more relevant to this discussion than the King James Version that simply says, "A measure of wheat for a penny, and three measures of barley for a penny."

5. DISTILLING PROVERBS OF HISTORY FROM THE HAITIAN WAR OF INDEPENDENCE

1. See Dupuy, pp. 112–16; and all of Moitt.

2. See Hilary Beckles, who says *The Black Jacobins* is one of those books of "historiographical decolonization" that inaugurated "an insider, creole, nationalist canon" in the Caribbean (777); see also Farred, "First Stop."

3. See also San Juan, p. 235; Blackburn, p. 87; Farred, "First Stop," p. 227.

4. I should make it clear that the Henry and Buhle text from which this phrasing is taken (114) is opposed to the kind of interpretation that is being discussed here.

5. See, for example, San Juan, pp. 227–35.

6. "The first African to 'pass through professional training' in Western historical scholarship" (Nwaubani 230).

7. For a discussion of the impact of Hegel on discursive constructions of Africa, see Taiwo.

8. More than fifty years earlier, Du Bois wrote in *The Souls of Black Folk,* "We must not forget that most Americans answer all queries regarding the Negro *a priori,* and that the least human courtesy can do is to listen to evidence" (96).

9. Hayden White says there is a strong correlation between tragic historical narratives, "mechanistic" explanations, and radical ideological intent (70).

10. See Adeeko, *Proverbs,* pp. 28–49.

11. This saying is a rewrite of Karl Marx in the first chapter of *The Eighteenth Brumaire of Louis Napoleon*: "Men make their own history, but they do not make it as they please; they do not make it under self-selected circumstances, but under circumstances existing already, given and transmitted from the past" (http://www.marxists.org/archive/marx/works/1852/18th-brumaire/ch01.htm).

12. This proverb, of course, speaks directly to the then-emerging middle class in the colonies—the class of Gandhi, Kenyatta, Nkrumah, Azikiwe—studying the ways and thoughts of their rulers. Like Toussaint, they are going to take advantage of their knowledge of the colonialists during the independence struggle.

13. Tony Martin, "C.L.R. James and the Race/Class Question."

14. Even Martin knew James believed that "the spontaneity of the masses [is] su-

perior to the dictates of the 'vanguard parties'" ("C.L.R. James and the Race/Class Question" 188).

15. James also describes bureaucrats as "privileged persons divorced from the masses and superior to the masses" (191).

16. No text theorizes this latter development better than Fanon's *The Wretched of the Earth.* See especially the chapter titled "The Pitfalls of National Consciousness," pp. 148–205.

6. SLAVE REBELLION AND MAGICAL REALISM

1. The words are Echevarria's (123), although he uses them to reiterate the opposite of what I am claiming for Macandal here.

2. See Murray and Rosalie Wax, "The Notion of Magic."

3. Sophie Oluwole says scientists should not quickly dismiss witchcraft's basic postulation that "the mind can affect other minds either by a kind of physical or non-physical radiation transmitted through brain waves" (33). See also Idowu; Idoniboye; and Mosley. Bodunrin disagrees with all of them.

4. See Horton; Barber, "How Man Makes God"; and also Olabimtan.

5. See Geschiere and also the essays, including the introduction, in Comaroff and Comaroff.

6. See Hallen and Sodipo, pp. 86–118.

7. See Thornton for a discussion of the role of "African soldiers" in the war.

8. Walter Rodney suggests that he is probably a Mandinka from Upper Guinea.

9. See Sokoloff for a structuralist explanation of the narrative movements.

7. SLAVERY IN AFRICAN LITERARY DISCOURSE

1. See Bolanle Awẹ́, "Praise Poems as Historical Data" and "Notes on Oríkì and Warfare in Yorubaland"; and Abimbola, "Ifa Divination Poems as Sources for Historical Evidence."

2. For an overview of the traditional views of African domestic slavery, see the essays collected in Miers and Kopytoff, especially chapter 1. For an overview of the revisions of the tradition, see Klein; and Frederick Cooper.

3. Ali Mazrui first uses this construction in "A Preliminary Critique" (5) and repeats it in "Black Orientalism?" (17) and "A Millennium Letter" (51). See also Asante, "Wonders," Mikell (33), and Agozino (45). Okolo does not disagree with Gates for depicting African participation in the slave trade but explains the involvement as an inevitable development (38). Inikori also uses a historicist explanation (31).

4. Historical anthropologists such as Rosalind Shaw are now suggesting that the "near-silence" of African oratures on great historical moments like slavery and colonialism should not be construed as signs of cultural amnesia. The past, Shaw says, "is remembered not only in words but also in images and non-discursive practical forms that go beyond words" (4). My assumption in this chapter is that the study of discursive genres need not be abandoned yet. After all, what is excluded from a text can be as important to meaning-making as what is excluded.

5. My primary area of exploration in African oral traditions is the Yorùbá sphere of influence.

6. For Awẹ́, "oríkì constitute some form of record of the past of the Yorùbá so-

ciety and most informants, especially the professional bards, seem to regard them as such" (333).

7. See Jan Vansina, pp. 173–78.

8. See chapter 4 of Babalola, *Content and Form of Yoruba Ijala.*

9. The poems may, of course, have been standardized before the emergence of the idea of the Yorùbá as one people. See Samuel Johnson, *History of the Yoruba.*

10. See chapter 6 of Barber's *I Could Speak.*

11. See Oroge, pp. 124–211.

12. In one section of the paragraph, she says two pages were removed. She reproduces six lines she managed to obtain from one Pa Adeniji of Iwo on pp. 335–36.

13. The connection between right and plot is taken from the dialogue between Àjàyí and the Olúmokò on pp. 127–28.

14. See chapter 1 of Soyinka's *Myth, Literature and the African World View* for a discussion of the Obatala-Ogun dichotomy in Yorùbá cosmology.

15. The best example would be found in Achebe's *Things Fall Apart*: "Our duty is not to blame this man or praise that, but to settle the dispute" (66).

16. Òyéwùmí's book disputes this interpretation.

17. More than one critic has found Fálétí's melodramatic ending irksome. See Olaniyan; and Isola, "Presenting Revolution" and "Indigo Revolt."

8. PRYING REBELLIOUS SUBALTERN CONSCIOUSNESS OUT OF THE CLENCHED JAWS OF ORAL TRADITIONS

1. Òyéwùmí suggests that the latter expression better reflects the Yorùbá worldsense (109).

2. Facts dramatized indicate that Ìṣọ̀lá's main sources are I. B. Akinyele's *Iwe Itan Ibadan* and Samuel Johnson's *History of the Yorubas.*

3. See Johnson's *History of the Yorubas,* pp. 391–94.

4. See Ìṣọ̀lá, *Ẹfúnṣetán,* pp. 3, 5, 45, 62.

5. See Barber, "Documenting."

9. REITERATING THE BLACK EXPERIENCE

1. Paulette White, Alexis Deveaux, Ntozake Shange, Gayl Jones, and Toni Cade Bambara are some of the writers included in the anthology.

2. In my view, the black women's era in twentieth-century American writing reached its peak with Morrison receiving the 1993 Nobel Prize for Literature.

3. Robert Stepto's *From Behind the Veil* appeared a year before "Meditations." In 1979, too, Stepto and Dexter Fisher edited *Afro-American Literature: The Reconstruction of Instruction,* arguably the first book to shepherd the terms of reading and teaching African American writing from the poststructuralist perspective.

4. See Rushdy, *Neo-Slave Narratives,* pp. 132–39; Stone, pp. 375–82.

5. See Rushdy, *Neo-Slave Narratives*; and Henderson, "(W)riting *The Work.*"

6. See Sánchez; Winchell; Davis, "Everybody Knows Her Name"; and McKible.

7. See Fowler; Davies; and Henderson, "Speaking in Tongues."

8. Meta-fictional historiography is from Linda Hutcheon. Works that analyze various aspects of this issue in *Dessa Rose* include Goldman; Sievers; McDowell; and the two articles by Henderson.

9. See Rushdy, *Neo-Slave Narratives* (144), for the probable historical origin of this name.

10. Fox-Good's essay discusses the significance of the cultural cooperation that makes the rescue possible.

11. "The mainstream has never run clean, perhaps never can," says Gayatri Spivak (2). On the bases of Black Studies see Asante, *The Afrocentric Idea*, pp. 1–23; on the influence of Black Power politics on the novel, see Rushdy, *Neo-Slave Narrative*, 135–39; Stone, 375–81.

12. Spillers believes that the perpetuation is actually ahistoricist (68).

13. See also Anne Goldman, p. 314.

14. This discussion has also benefited from Rushdy, *Neo-Slave Narrative*, pp. 139–47.

15. This event is loosely based on an event reported in *Niles Weekly Register*, 5 September 1829, pp. 18–19, and 26 December 1829, p. 277. "Meditations" retains the year 1829, but the novel shifts the events to 1847.

16. She uses this phrasing at Sutton Glen when Rufel asks why his master's wife was cruel to her: Dessa says, "'Cause she can'" (149).

17. Nemi's psychologism is possibly a critique of the theory of repressed sexuality Styron used to frame his Nat Turner story.

18. We should recall that Gray called Turner and his associates "diabolical actors" (40).

19. For discussions of the meaning of Dessa and Rufel's fraught relation, see Rushdy, "Reading Mammy" (also in *Neo-Slave Narratives*, pp. 147–58); McKible, p. 227; Porter, pp. 260–65; and Sánchez, pp. 28–31.

20. See also Leaming.

21. Suzan Harrison says the letter signifies "rebellion, revolt or renegade" (18). Guy Endore's *Babouk* records a similar punishment for a slave rebel (78). Perhaps the most probable source of Williams's depiction of Dessa's mutilation is the episode in Margaret Walker's *Jubilee* in which a runaway slave woman has the letter 'R' burned into her face. The novel also narrates the case of two slave women executed on Fourth of July celebrations for trying to kill their master. See chapter 11.

22. I took "writing" and "righting" first from Henderson, where writing is the main theme, and also from Carole Boyce Davies, where the difficulties of "righting" is the primary subject.

BIBLIOGRAPHY

Abimbola, Wande. "Ifa Divination Poems as Sources for Historical Evidence." *Lagos Notes and Records* 1 (June 1967): 17–26.

Achebe, Chinua. *Things Fall Apart.* London: Heinemann, 1962.

Adéẹ̀kọ́, Adélékè. *Proverbs, Textuality, and Nativism in African Literature.* Gainesville: University of Florida Press, 1998.

———. "Signatures of Blood in William Wells Brown's *Clotel.*" *Nineteenth-Century Contexts* 21.1 (1999): 115–34.

Agozino, Biko. "Wonders of the African Crisis." *Black Scholar* 30.1 (Spring 2000): 45–47.

Aidoo, Ama Ata. *The Dilemma of a Ghost: Anowa—Two Plays.* Essex: Longman, 1987.

Akinyele, I. B. *Iwe Itan Ibadan.* 3rd ed. Exeter: James Townsend, 1951.

Alexander, Eleanor. "A Portrait of Cinque." *Connecticut Historical Society Bulletin* 49.1 (Winter 1984): 30–51.

Alexis, Stephen J. "Of the Marvelous Realism of the Haitians." *Presence Africaine* 8–9 (June–Nov. 1956): 249–75.

Almedinger, David. F. "The Construction of the Confessions of Nat Turner." Greenberg 24–42.

Andrews, William L. "The Novelization of Voice in Early African American Fiction." *PMLA* 105 (1990): 23–34.

———. "The Representation of Slavery and the Rise of Afro-American Literary Realism 1865–1920." McDowell and Rampersad 62–80.

———. *To Tell a Free Story: The First Century of Afro-American Autobiography, 1760–1865.* Urbana: University of Illinois Press, 1986.

Aptheker, Herbert. *American Negro Slave Revolts.* New York: International Publishers, 1963.

———. "Maroons Within the Present Limits of the United States." *Maroon Societies: Rebel Slave Communities in the Americas.* Ed. Richard Price. New York: Anchor Books, 1973. 150–67.

Armah, Ayi Kwei. *The Healers.* Nairobi: East African Publishing House, 1978.

———. *Two Thousand Seasons.* London: Heineman, 1979.

Asante, Molefi K. *The Afrocentric Idea.* Philadelphia: Temple University Press, 1998.

———. "Wonders of the African World." *Black Scholar* 30.1 (Spring 2000): 8–9.

Awe, Bolanle. "Iyalode Efunsetan Aniwura (Owner of Gold)." *Nigerian Women in Historical Perspective.* Ed. Bolanle Awe. Ibadan: Sankore/Bookcraft, 1992. 55–71.

———. "Notes on Oriki and Warfare in Yorubaland." *Yoruba Oral Tradition: Poetry in Music, Dance, and Drama.* Ed. Wande Abimbola. Ile-Ife: Department of African Languages and Literatures, 1975. 267–92.

———. "Praise Poems as Historical Data: The Example of Yoruba Oriki." *Africa* 44.4 (1974): 331–49.

Babalola, Adeboye. *Àwọn Oríkì Orílẹ̀.* Glasgow: Collins, 1967.

———. *The Content and Form of Yoruba Ijala.* Oxford: Oxford University Press, 1966.

Babayemi, S. O. *Content Analysis of Oriki Orile.* Ibadan: Institute of African Studies, 1988.

Bahti, Timothy. "History as Rhetorical Enactment: Walter Benjamin's Theses 'On the Concept of History.'" *Diacritics* 9.3 (Sept. 1979): 2–17.

Bailyn, Bernard. "Considering the Slave Trade: History and Memory." *William and Mary Quarterly* 58.1 (Jan. 2001): 244–51.

Baker, Houston A. *Blues, Ideology, and Afro-American Literature: A Vernacular Theory.* Chicago: University of Chicago Press, 1984.

Bamgbose, Ayo, ed. *Yoruba Metalanguage: Ede Iperi Yoruba Vol. I.* Lagos: Nigeria Educational Research Council, 1984.

Barber, Karin. "Documenting Social and Ideological Changes Through Yoruba Oríkì." *Journal of the Historical Society of Nigeria* 10.4 (1981): 39–52.

———. "How Man Makes God in West Africa: Yoruba Attitudes Towards the Orisa." *Africa* 51.3 (1981): 724–45.

———. *I Could Speak Until Tomorrow: Oriki, Women and the Past in a Yoruba Town.* Edinburgh: Edinburgh University Press, 1991.

Bauer, Raymond A., and Alice Bauer. "Day to Day Resistance to Slavery." *Journal of Negro History* 27 (1942): 388–419.

Beckles, Hilary McD. "Capitalism, Slavery, and Caribbean Modernity." *Callaloo* 20.4 (1997): 777–89.

Behrendt, Stephen D., David Eltis, and David Richardson. "The Costs of Coercion: African Agency in the Pre-Modern Atlantic World." *Economic History Review* 44.3 (2001): 454–76.

Bell, Bernard W. *The Afro-American Novel and Its Tradition.* Amherst: University of Massachusetts Press, 1987.

Bell, Steven. "Carpentier's *El Reino De Este Mundo* in a New Light: Toward a Theory of the Fantastic." *Journal of Spanish Studies: 20th Century* 8 (1980): 29–43.

Benjamin, Walter. *Illuminations: Essays and Reflections.* Trans. Harry Zohn. Ed. Hannah Arendt. New York: Harper and Row.

Bentley, Nancy. "White Slaves: The Mulatto Hero in Antebellum Fiction." *American Literature* 65.3 (Sept. 1993): 501–22.

Bhabha, Homi K. *The Location of Culture.* London: Routledge, 1994.

Bienvenu, Germain J. "The People of Delany's *Blake.*" *CLA Journal* 36.4 (1993): 406–29.

Biko, Agozino. "Wonders of the African Crisis." *Black Scholar* 30.1 (Spring 2000): 45–47.

Blackburn, Robin. "*The Black Jacobins* and New World Slavery." Cudjoe and Cain 81–97.

Bodunrin, P. O. "Witchcraft, Magic and E.S.P.: A Defence of Scientific and Philosophical Scepticism." *Second Order* 7.1/2 (Jan./July 1978): 36–50.

Bontemps, Arna. "Arna Bontemps." *Interviews with Black Writers.* Ed. John O'Brien. New York: Liveright, 1973. 3–15.
———. *Black Thunder.* Boston: Beacon Press, 1968.
———. *Drums at Dusk.* New York: Macmillan, 1938.
———. "The Return." *The Poetry of the Negro 1746–1970.* Ed. Langston Hughes and Arna Bontemps. New York: Doubleday, 1970. 215–16.
Bradley, David. "On the Lam from Race and Gender." *New York Times Book Review* 3 Aug. 1986.
Brent, Linda (Harriet Jacobs). *Incidents in the Life of a Slave Girl.* 1861. Ed. Jean Fagan Yellin. Cambridge, Mass.: Harvard University Press, 1987.
Brown, William Wells. *Clotel, or the President's Daughter. Three Classic African American Novels.* Ed. William L. Andrews. New York: Mentor Books, 1990. 71–283.
Buck-Morss, Susan. "Hegel and Haiti." *Critical Inquiry* 26 (Summer 2000): 821–47.
Butler, Judith. *The Psychic Life of Power: Theories in Subjection.* Stanford: Stanford University Press, 1997.
Campbell, Jane. *Mythic Black Fiction: The Transformation of History.* Knoxville: University of Tennessee Press, 1986.
Carby, Hazel V. "Ideologies of Black Folk: The Historical Novel of Slavery." McDowell and Rampersad. 125–63.
———. "Proletarian or Revolutionary Literature: C.L.R. James and the Politics of the Trinidadian Renaissance." *South Atlantic Quarterly* 87.1 (Winter 1988): 39–52.
Carpentier, Alejo. "The Baroque and the Marvelous Real." Parkinson and Zamora 89–108.
———. *The Kingdom of This World.* Trans. Marriett de Onis. New York: Knopf, 1957.
———. "Prologue to *The Kingdom of This World.*" *Review: Latin American Literature and Arts* 47 (Fall 1993): 28–32.
Cecelski, David S., and Timothy B. Tyson, eds. *Democracy Betrayed: The Wilmington Race Riot of 1898 and Its Legacy.* Chapel Hill: University of North Carolina Press, 1998.
Césaire, Aimé. *Notebook of a Return to the Native Land.* Trans. Clayton Eshleman and Annette Smith. Middletown, Conn.: Wesleyan University Press, 2001.
Chanady, Amaryll. "The Territorialization of the Imaginary in Latin America: Self-Affirmation and Resistance to Metropolitan Paradigms." Parkinson and Zamora 125–44.
Chesnutt, Charles W. *The Marrow of Tradition.* Ann Arbor: University of Michigan Press, 1973.
Child, Lydia Maria. "Charity Bowery." *Liberty Bell* 1 (1839): 26–48.
Chrisman, Laura. "Journeying to Death: Paul Gilroy's *Black Atlantic.*" *Race and Class* 39.2 (1997): 51–64.
Clarke, John Henrik. *William Styron's Nat Turner: Ten Black Writers Respond.* Boston: Beacon, 1968.
Clifford, James. "Diasporas." *Cultural Anthropology* 9.3 (Aug. 1994): 302–38.
Comaroff, Jean, and John Comaroff. *Modernity and Its Malcontents: Ritual and Power in Postcolonial Africa.* Chicago: University of Chicago Press, 1993.
Cooper, Brenda. *Magical Realism in West African Fiction: Seeing with a Third Eye.* London: Routledge, 1998.
Cooper, Frederick. "The Problem of Slavery in African Studies." *Journal of African History* 20.1 (1979): 103–25.

Crane, Gregg D. "The Lexicon of Rights, Power, and Community in *Blake:* Martin R. Delany's Dissent from *Dred Scott.*" *American Literature* 68.3 (Sept. 1996): 527–53.

Cromwell, John. "The Aftermath of Nat Turner's Insurrection." *Journal of Negro History* 5.2 (Apr. 1920): 208–34.

Cruse, Harold. *The Crisis of the Negro Intellectual: A Historical Analysis of Black Leadership.* New York: Quill, 1967.

Cudjoe, Selwyn R., and William E. Cain, eds. *C.L.R. James: His Intellectual Legacies.* Amherst: University of Massachusetts Press, 1995.

Cullen, Countee. "Heritage." *The Black Poets.* Ed. Dudley Randall. New York: Bantam Books, 1971. 95–98.

Dain, Bruce. "Haiti and Egypt in Early Black Racial Discourse in the United States." *Slavery and Abolition* 14.3 (Dec. 1993): 139–61.

Daniels, Josephus. *Editor in Politics.* Chapel Hill: University of North Carolina Press, 1941.

Davies, Carole Boyce. "Mother Right/Write Revisited: *Beloved* and *Dessa Rose* and the Construction of Motherhood in Black Women's Fiction." *Narrating Mothers: Theorizing Maternal Subjectivities.* Ed. Brenda O. Daly and Maureen T. Reddy. Knoxville: University of Tennessee Press, 1991. 44–57.

Davis, Angela. "Reflections on the Black Woman's Role in the Community of Slaves." *Black Scholar* (Dec. 1971): 3–15.

Davis, Mary Kemp. "Arna Bontemps' *Black Thunder:* The Creation of an Authoritative Text of 'Gabriel's Defeat.'" *Black American Literature Forum* 23.1 (Spring 1989): 17–36.

———. "Everybody Knows Her Name: The Recovery of the Past in Sherley Anne Williams's *Dessa Rose.*" *Callaloo* 12.3 (Summer 1989): 544–58.

———. "From Death unto Life: The Rhetorical Function of Funeral Rites in Arna Bontemps' *Black Thunder.*" *Journal of Ritual Studies* 1.1 (1987): 85–101.

———. *Nat Turner Before the Bar of Judgment: Fictional Treatments of the Southampton Slave Insurrection.* Baton Rouge: Louisiana State University Press, 1999.

Dayan, Joan. "Paul Gilroy's Slaves, Ships, and Routes: The Middle Passage as Metaphor." *Research in African Literatures* 27.4 (Winter 1996): 7–14.

De Armas, Frederick A. "Metamorphosis as Revolt: Cervantes' *Persile y Sigismunda* and Carpentier's *El Reino De Este Mundo.*" *Hispanic Review* 49.3 (Summer 1981): 297–316.

De Lancey, Dayle B. "The Self's Own Kind: Literary Resistance in Sherley Anne Williams' *Dessa Rose.*" *MAWA Review* 5.2 (1990).

Delany, Martin. *Blake, or the Huts of America.* Boston: Beacon Press, 1970.

Delmar, P. Jay. "The Moral Dilemma in Charles Chesnutt's *The Marrow of Tradition.*" *American Literary Realism* 14.2 (1981): 269–72.

Demos, John. "The Antislavery Movement and the Problem of Violent 'Means.'" *New England Quarterly* 37 (1964): 501–26.

Diaz, Nancy G. "The Metamorphoses of Maldoror and Macandal: Reconsidering Carpentier's Reading of Lautreamont." *Modern Language Studies* 21.3 (Summer 1991): 48–56.

Dike, K. Onwuka. "African History and Self-Government 1." *West Africa* 28 Feb. 1953: 177–78.

———. "African History and Self-Government 2." *West Africa* 14 March 1953: 225–26.

———. "African History and Self-Government 3." *West Africa* 21 March 1953: 251.
Douglass, Frederick. *The Heroic Slave. Three Classic African American Novels.* Ed. William L. Andrews. New York: Mentor Books, 1990. 25–69.
———. *Narrative of the Life of Frederick Douglass, an American Slave: Written by Himself. The Classic Slave Narratives.* Ed. Henry Louis Gates Jr. New York: Mentor Books, 1987. 243–331.
Du Bois, W.E.B. "Criteria of Negro Art." *Within the Circle: An Anthology of African American Literary Criticism from the Harlem Renaissance to the Present.* Ed. Angelyn Mitchell. Durham, N.C.: Duke University Press, 1994. 60–68.
———. *The Souls of Black Folk.* Ed. David W. Blight and Robert Gooding-Williams. Boston: Bedford Books, 1997.
Dupuy, Alex. "Toussaint-Louverture and the Haitian Revolution: A Reassessment of C.L.R. James's Interpretation." Cudjoe and Cain 106–17.
Dutertre, Elizabeth. "Slave Religion and Slave Rebellions." *Le Sud et Autres Points Cardinaux.* Ed. Jeanne-Marie Santraud. Paris: Presses de l'Université de Paris-Sorbonne, 1984. 21–30.
Echevarria, Roberto G. *Alejo Carpentier: The Pilgrim at Home.* Ithaca: Cornell University Press, 1977.
Edmonds, Helen G. *The Negro and Fusion Politics in North Carolina 1894–1901.* Chapel Hill: University of North Carolina Press, 1951.
Edwards, Brent H. "The Uses of Diaspora." *Social Text* 19.1 (Spring 2001): 45–73.
Eggerton, Douglas R. *Gabriel's Rebellion: The Virginia Slave Conspiracies of 1800 and 1802.* Chapel Hill: University of North Carolina Press, 1993.
Ellison, Ralph, et al. "The Uses of History in Fiction." *Southern Literary Journal* 1.2 (1969): 58–90.
Emecheta, Buchi. *Joys of Motherhood.* London: Heinemann, 1979.
———. *The Slave Girl.* New York: George Braziller, 1977.
Endore, Guy. *Babouk.* New York: Vanguard Press, 1934.
Engels, Frederick. *Anti-Duhring.* Peking: Foreign Language Press, 1976.
Engler, Bernd, and Oliver Scheiding. "Re-Visioning the Past: The Historical Imagination in American Historiography and Short Fiction." Engler and Scheiding11–37.
———, eds. *Re-Visioning the Past: Historical Self-Reflexivity in American Fiction.* Trier: Wissenschaftlichen, 1998.
Ernest, John. *Resistance and Reformation in Nineteenth-Century African-American Literature: Brown, Wilson, Jacobs, Delany, Douglass, and Harper.* Jackson: University of Mississippi Press, 1995.
Faleti, Adebayo. *Omo Olokun Esin.* Ibadan: Heinemann Educational Publishers, 1993.
Fanon, Frantz. *Black Skin, White Masks.* Trans. Charles Lam Markmann. New York: Grove Press, 1967.
———. *The Wretched of the Earth.* Trans. Constance Farrington. New York: Grove, 1960.
Farred, Grant. "First Stop, Port-au-Prince: Mapping Postcolonial Africa through Toussaint L'Ouverture and His Black Jacobins." *The Politics of Culture in the Shadow of Capital.* Ed. Lisa Lowe and David Lloyd. Durham, N.C.: Duke University Press, 1997. 227–47.
———, ed. *Rethinking C.L.R. James.* London: Blackwell, 1996.
Finkelman, Paul. *Dred Scott v. Sandford: A Brief History with Documents.* Boston: Bedford Book, 1997.

Finnegan, Ruth. "A Note on Oral Tradition and Historical Evidence." *History and Theory* 9.2 (1970): 195–201.

Fisher, Dexter, and Robert Stepto. *Afro-American Literature: The Reconstruction of Instruction.* New York: Modern Language Association, 1979.

Flores, Angel. "Magical Realism in Spanish American Fiction." *Hispania* 38.2 (May 1955): 187–92.

Foley, Barbara. "History, Fiction, and the Ground Between: The Uses of the Documentary Mode in Black Literature." *PMLA* 95 (1980): 389–403.

———. *Radical Representations.* Durham, N.C.: Duke University Press, 1993.

Foot, Michael. "C.L.R. James." Cudjoe and Cain 98–105.

Fowler, Shelli B. "Marking the Body, Demarcating the Body Politic: Issues of Agency and Identity in *Louisa Picquet* and *Dessa Rose.*" *CLA Journal* 40.4 (June 1997): 467–78.

Fox-Good, Jacquelyn. "Singing the Unsayable: Theorizing Music in *Dessa Rose.*" *Black Orpheus: Music in African American Literature from the Harlem Renaissance to Toni Morrison.* Ed. Saadi Simawe. New York: Garland, 2000. 1–40.

French, Scot. *The Rebellious Slave: Nat Turner in American Memory.* Boston: Houghton Mifflin, 2004.

Frye, Northrop. *Anatomy of Criticism.* Princeton: Princeton University Press, 1957.

"Gabriel's Defeat." *The Liberator* [38] 17 Sept. 1831.

"Gabriel's Defeat." *Richmond Enquirer* [Richmond, Va.] 21 Oct. 1831.

Gandhi, Mahatma. *Hind Swaraj and Other Writings.* Ed. Anthony J. Parel. Cambridge: Cambridge University Press, 1997.

Gates, Henry Louis Jr. *Figures in Black: Words, Signs, and the "Racial" Self.* New York: Oxford University Press, 1987.

———. *The Signifying Monkey: A Theory of African American Literary Criticism.* New York: Oxford University Press, 1988.

———. *Wonders of the African World.* PBS Home Video, 1999.

Genovese, Eugene D. *Roll, Jordan, Roll: The World the Slaves Made.* New York: Vintage Books, 1972.

George, Marjorie, and Richard Pressman. "Confronting the Shadow: Psycho-Political Repression in Chesnutt's *The Marrow of Tradition.*" *Phylon* 48.4 (Winter 1987): 287–98.

Geschiere, Peter. *The Modernity of Witchcraft: Politics and the Occult in Postcolonial Africa.* Trans. Peter Geschiere and Janet Roitman. Charlottesville: University of Virginia, 1997.

Gibson, Nigel. "Dialectical Impasses: Turning the Table on Hegel and the Black." *Parallax* 8.2 (April 2002): 30–45.

Gikandi, Simon. "In the Shadow of Hegel: Cultural Theory in the Age of Displacement." *Research in African Literatures* 27.2 (Summer 1996): 139–50.

———. "Introduction: Africa, Diaspora, and the Discourse of Modernity." *Research in African Literatures* 27.4 (Winter 1996): 1–6.

Giles, James R., and Thomas P. Lally. "Allegory in Chesnutt's *Marrow of Tradition.*" *Journal of General Education* 35.4 (1984): 259–69.

Gilmore, Glenda. "Murder, Memory, and the Flight of the Incubus." Cecelski and Tyson 73–93.

Gilroy, Paul. *The Black Atlantic: Modernity and Double Consciousness.* Cambridge, Mass.: Harvard University Press, 1993.

Giovanni, Nikki. *Gemini: An Extended Autobiographical Statement on my First Twenty-Five Years of Being a Black Poet.* New York: Penguin Books, 1976.

Gleason, William. "Voices at the Nadir: Charles Chesnutt and David Bryant Fulton." *American Literary Realism* 24.3 (1992): 22–41.

Goldberg, Florinda F. "Patterns of Repetition in *The Kingdom of the World.*" *Latin American Review* 19 (July–Dec. 1991): 23–34.

Goldman, Anne E. "'I Made the Ink': (Literary) Production and Reproduction in *Dessa Rose* and *Beloved.*" *Feminist Studies* 16.2 (Summer 1990): 313–30.

Goldner, Ellen J. "Allegories of Exposure: *The Heroic Slave* and the Agonistics of Frederick Douglass." *Racing and (E)Racing Language: Living with the Color of Our Words.* Ed. Ellen J. Goldner and Safiya Henderson. Syracuse: Syracuse University Press, 2001. 31–55.

Goldstein, Leslie Friedman. "Violence as an Instrument for Social Change: The Views of Frederick Douglass (1817–1895)." *Journal of Negro History* 61.1 (Jan. 1976): 61–72.

Gordon, Lawrence. "A Brief Look at Blacks in Depression Mississippi, 1929–1934: Eyewitness Accounts." *Journal of Negro History* 64.4 (Autumn 1979): 377–90.

Gray, Thomas. *The Confessions of Nat Turner.* Ed. Kenneth S. Greeberg. Boston: Bedford Books, 1996.

Grayson, Sandra M. "African Culture as Tradition: A Reading of *Tales of the Congaree, Middle Passage,* and *Black Thunder.*" Diss. University of California, Riverside, 1994.

Greenberg, Kenneth S. "Name, Face, Body." Greenberg, *Nat Turner* 3–23.

———, ed. *Nat Turner: A Slave Rebellion in History and Memory.* New York: Oxford University Press, 2003.

Griffin, Jasmine Farah. "Textual Healing: Claiming Black Women's Bodies, the Erotic and Resistance in Contemporary Novels of Slavery." *Callaloo* 19.2 (1996): 519–36.

Guha, Ranaji. "The Prose of Counter-Insurgency." *Selected Subaltern Studies.* Ed. Ranajit Guha and Gayatri Chakravorty Spivak. New York: Oxford University Press, 1988. 45–86.

Gwendolyn, Mikell. "Deconstructing Gates' 'Wonders of the African World.'" *Black Scholar* 30.1 (Spring 2000): 32–34.

Habermas, Jürgen. *The Philosophical Discourses of Modernity.* Trans. Frederick G. Lawrence. Cambridge, Mass.: MIT Press, 1990.

Hackenberry, Charles. "Meaning and Models: The Uses of Characterization in Chesnutt's *The Marrow of Tradition* and *Mandy Oxendine.*" *American Literary Realism* 17.2 (1984): 193–202.

Hallen, Barry, and J. O. Sodipo. *Knowledge, Belief, and Witchcraft.* London: Ethnografika, 1986.

Hamilton, C. A. "Ideology and Oral Traditions: Listening to the Voices 'from Below.'" *History in Africa* 14 (1987): 67–86.

Hamilton, Cynthia. "A Way of Seeing: Culture as Political Expression in the Works of C.L.R. James." *Journal of Black Studies* 22.3 (March 1992): 429–43.

Harrison, Suzan. "Mastering Narratives/Subverting Masters: Rhetorics of Race in *The Confessions of Nat Turner, Dessa Rose,* and *Celia, A Slave.*" *Southern Quarterly* 35.3 (Spring 1997): 13–28.

Hayden, Harry. *The Story of the Wilmington Rebellion.* Wilmington, N.C.: n.p., 1936.

Hegel, G.W.F. *The Phenomenology of Mind.* Trans. J. B. Bailie. New York: Harper Torchbooks, 1967.

Henderson, Mae Gwendolyn. "Speaking in Tongues: Dialogics, Dialectics, and the Black Woman's Literary Tradition." *Changing Our Words: Essays on Criticism, Theory, and Writing by Black Women.* Ed. Cheryl Wall. New Brunswick: Rutgers University Press, 1991. 16–37.

———. "(W)Riting *The Work* and Working the Rites." *Black American Literature Forum* 23.4 (Winter 1989): 631–60.

Henry, Paget. *Caliban's Reason: Introducing Afro-Caribbean Philosophy.* New York: Routledge, 2000.

Henry, Paget, and Paul Buhle. "Caliban as Deconstructionist: C.L.R. James and Post-Colonial Discourse." Henry and Buhle, *C.L.R. James's Caribbean* 110–42.

———. *C.L.R. James's Caribbean.* Durham, N.C.: Duke University Press, 1992.

Higginson, Thomas W. *Black Rebellion: A Selection from Travellers and Outlaws.* Boston: Lee and Shepard, 1889. New York: Arno Press, 1969.

Hite, Roger. "'Stand Still and See the Salvation': The Rhetorical Design of Martin Delany's *Blake.*" *Journal of Black Studies* 5 (1974): 192–202.

Holmes, Eugene C. "Problems Facing the Negro Writer Today." *New Challenge* 2.2 (Fall 1937): 69–72.

Holmes, Kristine. "'This Is Flesh I'm Talking About Here': Embodiment in Toni Morrison's *Beloved* and Sherley Ann Williams' *Dessa Rose.*" *LIT* 6 (1995): 133–48.

Horton, Robin. "African Traditional Thought and Western Science." *Africa* 37.1–2 (Jan. and Apr. 1967): 50–71; 155–87.

Hurston, Zora Neale. *Their Eyes Were Watching God.* New York: Harper and Row, 1990.

Hutcheon, Linda. *A Poetics of Postmodernism: History, Theory, Fiction.* New York: Routledge, 1988.

Idahosa, Paul. "James and Fanon and the Problem of the Intelligentsia in Popular Organizations." Cudjoe and Cain 388–404.

Idoniboye, D. E. "The Idea of an African Philosophy: The Concept of 'Spirit' in African Metaphysics." *Second Order* 2.1 (Jan. 1973): 83–89.

Idowu, Bolaji E. "The Challenge of Witchcraft." *Orita: Ibadan Journal of Religious Studies* 4.1 (June 1970): 3–16.

———. "Religion, Magic and Medicine—with Special Reference to Africa." *Orita: Ibadan Journal of Religious Studies* 1.2 (1977): 62–77.

Inikori, Joseph. "'Wonder of the African World' and the Trans-Atlantic Slave Trade." *Black Scholar* 30.1 (Spring 2000): 30–31.

"Interesting Items." *Niles Weekly Register* 26 Dec. 1829: 277.

"The Internal Slave Trade." *Niles Weekly Register* 5 Sept. 1829: 18–19.

Irele, Abiola. "The African Imagination." *Research in African Literatures* 21.1 (1990): 49–67.

Isola, Akinwumi. *Efunsetan Aniwura: Iyalode Ibadan.* Ibadan: Oxford University Press, 1970.

———. "Indigo Revolt in *Basorun Gaa.*" *Research in Yoruba Language and Literature* 1 (Jan. 1991): 29–37.

———. "Presenting Revolution in *Omo Olokun Esin.*" *Research in Yoruba Language and Literature* 2 (1992): 51–58.

———. *Two Contemporary African Plays.* Trans. Niyi Oladeji. Dubuque: Kendall/Hunt Publishers, 1992.

Jackson, Richard. "Remembering the 'Disremembered': Modern Black Writers and Slavery in Latin America." *Callaloo* 13.1 (Winter 1900): 131–44.

James, C.L.R. *The Black Jacobins: Toussaint L'Ouverture and the San Domingo Revolution.* New York: Vintage, 1963.

———. *The C.L.R. James Reader.* Ed. Anna Grimshaw. Oxford: Blackwell, 1992.

———. "Lectures on The Black Jacobins." *Small Axe* 8 (Sept. 2000): 65–112.

James, Charles L. "On the Legacy of the Harlem Renaissance: A Conversation with Arna Bontemps and Aaron Douglas." *Obsidian* 4.1 (Spring 1978): 32–53.

Jeyifo, Biodun. *The Yoruba Popular Travelling Theatre of Nigeria.* Lagos: Nigeria Magazine, 1984.

Johnson, James Weldon. "The Dilemma of the Negro Author." *American Mercury* 15 (1928): 477–81.

Johnson, Samuel. *The History of the Yorubas: From the Earliest Times to the Beginning of the British Protectorate.* Lagos: C.M.S Bookshops, 1921.

Jones, Howard. "The Peculiar Institution and National Honor: The Case of the *Creole* Slave Revolt." *Civil War History* 21.1 (March 1975): 28–50.

Jones, Paul Christian. "Copying What the Master Had Written: Frederick Douglass's 'The Heroic Slave' and the Southern Historical Romance." *Southern Quarterly* 38.4 (Summer 2000): 78–91.

Jordan, Shirley. *Broken Silences: Interviews with Black and White Women Writers.* New Brunswick: Rutgers University Press, 1993.

Julien, Eileen. *African Novels and the Question of Orality.* Bloomington: Indiana University Press, 1992.

Karlsson, Ann-Marie Elisabet. "Signs in Blood: Racial Violence and Antebellum Narratives of Resistance." Diss. University of California, Berkeley.

Keith, Allyn. "A Note on Negro Nationalism." *New Challenge* 2.2 (Fall 1937): 65–69.

Kekeh, Andre-Anne. "Sherley Ann Williams' *Dessa Rose:* History and the Disruptive Power of Memory." *History and Memory in African-American Culture.* Ed. Geneviève Fabre and Robert O'Meally. New York: Oxford University Press, 1994. 219–27.

Kelley, Robin D. G. "The World the Diaspora Made: C.L.R. James and the Politics of History." Farred, *Rethinking* 103–30.

Kester, Gunilla Theander. *Writing the Subject: Bildung and the African American Text.* New York: Peter Lang, 1995.

Killens, John Oliver. *The Trial Record of Denmark Vesey.* Boston: Beacon Press, 1970.

King, Nicole R. "Meditations and Mediations: Issues of History and Fiction in *Dessa Rose.*" *Soundings* 76.2–3 (Summer/Fall 1993): 351–68.

Kirk, John. "Magic Realism and Voodoo: Alejo Carpentier's *The Kingdom of the World.*" *Perspectives on Contemporary Literature* 5 (1979): 124–30.

Kirk-Greene, A.H.M. "America in the Niger Valley: A Colonization Centenary." *Phylon* 23.3 (1962): 225–39.

Klein, Martin A. "Studying the History of Those Who Would Rather Forget: Oral History and the Experience of Slavery." *History in Africa* 16 (1989): 209–17.

Knadler, Stephen P. "Untragic Mulatto: Charles Chesnutt and the Discourse of Whiteness." *American Literary History* 8.3 (Fall 1996): 428–48.

Kojève, Alexandre. *Introduction to the Reading of Hegel.* Trans. James H. Nichols Jr. Ed. Allan Bloom. Ithaca: Cornell University Press, 1969.

Lamming, George. *The Pleasures of Exile.* Ann Arbor: University of Michigan Press, 1992.

Lazarus, Neil. "Is a Counterculture of Modernity a Theory of Modernity?" *Diaspora* 4.3 (1995): 323–39.

Leal, Luis. "Magical Realism in Spanish Literature." Parkinson and Zamora 119–24.

Leaming, Hugo P. *Hidden Americans: Maroons of Virginia and the Carolinas.* New York: Garland, 1995.

Levecq, Christine. "Philosophies of History in Arna Bontemps' *Black Thunder.*" *Obsidian III* 1.2 (Summer 2000): 111–30.

Levine, Robert S. *Martin Delany, Frederick Douglass and the Politics of Representative Identity.* Chapel Hill: University of North Carolina Press, 1997.

Linder, Douglas O. *Without Fear or Favor: Judge James Edwin Horton and the Trial of the "Scottsboro Boys."* University of Missouri–Kansas City Law School. 2000. http://www.law.umkc.edu/faculty/projects/FTrials/trialheroes/essayhorton.html.

Lopez-Springfield, Consuelo. "Through the People's Eyes: C.L.R. James's Rhetoric of History." *Caribbean Quarterly* 36.1/2 (1990): 85–97.

Macherey, Pierre. *A Theory of Literary Production.* Trans. Geoffrey Wall. London: Routledge and Kegan Paul, 1978.

Martin, Charles H. "White Supremacy and Black Workers: Georgia's 'Black Shirts' Combat the Great Depression." *Labor History* 18.3 (Summer 1977): 366–81.

Martin, Tony. "C.L.R. James and the Race/Class Question." *Race* 14.2 (1972): 183–93.

Marx, Jo Ann. "Myth and Meaning in Martin R. Delany's *Blake; or the Huts of America.*" *CLA Journal* 38.2 (Dec. 1994): 183–92.

Masilela, Ntongela. "The 'Black Atlantic' and African Modernity in South Africa." *Research in African Literatures* 27.4 (Winter 1996): 88–96.

Mathison-Fife, Jane. "*Dessa Rose:* A Critique of the Received History of Slavery." *Kentucky Philological Review* 8 (1993): 29–33.

Matory, J. Lorand. "The English Professors of Brazil: On the Diasporic Roots of the Yorùbá Nation." *Comparative Studies in Society and History* 41.1 (1999): 72–103.

Mazrui, Ali A. "Black Orientalism? Further Reflections on 'Wonders of the African World.'" *Black Scholar* 30.1 (Spring 2000): 15–18.

———. "A Millennium Letter to Henry Louis Gates, Jr.: Concluding a Dialogue." *Black Scholar* 30.1 (Spring 2000): 48–51.

———. "A Preliminary Critique of the TV Series by Henry Louis Gates, Jr." *Black Scholar* 30.1 (Spring 2000): 5–6.

Mbembe, Achille. *On the Postcolony.* Berkeley: University of California Press, 2001.

McDowell, Deborah E. "Negotiating between Tenses: Witnessing Slavery after Freedom—*Dessa Rose.*" McDowell and Rampersad 144–63.

McDowell, Deborah E., and Arnold Rampersad, eds. *Slavery and the Literary Imagination: Selected Papers from the English Language Institute, 1987.* Baltimore: Johns Hopkins University Press, 1989.

McGowan, Winston. "African Resistance to the Atlantic Slave Trade in West Africa." *Slavery and Abolition* 11.5 (1990): 5–29.

McKible, Adam. "'These Are the Facts of the Darky's History': Thinking History and Reading Names in Four African American Texts." *African American Review* 28.2 (1994): 223–35.

McKoy, Sheila Smith. "Riot: Episodes of Racialized Violence in African and African American Culture." Diss. Duke University, 1994.

Meacham, Gloria Horsley. "Selected Nineteenth Century Interpretations of Organized Slave Resistance: Black Character Consciousness as Represented in the Fictional Works of Harriet Beecher Stowe, Herman Melville, and Martin Robinson Delany and Related Historical Sources." Diss. Cornell University, 1980.

Miers, Suzanne, and Igor Kopytoff. *Slavery in Africa: History and Anthropological Perspectives.* Madison: University of Wisconsin Press, 1977.

Mikell, Gwendolyn. "Deconstructing Gates' 'Wonders of the African World.'" *Black Scholar* 30.1 (Spring 2000): 32–34.

Mills, Bruce. "Lydia Maria Child and the Endings to Harriet Jacobs's *Incidents in the Life of a Slave Girl.*" *American Literature* 64.2 (June 1992): 255–72.

Minus, Marian. "Present Trends of Negro Literature." *Challenge* 2.1 (Spring 1937): 9–11.

Moitt, Bernard. "Transcending Linguistic and Cultural Frontiers in Caribbean Historiography: C.L.R. James, French Sources, and Slavery in San Domingo." Cudjoe and Cain 136–60.

Mosley, Albert. "The Metaphysics of Magic: Practical and Philosophical Implications." *Second Order* 7.1 and 7.2 (Jan./July 1978): 3–19.

Nowak, Bronislaw. "The Slave Rebellion in Sierra Leone in 1785–1796." *Hemispheres* 3.3 (1986): 151–69.

Nwaubani, Ebere. "Kenneth Onwuka Dike, *Trade and Politics,* and the Restoration of African History." *History in Africa* 27 (2000): 229–48.

Ogunsina, Bisi. *The Development of the Yoruba Novel: 1930–1975.* Ibadan: Gospel Faith Mission Press, 1992.

Okolo, Amechi. "My Response to 'A Preliminary Response to Ali Mazrui's Critique.'" *Black Scholar* 30.1 (Spring 2000): 35–38.

Olabimtan, Afolabi. "Symbolism in Yoruba Traditional Incantatory Poetry." *Nigeria Magazine* 114.35–42 (1974).

Olaniyan, Tejumola. "Adebayo Faleti." *Perspectives on Nigerian Literature: 1700 to the Present.* Ed. Yemi Ogunbiyi. Lagos: Guardian Books, 1988. 137–41.

Olatunji, Olatunde O. *Features of Yoruba Oral Poetry.* Ibadan: University Press Limited, 1984.

Olney, James. "'I Was Born': Slave Narratives, Their Status as Autobiography and as Literature." *Callaloo* 7.1 (Winter 1984): 46–73.

Oluwole, Sophie B. "On the Existence of Witches." *Second Order* 7.1 and 7.2 (Jan./July 1978): 20–35.

Oroge, Adeniyi. "The Institution of Slavery in Yorubaland with Particular Reference to the Nineteenth Century." Diss. University of Birmingham, 1971.

Osagie, Iyunolu Folayan. *The Amistad Revolt: Memory, Slavery, and the Politics of Identity in the United States and Sierra Leone.* Athens: University of Georgia Press, 2000.

Ouologuem, Yambo. *Bound to Violence.* Trans. Ralph Manheim. London: Heinemann, 1977.

Òyéwùmí, Oyèrónkẹ́. *The Invention of Women: Making an African Sense of Western Gender Discourses.* Minneapolis: University of Minnesota Press, 1997.

Parkinson, Louis, and Wendy B. Faris Zamora, eds. *Magical Realism: Theory, History, Community.* Durham, N.C.: Duke University Press, 1995.

Patterson, Orlando. *Slavery and Social Death: A Comparative Study.* Cambridge, Mass.: Harvard University Press, 1982.

Peel, J. D. Y. *Religious Encounter and the Making of the Yoruba.* Bloomington: Indiana University Press, 2000.

Peterson, Carla L. "Capitalism, Black (Under)Development, and the Production of the African-American Novel in the 1850s." *American Literary History* 4.4 (Winter 1992): 559–83.

Peterson, Dorothy R. "Rev. of *Black Thunder* by Arna Bontemps." *Challenge* 1.5 (June 1936): 45–46.

Piersen, William D. "White Cannibals, Black Martyrs: Fear, Depression, and Religious Faith as Causes of Suicide among New Slaves." *Journal of Negro History* 62.2 (1977): 147–59.

Piot, Charles. "Atlantic Aporias: Africa and Gilroy's Black Atlantic." *South Atlantic Quarterly* 100.1 (Winter 2001): 155–70.

Porter, Nancy. "Women's Interracial Friendships and Visions of Community in *Meridian, The Salt Eaters, Civil Wars,* and *Dessa Rose.*" *Tradition and the Talents of Women.* Ed. Florence Howe. Urbana: University of Illinois Press, 1991. 251–67.

Prather, Leon H. Sr. "We Have Taken a City: A Centennial Essay." Cecelski and Tyson 15–41.

Rabbit, Kara M. "C.L.R. James's Figuring of Toussaint-L'Ouverture: *The Black Jacobins* and the Literary Hero." Cudjoe and Cain 118–35.

Rampersad, Arnold. Introduction. *Black Thunder.* By Arna Bontemps. Boston: Beacon Press, 1968. vii–xx.

Rathbone, Richard. "Some Thoughts on Resistance to Enslavement in West Africa." *Slavery and Abolition* 6.2 (1985): 11–22.

Reagan, Daniel. "Achieving Perspective: Arna Bontemps and the Shaping Force of Harlem Culture." *Essays in Arts and Sciences* 25 (Oct. 1996): 69–78.

———. "Voices of Silence: The Representation of Orality in Arna Bontemps' *Black Thunder.*" *Studies in American Fiction* 19.1 (Spring 1991): 71.

Reid-Pharr, Robert. "Violent Ambiguity: Martin Delany, Bourgeois Sadomasochism, and the Production of Black Masculinity." *Representing Black Men.* Ed. Marcellus Blount and George P. Cunningham. New York: Routledge, 1996. 73–94.

Reilly, John M. "The Dilemma in Chesnutt's *The Marrow of Tradition.*" *Phylon* 32 (1971): 31–38.

Richardson, David. "Shipboard Revolts, African Authority, and the Atlantic Slave Trade." *William and Mary Quarterly* 58.1 (Jan. 2001): 69–91.

Rodney, Walter. "Upper Guinea and the Significance of the Origins of African Enslaved in the New World." *Journal of Negro History* 44.4 (Oct. 1969): 327–45.

Roe, Jae H. "Keeping an 'Old Wound' Alive: *The Marrow of Tradition* and the Legacy of Wilmington." *African American Review* 33.2 (1999): 231–43.

Roh, Franz. "Magic Realism: Post-Expressionism." Parkinson and Zamora 15–31.

Rucker, Walter C. "'The River Floweth On': The African Social and Cultural Origins of Slave Resistance in North America, 1712–1831." Diss. University of California, Riverside, 1999.

Rushdy, Ashraf H. A. *Neo-Slave Narratives: Studies in the Social Logic of a Literary Form.* New York: Oxford University Press, 1999.

———. "Reading Mammy: The Subject of Relation in Sherley Ann Williams' *Dessa Rose.*" *African American Review* 27.3 (1993): 365–89.

Sadler, Lynn Veach. "The Figure of the Black Insurrectionist in Stowe, Bouvé, Bontemps, and Gaithier: The Universality of the Need for Freedom." *MAWA Review* 2.1 (June 1986): 21–24.

———. "The Sea in Selected American Novels of Slave Unrest." *Journal of American Culture* 10.2 (Summer 1987): 43–48.

———. "The West Indies as a Symbol of Freedom in Johnston's *Prisoners of Hope* and

The Slave Ship and in Bontemps' *Black Thunder.*" *Jack London Newsletter* 15.1 (Jan.–Apr. 1982): 42–48.

Sale, Maggie. "Critiques from Within: Antebellum Projects of Resistance." *American Literature* 64.4 (Dec. 1992): 695–718.

———. *The Slumbering Volcano: American Slave Ship Revolts and the Production of Rebellious Masculinity.* Durham, N.C.: Duke University Press, 1997.

San Juan, E. Jr. *Beyond Postcolonial Theory.* New York: St. Martin's Press, 1998.

Sánchez, Marta E. "The Enstrangement Effect in Sherley Anne Williams' *Dessa Rose.*" *Genders* 15 (Winter 1992): 20–36.

Sander, Reinhard W. "C.L.R. James and the Haitian Revolution." *World Literature Written in English* 26.2 (Autumn 1986): 277–90.

Scheub, Harold. "A Review of African Oral Traditions and Literature." *African Studies Review* 28.2/3 (1985): 1–72.

Schuler, Monica. "Akan Slave Rebellions in the British Caribbean." *Savacou* 1.1 (June 1970): 8–31.

Sekoni, Ropo. *Folk Poetics: A Sociosemiotic Study of Yoruba Trickster Tales.* Westport, Conn.: Greenwood Press, 1994.

Shaw, Rosalind. *Memories of the Slave Trade: Ritual and Historical Imagination in Sierra Leone.* Chicago: University of Chicago Press, 2002.

Sidbury, James. "Reading, Revelation, and Rebellion: The Textual Communities of Gabriel, Denmark Vesey, and Nat Turner." Greenberg 119–33.

Sievers, Stefanie. "Escaping the Master(')s Narrative? Sherley Anne Williams's Rethinking of Historical Representation in 'Meditations on History.'" *Re-Visioning the Past: Historical Self-Reflexivity in American Short Fiction.* Engler and Scheiding 365–81.

Sodipo, J. O. "Notes on the Concept of Cause and Chance in Yoruba Traditional Thought." *Second Order* 2.2 (July 1973): 12–20.

Sokoloff, Naomi. "The Discourse of Contradiction: Metaphor, Metonymy and *El Reino de Este Mundo.*" *Modern Language Studies* 16.2 (1986): 39–53.

Solomon, William. "Politics and Rhetoric in the Novel in the 1930s." *American Literature* 68.4 (Dec. 1996): 799–818.

Soyinka, Wole. *Myth, Literature, and the African World.* Cambridge: Cambridge University Press, 1976.

Spear, Thomas. "Oral Traditions: Whose History?" *History in Africa* 8 (1981): 165–81.

Spielberg, Steven, dir. *Amistad.* Dreamworks Pictures, 1997.

Spillers, Hortense J. "Mama's Baby, Papa's Maybe: An American Grammar Book." *Diacritics* 17.2 (Summer 1987): 65–81.

Spindler, William. "Magic Realism: A Typology." *Forum for Modern Language Studies* 39.1 (1993): 75–85.

Spivak, Gayatri Chakravorty. *A Critique of Postcolonial Reason: Toward a History of the Vanishing Present.* Cambridge, Mass.: Harvard University Press, 1999.

Stepto, Robert B. *From Behind the Veil: A Study of Afro-American Narrative.* Urbana: University of Illinois Press, 1991.

———. "Storytelling in Early Afro-American Fiction: Frederick Douglass' 'The Heroic Slave.'" *Georgia Review* 36.2 (Summer 1982): 355–68.

Sternsher, Bernard. "Great Depression Labor Historiography in the 1970s: Middle-Range Questions, Ethnocultures, and Levels of Organization." *Reviews in American History* 11.2 (June 1983): 300–19.

Stone, Albert. *The Return of Nat Turner: History, Literature, and Cultural Politics in Sixties America.* Athens: University of Georgia Press, 1982.

Styron, William. *The Confessions of Nat Turner.* New York: Random House, 1967.

Sundquist, Eric J. *The Hammers of Creation: Folk Culture in Modern African-American Fiction.* Athens: University of Georgia Press, 1992.

———. *To Wake the Nations: Race in the Making of American Literature.* Cambridge, Mass.: Harvard University Press, 1993.

Sundstrom, William A. "Last Hired, First Fired? Unemployment and Urban Black Workers during the Great Depression." *Journal of Economic History* 52.2 (June 1992): 415–29.

Sutherland, Efua. *The Marriage of Anansewa; Edufa: Two Plays.* Essex: Longman, 1987.

Taiwo, Olufemi. "Exorcising Hegel's Ghost: Africa's Challenge to Philosophy." *African Studies Quarterly* 1.4 (1998). http://web.africa.ufl.edu/asq.

Thornton, John K. "African Soldiers in the Haitian Revolution." *Journal of Caribbean History* 25.1 and 25.2 (1991): 58–80.

Todorov, Tzvetan. "Living Alone Together." *New Literary History* 27.1 (1996): 1–14.

Tragle, Henry Irving. *The Southampton Slave Revolt of 1831: A Compilation of Source Material Including the Full Text of the Confessions of Nat Turner.* New York: Vintage Books, 1973.

Turner, Darwin. "Black Fiction: History and Myth." *Studies in American Fiction* 5 (1977): 109–26.

Unruh, Vicky. "The Performing Spectator in Alejo Carpentier's Fictional World." *Hispanic Review* 66.1 (Winter 1998): 57–77.

Urban, C. Stanley. "The Africanization of Cuba Scare, 1853–1855." *Hispanic American Historical Review* 37.1 (Feb. 1957): 29–45.

Vansina, Jan. *Oral Tradition as History.* Madison: University of Wisconsin Press, 1985.

Wade, Richard C. "The Vesey Plot: A Reconsideration." *Journal of Southern History* 30.2 (May 1964): 143–61.

Walker, Margaret. *Jubilee.* New York: Bantam Books, 1966.

Walter, Krista. "Trappings of Nationalism in Frederick Douglass's The Heroic Slave." African American Review 34.2 (Summer 2000): 233–47.

Washington, Mary Helen, ed. *Midnight Birds: Stories of Contemporary Black Women Writers.* New York: Anchor Books, 1980.

Watson, Ruth. "Murder and the Political Body in Early Colonial Ibadan." *Africa* 70.1 (2000): 25–47.

Watt, Ian P. *The Rise of the Novel: Studies in Defoe, Richardson and Fielding.* Berkeley: University of California Press, 1967 (1957).

Wax, Darold. "Negro Resistance to the Early American Slave Trade." *Journal of Negro History* 51.1 (1966): 1–15.

Wax, Murray, and Rosalie Wax. "The Notion of Magic." *Current Anthropology* 4.5 (Dec. 1963): 495–518.

Weil, Dorothy. "Folklore Motifs in Arna Bontemps' *Black Thunder.*" *Southern Folklore Quarterly* 35.1 (March 1971): 14.

White, Hayden. *Tropics of Discourse: Essays in Cultural Criticism.* Baltimore: Johns Hopkins University Press, 1978.

White, Roger W. "'Stand Still and See the Salvation': The Rhetorical Design of Martin Delany's *Blake.*" *Journal of Black Studies* 5.2 (Dec. 1974): 192–202.

Whites, LeeAnn. "Love, Hate, Rape, Lynching: Rebecca Latimer Felton and the

Gender Politics of Racial Violence." Cecelski and Tyson 143–62.
Williams, Lorna V. "The Utopian Vision in Carpentier's *El Reino De Este Mundo.*" *Journal of Caribbean Studies* 2.1 (1981): 129–39.
Williams, Sherley Anne. *Dessa Rose.* New York: Berkley Books, 1987.
———. "The Lion's History: The Ghetto Writes B(l)Ack." *Soundings* 76.2–3 (Summer/Fall 1993): 243–60.
———. "Meditations on History." *Midnight Birds: Stories of Contemporary Black Women Writers.* Ed. Mary Helen Washington. New York, 1980. 200–48.
Winchell, Donna Haisty. "Cries of Outrage: Three Novelists' Use of History." *Mississippi Quarterly* 49.4 (Fall 1996): 727–42.
Wintz, Cary D. "Race and Realism in the Fiction of Charles W. Chesnutt." *Ohio History* 81 (1981): 122–30.
Wish, Harvey. "American Slave Insurrections before 1861." *Journal of Negro History* 22.3 (July 1937): 299–320.
———. "The Slave Insurrection Panic of 1856." *Journal of Southern History* 5 (May 1939): 206–22.
Wolkomir, Michelle J. "Moral Elevation and Egalitarianism: Shades of Gray in Chesnutt's *The Marrow of Tradition.*" *CLA Journal* 36.3 (March 1993): 245–59.
Wright, Richard. "Blueprint for Negro Writing." *New Challenge* 2.2 (Fall 1937): 53–65.
———. *Native Son.* New York: Harper and Row, 1966 (1940).
———. "A Tale of Folk Courage." *Partisan Review and Anvil* April 1936: 31.
Yarborough, Richard. "Race, Violence, and Manhood: The Masculine Ideal in Frederick Douglass's 'The Heroic Slave.'" *Frederick Douglass: New Literary and Historical Essays.* Ed. Eric J. Sundquist. Cambridge: Cambridge University Press, 1990. 166–88.
———. "Violence, Manhood, and Black Heroism: The Wilmington Riot in Two Turn-of-the-Century African American Novels." Cecelski and Tyson 225–51.
Young, Pauline. "Rev. of *Black Thunder* by Arna Bontemps." *Journal of Negro History* 22 (1937): 355–56.
Zeugner, John. "A Note on Martin Delany's *Blake,* and Black Militancy." *Phylon* 32.1 (1971): 98–105.

INDEX

ADÉLÉKÈ ADÉẸ̀KỌ́

is Associate Professor of English and Chair of the Department of Comparative Literature at the University of Colorado, Boulder. His articles on African and African American literatures have appeared in many journals, including *Research in African Literatures, Critique, Nineteenth Century Contexts,* and *Dialectical Anthropology.* He is author of *Proverbs, Textuality, and Nativism in African Literature* (1998). Adéẹ̀kọ́ attended Obafemi Awolowo University, Ile-Ife in Nigeria and the University of Florida, Gainesville. He is co-editor of *West Africa Review.*